CAR
[CONFIDENTIAL]

INSIDER SECRETS ABOUT AUTOMOBILE OWNERSHIP, CAR MAINTENANCE AND ROAD SAFETY

SHAHE KOULLOUKIAN
AUTO INDUSTRY AMBASSADOR, INSIDER AND EDUCATOR

PRAISE FOR CAR CONFIDENTIAL

"To be asked to contribute a review for this book is more than a surprise. While I have enthusiastically driven everything from Mustangs to Mercedes, I selected them almost exclusively by design and reputation since everything under their hoods was and still is a highly classified mystery to me. Admitting that may create a question about my masculinity, but I can live with that. It's living confidently with the car I have and the knowledge I don't have that is the basis for my deep appreciation for Car Confidential *by Shahe Koulloukian, a name I use to test my vision when visiting my ophthalmologist.*

I live in a big city with lots of automobile experts, but when I want one to guest on my television program, I only want to talk to Shahe. Even more personally, when I need information about our family cars, I only want to talk to Shahe. Buying or selling a car, repairing a car, trading in a car...first I talk to Shahe. Actually, I don't have to talk to Shahe quite as often because all I have to do now is read this book... you too, your wife and most especially your kids.

So, what does a guy named John Patrick Michael McMahon know since there's no such thing as an Irish car? Well, the reason for that is they thought an automobile named Guinness Speedster might have a marketing problem. So there!"

—Pat McMahon
Hall of Fame Broadcaster

"I must admit that I am your typical car owner. I love my vehicles, but I really don't know enough about what's going on under the hood to know if I am being ripped off or not during maintenance or other issues. Okay, I'll say it, I'm naïve and ignorant. BUT... after reading this incredible book Car Confidential *I really feel 'in the know.'*

Shahe Koulloukian is the perfect INSIDER to educate and enlighten a car owner like me. His knowledge and experience are to be TOTALLY trusted! He also wrote this book in a style and manner with easy and understandable terms that spoke to me. His awareness of buying vehicles, maintaining them, and keeping us safe in them is definitely remarkable.

I highly recommend this book to EVERYONE! Our relationship with our cars is an important one in our lives. Shahe 'has our back'! Let him educate and inspire you like he did me."

—Glenn Scarpelli
Actor, best known for *One Day at a Time*,
CEO and Host, *Sedona NOW TV*

"Shahe Koulloukian is the rarest of individuals…he's a mechanic you trust!!! There's no smoke, no mirrors, no hidden fees.

What he does, better than any mechanic I've ever encountered is give you 'truthful options,' then works with you to make the best decision for YOU. So, when he writes a book that will empower you to be a better car owner, you don't just buy Car Confidential *for yourself... you purchase it for everyone you know that has a car!!!"*

—Segun Oduolowu
Entertainment Journalist on *NBC Access Live, Today Show* and current *Host of Boston Globe Today*

"Car Confidential *is written with the exact same care and thoroughness that my vehicles and I have experienced every time I have visited Shahe at Mazvo Auto.*

The content reflects the admirable authenticity and honesty much needed in an industry that many don't trust, but you can always find with Shahe."

—Brett Labit
Founder and CEO of Tribe Up

"In today's fast-paced world, where we rely heavily on automobiles for our daily lives, having a trusted friend who can provide sage advice on all things automotive is truly a treasure. For over three decades, Shahe Koulloukian has been that invaluable friend to me and my family. His wisdom and expertise in the automotive industry have consistently guided us in making informed decisions about our vehicles. Now, with the release of his book, Car Confidential, *Shahe extends his priceless knowledge to a wider audience, transforming the reader into a responsible and savvy car owner.* Car Confidential *is more than just a book; it's a guide that equips readers with the fundamental knowledge and insights required to navigate the complex world of car ownership successfully. Much like having a doctor or lawyer in the family, having Shahe's wealth of knowledge at your fingertips through this book is a game changer.*

One of the book's key strengths is its focus on empowerment. Shahe empowers readers by arming them with essential information about vehicle ownership. Whether you're a first-time car owner or someone with years of experience, the book's central message is that owning a car is not just an emotional affair; it's a rational decision that requires careful consideration and a commitment to responsible ownership. This perspective resonates with those who advocate for truth and honesty in all aspects of life, including the automotive industry. Shahe Koulloukian's commitment to transparency and integrity shines through every page of the book. Additionally, he provides practical tips and actionable advice that readers can implement immediately, making the book a valuable resource for both novices and seasoned car owners.

In conclusion, Car Confidential *by Shahe Koulloukian is must-read for anyone looking to enhance their understanding of the automotive world and become a more responsible car owner. Shahe's dedication to truth, honesty, and empowerment shines brightly throughout the book, making it a trustworthy and essential guide for all car enthusiasts. With this book in your hands, you'll have the wisdom of a lifelong friend and automotive expert by your side, ready to assist you on your journey to becoming a savvy and responsible car owner."*

—Chris Hutson
Film and Television Industry (More importantly, someone who wants a safe and reliable vehicle for his family.)

"Shahe knows more about cars than any guest I've ever booked. But what sets him apart is his humanity, sense of humor, and genuine desire to help others.

He never makes people feel dumb for not knowing something. Instead, he takes his time explaining what needs to be done, and even more time teaching how to prevent it.

Almost every day, I use his insider tips, whether it's which direction to park my car or how to fix a chipped windshield.

Like all other drivers he encounters, I don't just trust him, I feel empowered. This is the connection that sets Shahe apart."

—Ed Roth
Executive Producer

"Shahe's book Car Confidential *is by far the most informative and interesting book that I have ever come across. Anyone who owns a vehicle of any kind should have a copy of this book on hand. Shahe educates the reader, gives great advice on how to be a better owner, how to communicate with your mechanic, how to find the right mechanic plus lists all the dos and don'ts of driving, owning, and maintaining your vehicle.*

I personally liked the section that talked about tires and brakes. That is one thing you do not want a budget price on. I have been in the automotive business, on the sales side for over thirty years, and I am appalled at how many people I see letting their tires run down with no tread and keep driving on them or put after-market brakes on to save a few bucks. Tires and brakes are too important to the vehicle's safety to procrastinate or cut corners on.

Shahe also makes the information easy to access when you need it with sections called Insider Files, Key Takeaways, Pit Stop Lessons, and Fuel for Thought reminders that are listed and highlighted within each chapter so the reader can find what they are looking for without reading the whole book again.

Car Confidential *should be included in the driver's training for every new driver on the road. A true must read for all vehicle owners everywhere!"*

—Terri Lynn Murphy, Author
Automotive Professional in Sales, Management, and Sales Training

"So, I still haven't read all of the pages, however, I think writing the book was very incisive and profound. It actually holds attention. I've been driving for many years, in spite of my youth.☺ However, there are things about a car that I'd never thought about or took for granted.

For those of us who are experienced drivers, or experienced car owners, thanks for the reminders. I also think every new driver or new car owner should be given a copy of this book!"

—C. Anthony Williams
CEO, Orion Protective Service LLC

CAR

CONFIDENTIAL

Insider Secrets About Automobile Ownership, Car Maintenance and Road Safety

Shahe Koulloukian

GLOBAL WELLNESS MEDIA
STRATEGIC EDGE INNOVATIONS PUBLISHING
LOS ANGELES, TORONTO, MONTREAL

For permission requests, send an email to book@carconfidential.net

First Edition. Published by:
Global Wellness Media
Strategic Edge Innovations Publishing
440 N Barranca Ave #2027
Covina, California, 91723
(866) 467-9090
StrategicEdgeInnovations.com

Publisher's Note: The views expressed in this work are solely those of the authors and do not necessarily reflect the views of the publisher, and the publisher hereby disclaims any responsibilities for them.

Editors: Bobbie Walton, Eric D. Groleau
Book Design: Global Wellness Media
Illustrations: Theresia Staudinger, Global Wellness Media
Cover Design: Eric D. Groleau

Car Confidential / Shahe Koulloukian. — 1st ed. [128P4]
ISBN: 978-1-957343-14-3 (Kindle)
ISBN: 978-1-957343-15-0 (Paperback)

TABLE OF CONTENTS

SECTION 1
OWNERSHIP

SECTION 2
MAINTENANCE

SECTION 3
ROAD SAFETY

DISCLAIMER

The information provided here is not meant to replace a professional inspection or repairs by a licensed technician. Any health information supplied is not intended as a substitute for expert medical advice. The author's personal experience and other real-life examples are used to create this book. In certain cases, names have been changed to protect privacy (like Uncle Dent and Cousin Ding).

The author has made the best efforts to ensure that the information in this book is correct at the time of publication. He does not assume and hereby disclaims any liability to any party for loss, damage, or disruption due to errors or omissions, whether by negligence, accident, or any other reason.

DEDICATION

Welcome, dear readers. To begin right, I would like to introduce those I admire, and believe deserve my dedication. First, my late father, Hagop Koulloukian, inspired my passion by teaching me to listen and to shake every hand that crosses my path. This ultimately guided me to becoming who I am today. My beautiful wife Lena has been the love of my life for three blissful decades. She taught me to accept that perfection is just a myth, while always making sure I felt loved and taken care of, something for which I will forever be truly thankful. My two beloved sons, Hagop and Janno, bring me much happiness and inspiration. Your boundless energy and love fill my heart with pride; I thank the stars above for entrusting me with such incredible sons. To my devoted mother, Azad, whose dedication, compassion, and kindness kept our family together after my father's passing. Your strength taught me resilience. Now I carry your spirit with me everywhere I go. And, finally, to my brother Alex who is always there as my biggest cheerleader, lending an infectious energy that gives me strength. You have always provided me with genuine support and sincere enthusiasm during every challenge or victory in life. Thank you for always being there for me.

Let's go back to where everything began, dearest friends. From Day One I set out as an advocate of truth, working tirelessly and passionately toward empowering consumers with helpful knowledge. Mazvo Car Care came to be, my words echoing far beyond its walls to educate and ignite minds. I sometimes push political correctness boundaries, but that only proves truth is bold and unyielding. So, if it causes some controversy I say, "Suck It Up!" My pledge to let truth matter remains strong every day.

Now that we've taken care of the formalities, let me focus my attention on why we're all here — YOU. This book is dedicated to all of you. May its contents assist you in becoming better car owners while navigating life with greater knowledge and ease. When something resonates with you personally, share it with someone else who could gain from its knowledge. Its reach increases exponentially when shared. Let's join forces and experience all the joys and triumphs together. After all, it's not about reaching our destination, but about the experience itself. Stay buckled up. Our road ahead promises both knowledge and laughter. Let's travel it together as we cherish memories and welcome new experiences as enthusiastic car owners.

FOREWORD

From 1965 to 1970, Flagstaff, Arizona was a quintessential, small college town; a little open-minded here, a little parochial there. Flagstaff also enjoyed the distinction of being the largest population center in Arizona situated along Interstate 40, which loosely follows the path of old Route 66. The town still enjoys this distinction. One of the most important aspects of the Flagstaff business community is services to the highway travelers. My best friend at the time worked for one of those service stations in the eastern part of town, just off the interstate. He told me this story, which he claimed to have witnessed firsthand.

A lady traveling with two young children pulled into the service station on a summer afternoon and told another employee that she detected a burning smell she thought may be coming from under her hood. The young man helping her stared under the hood, pulled a small wrench from his pocket, freed the battery from its wires and brackets, and pulled the battery away from its moorings. He then ran some twenty feet away and tossed the battery about eight feet in the air. When it landed on the asphalt drive, the case fractured, and a foaming, smoking liquid erupted from the broken shell. High drama. He returned to the car and, addressing the woman with the most serious countenance he could muster, he announced that, while he didn't like to brag, he had probably just saved her life.

The result, of course, was the sale of a new premium battery to a customer who probably did not need it. The worst part, one could only imagine, must have been the warm feelings of gratitude the customer felt as she pulled back onto I-40. That young man's heroic behavior had rescued her from the jaws of a disaster. She may have lived her entire life unaware of his duplicity. It was simply criminal.

During this same time frame, 1967 to be precise, Shahe Koulloukian was born in Beirut, Lebanon. He was one of the multitudes of

Armenians born in the city that used to be known as the Paris of the Middle East. Why were so many Armenians born far from their original homeland? The simple answer is the Ottoman Turks. In April of 1915, the Ottoman Turks fancied themselves fez wearing Nazis. This occurred ten years before being a Nazi was even fashionable. In fact, the word Nazi did not exist then, but the Turks didn't care. They were trend setters. And like all good Nazis, they dehumanized a successful minority who lived among them and blamed them for all their problems. The result was the Armenian genocide, where over a million people were driven from their homes and murdered. Many, however, escaped and they scattered to the four winds. Wherever this proud group of people landed, they rebuilt their lives and became successful. It's hard to find a silver lining in the tragic cloud of genocide, but I can think of one serendipitous result: America got Shahe.

This photo of Khor Virap Monastery, built in 642, with Mount Ararat as a backdrop, is both personally and culturally meaningful. It symbolizes Armenian perseverance and resilience.

Shahe Koulloukian comes as close to the definition of Renaissance Man as any person I have ever known. This is no small compliment. The credentials are impressive. He speaks several languages including

Turkish, which is wonderful irony. He is a Cordon Bleu trained chef, an actor, and a stand-up comedian (have you ever noticed how many comedians come from the ranks of persecuted peoples?) As if that weren't enough, Shahe is also a successful entrepreneur. He owns and operates a catering business, a food truck, and an auto repair business. His knowledge of all things automotive is more than impressive. (Most of his success he owes to his wife, Lena. She paid me to say this, but it's still true.) Shahe is also an excellent teacher. He comes by this naturally with no formal training, but he is a teacher because he knows his subject and has excellent communication skills. He has held classes in automotive maintenance for interested clients, their spouses, and their kids.

Shahe has heard the stories of hapless motorists like the one shared with you here. He's heard it, and seen it, probably thousands of times. So, he wrote this book to help the people who depend on cars nearly every day of the week, but don't know much about them. In other words, most of us. He has actually helped thousands of people like the woman with the battery.

This man's approach is unique and layman friendly. He does not leave the readers scratching their heads with mountains of technical data or running for the dictionary. Some writers seem to take great pleasure in using big words and complicated forms, as if to say, "Look how smart I am." Shahe does not do that. He demonstrates his considerable intelligence by explaining complicated processes in simple terms, like, "Don't drive even another thousand feet if your oil light comes on. If you do, you will be sitting in a four-thousand-pound paperweight." Paperweights can be had for considerably less money than a Honda Accord. I was reminded about simplicity when I heard Linus Pauling speak at my college. Linus Pauling won a Nobel Prize in chemistry, but never mind. His talent with his students lay in his ability to express the beautiful symmetry of chemistry and biology in terms that even a clueless undergraduate like myself could appreciate. I came to understand this fact: When you really understand something, you can teach it. Albert Einstein famously quipped, "If you can't teach it, you don't understand it well enough." Shahe can teach it.

This book presents an easy to embrace philosophy of car ownership. Yes, I said, "philosophy." The reader is reminded that they do not "love" their car. They depend on it. All the sexiness of leather seats, sound systems where the bass gives the driver a back massage, or a high-performance engine, fade into the ethers of everyday concerns. There are tips on driving in the rain, avoiding auto theft, and the omnipresent auto insurance decisions. The list is long and valuable.

There are legions of drivers who will benefit from this book. Enjoy it. Absorb it. Laugh with it. And remember, a "throw-out bearing" is not a piece of metal a technician tosses in the trash.

James Ware
Professor of Biology
The University of Arizona and
Gateway Community College

PREFACE

It seems my future in automobile craftmanship was stitched in destiny at a very young age. I learned the importance of high-quality work and attention to detail from my father, a fourth-generation cobbler who began designing and handcrafting custom leather shoes in Lebanon. He also ignited my entrepreneurial spirit as he later fabricated shoes in his various factories located across three continents.

My great-uncle (my grandfather's brother) was also an accomplished craftsman of leather whose talents caught the attention of Ferrari. The prestigious company hired him to hand stitch the steering wheels for all cars sold in California.

I was inspired by this attention to detail and learned to emulate my great-uncle's dedication to quality work. Meanwhile, my beloved mother developed expertise in sewing car covers, shifter-knob shields and bras exclusively for Jensen-Healey and Austin-Healey cars. Just picturing my petite mother devoting her expertise to these iconic British car brands still evokes profound admiration in me.

Therefore, my family instilled in me an ethical responsibility to provide quality work. It is a driving force propelling me every day.

I've always been a bit of a mixed breed when it comes to all the facets of life that I happen to be involved in. From traveling the world, to stand-up comedy, to acting in feature films, to being a professional chef, to being happily married for three decades, to having two amazing sons, to having a supportive family, to maintaining a valued circle of friends, to owning and operating my own food truck, to owning and operating my auto repair shop... Okay. Okay, that's quite a mouthful. (It's true, so I'm not bragging! 😊)

Apparently, that wasn't enough. I had to push it a little more by authoring my first book, *Car Confidential*. I've been working on this book for over three years because I believe it's important to share these facts. It's all about grit gained from what I've seen and experienced in the automotive industry since I was 13 years old.

This book isn't about teaching you how to work on your car or about giving you quick tips on how to make it go faster or look sexier. It's about empowering you to be a better car owner so that you not only grasp your ownership responsibilities but also overcome your worries. It's a book that every new car driver and old car owner should have. I don't claim to be the first to offer this information; instead, I'm thrilled to be providing you with knowledge I have gained over 40 years in the business.

I can't tell you how excited I am to be sharing this with you. I hope the book will help you become your own first line of defense to protect yourself. As a consumer advocate, I believe the truth must be heard, and I hope it will resonate as you read this book.

Shahe Koulloukian

INTRODUCTION

Car Confidential is an empowering tool to help you comprehend the relationship with your car, from the thrilling and emotional moment you bought it to the financial and sensible realization of your ownership commitment and obligations.

Understanding vehicles may be difficult, especially because each car owner views theirs as an extension of themselves. In some situations, we might notice that cars can shape the personality of their owners.

HOW TO READ THIS BOOK

The book is divided into three sections that address key aspects of car ownership. They are owning it, maintaining it and overall car safety. There may be some crossover between sections, but this book ultimately addresses the core topics you need to know to hit the roads safely and responsibly.

The ownership section covers the period during which you begin owning your car, and accepting the responsibilities related to that. This also includes determining how you are going to use the car and which features are important to you. It is critical to select a vehicle that fits your needs and budget as well as your lifestyle.

The maintenance section covers the responsibilities for tasks involved in keeping your vehicle in excellent running condition. This includes routine maintenance, like oil changes, tire rotations, and brake inspections. It also includes dealing with any repairs that are required due to wear and tear or damage. This is not a 'How-To' book; there are many technical books focused on specific aspects of maintenance. My goal here is to educate you on important aspects so you can understand them. You certainly don't have to become a mechanic, but knowing some terms and how repair shops work will help you build a better relationship with your mechanic and be better served.

The safety section covers your responsibilities, for both your own and other people's safety, while driving your car. This includes performing regular safety checks. It also entails embracing preventive measures such as following traffic laws, avoiding distractions, and driving defensively.

These three aspects of car ownership are interconnected and play an important role in the overall driving experience. They will help you maximize the enjoyment of your car while minimizing risks and costs associated with that privilege.

Car Confidential is not a book to be read from cover to cover in one sitting. Instead, it should serve as a resource that you can consult whenever you have questions about your car. It is the ideal companion for all car owners, especially new drivers.

Stories have always been powerful tools of education. They impart lessons, as the old sales quote states: "Facts tell, stories sell." To better convey information, while keeping it entertaining, each chapter is preceded by a story featuring the Smiths. They are a fictional family, representing the wide spectrum of clients and situations I have encountered, and real car ownership issues my clients have experienced. These stories allow me to weave lessons into each chapter. The gray page tales also serve to introduce topics covered in the following chapter with some insight into its topic area.

In addition to these stories, you'll discover **'Insider Files'** scattered throughout the book. These valuable gems from the industry could save you headaches, hassle and potentially lots of money. One such golden nugget helped one of my clients save an incredible $10,000 when I explained that the insurance should cover those major repairs. After reviewing the policy and discussing the issue with an agent, the repairs were eventually covered. (Ironically, this client was a famous lawyer who reviews contracts for a living! What's that saying about shoemakers?)

If you're crunched for time or just want to recap, each chapter ends with Key Takeaways. Think of them as your rearview 'review' mirror, highlighting important lessons you don't want to miss. It's your fast track to understanding the essentials.

It is my deepest desire to help you stay safe, knowledgeable, and happy with your automobile decisions. This book has been written to cater to busy car owners who may not have the time to read every detail in one sitting. The information has been structured in a concise manner, with boxes highlighting important details. This ensures that, even in a hurry, readers can easily pick up the information they need.

I am delighted to introduce you to *Car Confidential.* I hope that it is not only informative, but also motivating. It should remind you that your vehicle is a tool — nothing more.

Driving can bring a sense of freedom and independence, but let's face it — it can also feed vanity. Car owners want to be seen and recognized, but no one really pays attention. Vehicles play an important role in our everyday lives and are part of our personal identity. We can prioritize the upkeep, maintenance, and safety in a way that ensures they will continue to serve us well and contribute positively to our daily routine.

My goal is to keep you secure, informed, and content with decisions related to your vehicle. So, if you're ready to take control of your ownership experience, take a deep breath, clear your distractions and let's start the journey toward empowerment and responsibility.

ADDITIONAL MATERIALS
AND RESOURCES

Access Your Additional Materials and Resources
Referenced Throughout This Book at
https://carconfidential.net/ccbonus

Section 1

OWNERSHIP

"Being an engaged car owner means being an intelligent and strategic driver."
—Shahe Koulloukian

Meet the Smiths

*A*s an ardent Corn Huskers supporter, Christopher Smith never imagined himself spending much time with someone who didn't share the same passion for his team. Yet one day, as the sun sank over Nebraska's plains, he was drawn to Victoria, an Iowa native. Despite her affection for the Hawkeyes, something was born, and neither could have predicted that their bond would endure for 15 eventful years.

The Smiths had many passionate discussions about football over the years. They also had their share of conflicts about many things, including cars. Maintenance costs frequently served as tests for their relationship, but they never allowed minor difficulties to take over. Instead, they saw these challenges as bumps in the road and used them as opportunities to grow as a couple and as individuals. Even though Victoria may not share Christopher's passion for automobiles, their combined personalities make them excellent car owners.

As they traveled through exciting adventures, the Smiths learned that cars frequently lead to a transitory sense of significance. They often felt uninformed of their cars' genuine worth beyond its price tag, especially when the emotions linked with their acquisition faded. Fortunately, they remain strong and empowered by consistently advancing their knowledge.

Let the engines rev and the football rivalries flare as the Smiths begin their car ownership journey, showing us all that love, laughter and unity can make each ride more pleasant, pleasurable and, most importantly, safe.

Chapter 1

OWN YOUR CAR LIKE A BOSS

It's always a good idea to review the fundamental aspects of car ownership and driving. The first step is realizing that having a car is a lot of work, a lot of money, and a lot of responsibility. No matter how you got your hands on a car — a gift, a loan, or via hard work and saving — knowing the basics of its features is essential. A car is a significant long-term commitment, which you'll quickly come to appreciate. To preserve your asset, you need to nourish it with regular maintenance. Delayed maintenance could lead to serious problems and expensive repairs down the line. This is like maintaining a healthy body.

It's important to understand the relationship between the exciting and emotional moment when you purchased your vehicle and the financial and sensible moment when you began to understand ownership responsibility.

EMOTION VS. LOGIC

Occasionally assess your emotions about your vehicle and have a heart-to-heart with it. Sit down with that hunk of metal and define your relationship. You should be straightforward and explain that you depend on it.

If you own your vehicle and are content with the way it works, you have a level of peace that no high-end luxury vehicle could provide. That might sound like a strange statement but it's quite simple. When you're driving a luxury vehicle, you're only borrowing the credibility of that car. If you keep your vanity separate from the ownership of a car, you'll be amazed at how much calm flows into your space.

Allow yourself to let go of your emotional attachment to your car. This is an important distinction because it is a depreciating asset. Its sole purpose is transportation, nothing more. Keep in mind that the single most important reason many people enjoy cars is they provide an instant and unequaled sense of independence. This freedom allows us to take the keys, get in the driver's seat, and go wherever we want, whenever we want, without anything or anyone getting in the way. Keep in mind, the feelings of safety and dependability are more important than the vehicle itself.

Buying a vehicle can shape how others perceive you. Don't let that influence your decisions. Instead, strive to differentiate needs versus desires and select something that brings peace of mind. Think back to when you bought the vehicle; did you really understand what was purchased or did you just choose out of desperation or vanity?

BEYOND SHINY AND NEW

Consumers often fail to consider their age or life circumstances when shopping for a new car. Before making purchase decisions, ask yourself important questions, such as "Will this be my last car?" Consider where you stand in life regarding work, retirement, and other factors. For example, are you a snowbird spending winters in warmer climates? How much will you use that new car? Once you review your situation, you will better understand the requirements you have and the features which are important to you.

Embracing Car Ownership with Wisdom

This information is not intended to discourage you from purchasing or selling your vehicle, but rather to provide you with an understanding of what it means to be a car owner. No matter the condition of your car, there will come a day when you wonder whether it is time to sell. Before taking that step, pause and consider all available information. Several factors help identify the best time to sell a car, and they're not all related to getting the most money from a prospective buyer. Let's explore that journey.

UNVEILING YOUR CAR'S TRUE BIRTHDAY

Have you ever wondered when your car was born? You most likely know the year, that's a given, but you might want to dig deeper to find its actual birth date. Don't worry, you won't need a cake or candles. It's not like a pet that you want to find another opportunity to spoil on a specific date. (Although car whisperers have said that vehicles love to be pampered, so a wash or maintenance is always a good idea for a special occasion.)

It's important to understand the distinction between the birth date, when the vehicle was made, and the anniversary date, the moment when you signed the contract and began your relationship with it. The discrepancy might seem trivial, but it could be used against you in some situations.

The 'Birth Date' of a car is easy to find. There is a sticker on the door jamb indicating the exact production date of that vehicle. Most people might only have a general recollection of the anniversary date of when they originally purchased their car, which is referred to as the 'in-service' date.

This is important information as the date that typically determines the start of warranty coverage is the day when the vehicle was first sold and registered to a consumer. This is the norm used by most manufacturers to structure their warranties.

Unfortunately, some dealers or their employees might make their own interpretation or simply not follow or understand the proper rules for warranties. I have witnessed many instances where clients have been told that aspects of their warranties begin on the date written on the door sticker, the birth date. This might seem trivial at first, yet it can make a huge difference if the car was purchased months after it was manufactured.

When dealerships receive cars, some sit on their lots for a long period of time. Imagine if a vehicle spends nine or ten months before being sold. If the dealer follows the production date for warranty coverage, the client then loses almost a year of warranty. Unfortunately, this happens on a regular basis, and unsuspecting owners end up paying for repairs or parts that should have been covered.

Question everything if you feel you're not covered for something that you believe should be. Also don't always assume the worse or wrongdoing. Errors do happen, so it is best to inquire and discuss with the mindset that the misunderstanding is from a mistake rather than nefarious intentions.

Here are a few key points to consider when it comes to getting your vehicle covered under its new purchase warranty.

Misunderstanding or Miscommunication: Misinterpretations often arise at dealerships when an employee is either under-educated or incorrectly communicates information to customers. Consumers should always keep a copy of their warranty agreement so they can compare it with what they are told.

Deceptive Practices: Although rare, some dealerships might engage in fraudulent practices. Such bad actors could falsify the warranty to exclude certain repairs. If customers feel misled or coerced into making repair decisions without having the complete information, they should contact their automobile manufacturer or seek legal advice.

Specific Manufacturer Stipulations: Although warranties typically begin with the in-service date, special limitations or exclusions may apply depending on the manufacturer or guarantee type. Always read your paperwork thoroughly.

If a dealership states that their warranty is based on production date rather than in-service date, the consumer should:

Check Warranty Documentation: Warranty coverage information can be found in the owner's manual or in the original contract documents.

Contact the Manufacturer: They can offer guidance regarding the effective date and terms of a warranty agreement. Their consumer inquiry hotline could provide an authorization number for the dealership to do the repairs required if they are covered under warranty.

Seek Legal Advice: You should consider seeking legal guidance regarding the effective date and terms of a warranty agreement.

THE INTERSECTION BETWEEN NEEDS AND WANTS

When considering a new car to hit the open road, take a second to map the intersection between your wants and needs. I will shed some light on the murky waters that you might find yourself in while exploring car purchasing options. This is important as people often dream of vehicles; yet they might never get to truly use their capabilities or potential.

Imagine that turbo vehicle you're considering while driving in your gated community with 15 mph speed bumps at every corner. Perhaps you don't have such bumps on the road, yet your daily commute includes many streets with low-speed limits. Unfortunately, unless timing yourself on an open racing circuit where no speed restrictions exist, that overpriced turbo will never reach its full boost potential.

Have you found yourself wanting an eight-passenger 4x4, yet you might only use it with three people most of the time, perhaps five when bringing the neighbors' kids to soccer? Are you ever driving anywhere that requires using four-wheel drive? If you only need these features for a couple of occasions a year, they might be an expensive proposition as some of them could cost thousands of dollars.

It's common to see people dreaming of driving a convertible car, yet living in an extremely hot or cold climate state might restrict them to three or five months of open-top driving per year.

So, I pose this question to anyone considering a new vehicle, "Do you really want it, or do you really need it?"

KEY TAKEAWAYS

- **Practical Ownership Over Prestige:** Accept that the value of any vehicle lies with its reliability rather than with any status it confers. It should serve your life, not define it.

- **Understand the Date of Service:** Being aware of terms can protect you from unexpected repair expenses that should be covered under warranty agreements.

- **Vehicle Emotional Intelligence:** Be ready to differentiate emotional desires from practical needs to determine its true purpose. A wise purchase often occurs where necessity overrules desire.

- **The Cost of Extras:** Carefully consider any additional features or capabilities offered. Don't allow potential use to outweigh actual use. Overspending on superfluous features is more than an economic misstep.

INFORMATION IN MIRRORS IS MORE EMPOWERING THAN IT MAY APPEAR!

When Relationships Dwindle

*A*fter a busy day at work, Christopher stopped for a quick Costco run. He should have noticed that the car next to him had backed in; yet he was in a rush. In hindsight, it was predictable that its owner might push a cart in the tight space between the cars to put stuff in the trunk.

"Come on! Enough already. I don't care about this car anymore!" he yelled upon seeing the fresh three-inch scratch on the back passenger door. Clearly, he had no concept of his car's real worth to him.

It was yet another issue plaguing his beloved car. He had turned a blind eye to the mischievous door ding on the passenger side for a while, but this was now too much to take in.

After the follow-up outburst back home, Victoria intervened by reminding her husband about the monthly payments remaining on their loan agreement.

Thoughts of purchasing a brand new car occasionally seduced them but their savvy instincts usually kicked in quickly. This time Christopher needed a reality check and to show some gratitude for the wheels they already owned instead of longing for something different. Fortunately, they consulted their trusted repair shop owner and mechanic, Dennis, who guides them as they develop wise ownership expertise.

Following an enlightening conversation with Dennis, the Smiths learned the importance of being sensible with their vehicle's ownership responsibilities. Christopher also discovered that a simple fix could cover the damage, and this helped him to appreciate what he already possessed instead of feeling entitled to more. Truth be told, he was deeply attached to his car but had no idea that he held the key to unlocking its true value.

With their newly acquired understanding, the Smiths continued to proudly own their cars while making informed choices to ensure they will enjoy them for the long road ahead.

Chapter 2

THE JOURNEY OF SELLING AND BUYING YOUR CAR

Every automobile owner eventually must face the difficult decision of whether to part ways with their dependable four-wheel friend. Convincing potential buyers to purchase your used car may not be easy, so let's approach it with optimism and confidence. When selling your vehicle, consider why you wish to do so before diving too deeply into the process. Needs change over time so perhaps your car no longer fulfills those requirements.

To make an easy transition to something different requires understanding your needs. Consider the investments of time and money into your current vehicle. Once it becomes necessary to change, do so with full conviction.

Knowing the difference between emotional and rational decisions can help you avoid making unwise purchases. Are you prepared to head into the dealership after deciding on a vehicle that meets your needs? This should only happen after taking your financial situation into consideration.

🏁 PIT STOP LESSON 🏁

EXTENDED WARRANTY TIP

It's important to know that an extended warranty can be transferred or cancelled when a vehicle is sold. Additionally, some policies may offer prorated refunds within the first year if no claims have been submitted.

A confident approach is necessary at this point in the car-buying process. By sticking to your priorities and being an informed buyer, you will prove yourself to be a savvy shopper who knows exactly what you want. Let me help you walk through specific questions designed to give you mastery over car ownership.

 FUEL FOR THOUGHT

MESSY CONVERTIBLE HAIRDO

Although convertible ownership may bring you great joy, not everyone shares your enthusiasm. Since the convertible function only appeals to certain individuals, your pool of potential purchasers shrinks accordingly.

Remember that some people can't handle the wind noise when driving at high speeds.

This doesn't mean you shouldn't buy one. I'm simply suggesting that you consider every aspect before making that decision.

DID YOU KNOW?

Selling or buying used cars can be both thrilling and daunting — we all understand this. As an automotive industry veteran, I know the importance of providing car owners with the information necessary for making rational decisions when trading-in, selling or simply valuing used cars. Knowing the true worth of a vehicle gives confidence when negotiating successfully. Managing these transactions requires knowing strategies for negotiating with dealers or private buyers.

As we explore what it takes to negotiate the best bargain possible for your car, we'll present practical steps you can use to navigate the process. So, buckle up! It's time for smart choices that will leave you satisfied when selling, buying, or trading cars.

PARTING IS SUCH SWEET SORROW

Car-owning dilemmas are ever present. Perhaps you are beginning your car ownership journey and you're trying to figure out if you should consider a pre-owned vehicle. Consumers often lack the details associated with buying, selling, and keeping used cars. The common question is, if not now, when is the best time to sell? Here are a few key points to use in making these decisions.

Before You Need To

Though it might seem odd, the ideal time to sell your car is before it becomes urgent. That way you have time to make a decision that doesn't feel forced. Consider all options without being pressured into making a decision that could leave your vehicle broken down on the side of a highway.

If a major repair, financing issue, or life event forces you to sell your car suddenly, a time crunch may force you into selling doing so when market conditions aren't ideal. Selling or trading-in a non-running car may turn away potential buyers or produce bargain-basement offers from potential sellers.

When Everything Is Working

Optimally, selling a car should only occur when everything is running smoothly with no service lights on the dash. Imagine yourself as one of your prospective buyers: they would want to deduct from the purchase price any cost associated with repairs or maintenance that might be needed. That is if they even make an offer.

An owner's forum online can indicate when similar cars typically experience major failures. It would be wise to follow your intuition if something feels amiss or you've been dealing with repeated breakdowns of the vehicle you own. Selling it would likely be the wisest course.

When It's the Right Season

In general, spring and summer are the optimal times to sell a used car because most buyers and sellers are in the market. This gives you the highest chance of receiving top dollar. Winter holidays and colder parts of the year present another challenge to consumers' finances. Families are busy during this season and budgets tend to be stretched. Dealers promote new car sales aggressively for Black Friday in a push to reach their sales goals before year's end. Their lots are typically full of used cars, so they are unlikely to offer top dollar for your trade-in.

Also consider how well suited the type of car you're selling is at different times and in various locations. For example, selling a convertible in Arizona's hot summer heat would likely prove challenging, while selling an SUV may prove easier. One effective way of gauging market demand is online advertising. If there are numerous vehicles like yours on the local market, perhaps waiting before selling may be wise. Having limited competition may increase your odds of receiving higher offers.

When Your Needs Change

There can be any number of reasons that why a car doesn't might no longer meet your needs. Selling your vehicle and selecting one more suited to your lifestyle would be another good reason for selling it. Many life events can compel owners to switch cars. Starting a family or becoming an empty nester are just two examples. Luckily, such life changes often give enough lead time to make the decision to sell. This enables you to determine when market demand will be highest for a sale.

Maintaining an automobile that doesn't work for you comes at a high price. Even though the mileage might not vary much, upkeep, insurance and parking must still be paid and any depreciation in value must still be factored into monthly costs.

Before You Default on Your Auto Loan

If you are on the verge of defaulting on a car loan and having your car repossessed, it is almost always better to sell the vehicle and pay off as much of the loan as you can. That's true even if you owe more than your car is worth.

If the value of your car exceeds its loan balance, you could use that extra money toward another car. If, however, its balance exceeds its value, you still owe the bank any outstanding balance. To reduce the difference and keep more cash in your pocket, you could sell the car privately instead of trading it in or letting the bank take it back.

If you default on a loan and your lender repossess your car, they are likely to sell it at auction and apply the proceeds toward paying your balance. Unfortunately, auctions typically don't yield as much money as private-party sales would. This is because fees taken by auction companies and repossession agencies will add directly to your balance.

Before You Hit "Mileage Milestones"

Remember, each vehicle is marked by important milestones which usually align with the expiry of key warranties. Basic and powertrain warranties often have different time frames. The end of their coverage represents important milestones, such as 36,000, 50,000, or 100,000 miles as well as year milestones of 3, 8, or 10 years.

Vehicles under warranty also have mileage markers as they might require important scheduled maintenance to keep their coverage and some of those could represent significant expenses.

When approaching significant milestones, a vehicle's market value can drop substantially as car shoppers know that repairs may then cost cash out-of-pocket. By understanding these time frames, you can get the best value for your vehicle.

It is wise to research the top mechanical issues for your vehicle and their average timeline. If it is common to see timing belts fail at 70,000 miles, you won't get the best price for a vehicle nearing this milestone unless maintenance records show that it's been changed. Imagine yourself as the buyer. Would you spend top dollar on a car knowing that it may experience major mechanical failure soon after transferring ownership?

To gauge the significant milestones and evaluate the resale value of your vehicle, consult the resource section at the end of the book for a list of useful websites.

Before It Gets Another Year Older

Mileage isn't the only factor reducing a vehicle's value. New model years can also cause this as consumers value cars that are one or two years newer. Remembering that car model years don't correspond directly with calendar years; it is better to sell before another automobile birthday rolls around. To maximize sales before this occurs, have it on the market by the end of summer at latest.

When You No Longer Feel Safe

If your mechanic advises that your old vehicle is no longer safe to drive, that would be an opportune time to consider change changing it. New vehicles offer significantly greater protection in collisions compared to their counterparts from years past. Many will include new passive features like electronic stability control, airbags, and antilock brakes. Modern cars also often provide advanced driver assistance and safety technologies designed to prevent or minimize accidents.

If you live in a four-season state with frequent snow and icefall, or require being at work regardless of weather, changing from your old car to an all-wheel-drive crossover could be a safer option.

When You Have Positive Equity

An effective strategy is to sell the vehicle when the value surpasses your debt obligation. The positive equity will provide funds that can go toward purchasing your next vehicle. Even if it takes several more payments before reaching positive equity territory, the delay will likely pay off in the long run.

No doubt we've all seen ads offering to pay off existing loans when trading your current car in for a new one. That amount may roll into your new loan and put you underwater. This approach to car purchasing should never be considered.

Make sure to consider market conditions, the state of your used car and any life changes that would make selling it an advantageous, or inadvisable, choice.

LOVE AT FIRST SIGHT

Every car owner, at some point, faces the question, "When should I change my ride?" Car enthusiasts will often succumb to the lure of purchasing an entirely new car as new models offer fresh designs, cutting-edge features and other enhancements. This is why it is easy to become distracted from remembering what comes with car ownership.

The following tips will help you reconnect with the core aspects of car ownership.

Audit Your Needs

Start by considering your purpose when purchasing a vehicle, prioritizing functionality as the main goal. Although flashy features such as sunroofs, racks on roofs, step sides, 4x4, eight-passenger seating all may look appealing, they do nothing if driving alone and only taking occasional off-road excursions. Renting could save money and make more sense than purchasing something specially tailored to such trips — which is why functionality and needs must come first.

Understand What You're Buying

When you understand your needs, have gone through your audit process, and decided on a vehicle, make sure to research its estimated resale value. If the model you're considering doesn't have strong resale demand, that could indicate a poor choice.

Do the Math

Once you get past all your emotional impulses and desires, buying a vehicle becomes simple. Contact your insurance company and inquire about how much automobile coverage would cost if you purchased specific makes, models, or years. Remember to consider the extra fees, such as tax, title, license, and document fees. These could go as high as $3,000 depending on rates in your state. Therefore, you might want to look at cars between $7,000–8,000 if you have a $10,000 budget.

Do Your Part

If you're about to purchase a vehicle, you need to follow a few 'smart' steps.

Step 1: Go look at the vehicle and take it for a good test drive, not just around the block. Drive on the highway at speeds of 60–70 mph and listen to recognize anything unsettling. (This is not the time to blast the stereo.)

Step 2: Get a CarFax evaluation. If you're buying from a dealership, they will provide one for free if you ask. Otherwise, they are inexpensive, and you can prepay three or five CarFax reports at a discounted rate.

Step 3: Make sure to have your trusted auto repair shop perform a full buyer's inspection of the vehicle before you buy it. An expensive on-board-diagnostic reader (OBD) might seem like a good option, but it will only tell you if the vehicle has a current error code. A buyer's inspection will go through the vehicle from bumper-to-bumper and advise you of anything that should be done now or soon. From brakes and tires to body damage, you will know it all before you buy it. The cost will usually be under $100, so it is money well spent.

THE TCO FORMULA

How Do I Know My True Cost of Ownership?

Standard repair and maintenance costs for Asian and American vehicles typically fall within an estimated annual repair range of $800–$1,100. This represents a monthly budget between $66–$91. For European cars, that range would be between $1,800 to $3,200 per year, or $150 to $266 per month.

The Total Cost of Ownership formula (TCO) provides an easy way to determine the real cost associated with owning your car. Simply add all maintenance and repair receipts for the last three years and divide the total by 36. This represents your monthly average.

Take into consideration that a typical new car payment, without insurance, is usually over $500. (This amount will obviously vary based on your down payment, loan terms, and credit score.) If your monthly TCO average falls between $100 and $200, that puts you far ahead and you should ask yourself, honestly, "Do I really require another car?"

🏁 PIT STOP LESSON 🏁

A YEARLY MISSION

Act like an IRS agent at least once every year. Start by acknowledging that the monthly average for car payments, before insurance, exceeds $500. Follow the TCO formula to assess your own situation.

DON'T LET EMOTIONS BUY YOUR NEXT CAR

Buckle up, dear friends! As we embark upon this exciting car shopping journey, emotions may take the wheel. That said, don't panic; I will help guide you through this rollercoaster of emotions to ensure that you make an informed decision.

Now, you might be thinking, "Wait, are you throwing another one of those fancy esoteric concepts at me?" No. This is all too real. Managing emotions when making car purchases can be like mastering yoga poses. Practice and discipline are needed. Don't believe me? OK, try answering these questions:

- How much does your current or the newer vehicle you want weigh?
- What type and grade of oil does the engine use?
- What type and size of tires does it require?
- Does it have a spare tire?
- What type of warranty comes with the car?

When I ask my clients, "Why did you purchase this car?" I am usually met with answers such as, "Oh man, it's such a sexy color and it has leather. Plus, I heard that it won several awards." Although it might be hard to admit for some people, the reality is that they often buy because they like the color, the look and style, features, or popularity.

Hold on tight to that steering wheel of decision-making and regain control over your emotions to select a car that truly meets both your needs and budget. Now is your time to show them who's the boss.

QUESTIONS YOU SHOULD ASK BEFORE BUYING

People often make snap judgments based solely on superficial criteria, such as "I love the look and color!" or "I can't stop talking about it." When buying cars, it can be easy to make hasty decisions solely based on emotion. That can often lead us down an expensive path if unexpected repairs and maintenance needs surface. It is important to take some time to answer the following questions.

What Does the Car Weigh?

Weight has a lot to do with fuel consumption. Sure, you want the big 4x4 SUV, but are you ready to fuel up two or three times a week?

What Type of Tire Does It Need?

Your first thought may be: who cares? After all, this has no bearing on buying a brand-new car. Well, you may be amazed to learn that most new vehicles come standard with moderately priced tires that cost between $100 and $300 each, while some vehicles could require tires that easily triple those amounts.

Unfortunately, you do not always have a choice when it comes to selecting the type of tires to use on your car. It might not be possible to downgrade due to engineering specifications and safety precautions.

At some point in time, new tires will become necessary. It's important to know the replacement costs and budget for them.

Does It Have a Spare Tire?

Nearly a third of new vehicles no longer come with a spare tire as standard equipment. This is one trick that automakers use to reduce the weight (and cost) of cars under the pretext of improving fuel economy. But what happens if you're on the side of the road with a flat tire? Unless you have the run-flat tire mentioned above, you better have roadside assistance or towing coverage through your insurance.

🏁 PIT STOP LESSON 🏁

RUN-FLAT SPARES

Many high-end cars now come equipped with run-flat tires. They act as spare tires and make driving safer by allowing drivers to reach a repair facility.

What's the Engine Size?

What are you searching for? Is it power, torque, or fuel economy? Take a close look at the numbers. Larger engines typically mean more power and a rush of adrenaline as you speed along highways. Yet do not underestimate the power of smaller engines, especially when coupled with newer technologies and fuel injection.

Larger engines come with special considerations as they could increase both your fuel consumption and ownership costs significantly. As you start shopping for a car, engine size should be of primary consideration. Knowing your true needs will help you avoid overspending on non-essentials.

What Safety Features Does It Have?

This is a topic that is not frequently discussed at the time of negotiating the price of the car you're interested in. Unfortunately, it usually comes up after someone is hurt during a collision. Do you know if the vehicle you're about to buy has the following features?

- Anti-Lock Braking System (ABS)
- Curtain Airbags
- Electronic Stability Control
- Driver Attention Detection
- Active Braking Systems
- Intelligent Speed Assist (ISA)
- Active Cruise Control
- Thorax Airbags with Head Protection.

While none of these features is necessary, some might be nice to have. Consider them when comparing vehicle makes or years. The same model might include different safety options in a later year.

What Is the Factory Warranty and What Does It Cover?

Here is something they don't want you to know: the standard 3-year/36,000 miles bumper-to-bumper warranty is just the tip of the iceberg. It means that almost everything between bumpers is fully covered, except for routine oil changes, scheduled maintenance and anything that is considered wear, like tires, belts, hoses, brakes, and filters. Sure, an extended warranty may be offered during negotiations but hold tight because there's more going on behind the scenes. You may not need it as all vehicles come with powertrain/drivetrain warranties that provide extensive coverage on top of the standard manufacturer's warranty. In the negotiation process, the salesperson won't remind you about the coverage already included, and you won't know to ask.

While the factory warranties have their own set of constraints, powertrain warranties provide greater coverage. They safeguard the engine, transmission, and drivetrain. Furthermore, some manufacturers offer extensive powertrain coverage up to 10 years or 100,000 miles. That's real peace of mind.

Do You Really Need an Extended Warranty?

Your driving habits will determine how important extended coverage will be. Sometimes it is vital while in other instances it might simply be a waste of money. Speak with the salesperson regarding each detail of the extended coverage and conduct an in-depth examination to determine its relevance for your situation. If you drive under 10,000 miles a year, skip it. If you have a family with kids and pets, you may use the vehicle to its full potential until the wheels fall off. You should then consider the extended warranty, as the vehicle will likely have breakdowns at some point.

It's important to know that extended warranties can also be purchased through third-party entities like credit unions, AAA, and Costco. These alternatives are worth considering as they might provide more flexibility and ensure that your investment remains protected.

Furthermore, an extended warranty doesn't need to be immediately purchased with the vehicle; rather it can be set up at any time while the original factory warranty is still active. This provides you with extra time to decide, without any pressure, how your vehicle should be protected.

What's the Resale Value?

You might think the best part of buying a car is the thrill of the drive, the purr of the engine, or the gleam of that fresh-off-the-lot paint job. And hey, that's all well and good. But please pay attention, because I'm about to drop a gearhead gospel that your average home-economics professor or late-night infomercial guru isn't going to tell you.

The second you buy a car, you ought to give some thought about selling it. That's right. You see, not all cars are created equal, and I'm not just talking about horsepower and cup holders, but about resale value — the real MVP of car ownership.

Your car's resale value is your silent partner, always there, whispering sweet financial forecasts into your ear. So, let me give you a piece of sage advice that I've emphasized ad-nauseum over the years. Get into the mindset of a seller before you become a buyer. Do your homework. Find out which brands are the blue-chip stocks of the car world and which ones are the risky day trades. Know what you're getting into. If you don't, trust me, you might find out the hard way what 'upside down' really means.

 PIT STOP LESSON

DEPRECIATION QUICK-START

Your new car's value drops immediately after leaving the dealership lot. On average, vehicles lose at least 10% of their value on the first day.

FROM DREAM CAR TO RESALE NIGHTMARE

Vehicles lose value the minute you drive off from the dealership. One of my clients had the most brutal experience of this harsh reality when he decided to buy his wife a Mercedes as an anniversary present.

When he asked my opinion before buying the vehicle, I explained that they are great cars, but the model he was considering, selling for $105,000, didn't have a great resale value. His intent for purchasing it was genuine and sincere, so he seemed disappointed to hear my advice. He said, "She just LOVES this make and model!" and added something along the lines that she was likely to keep it forever and won't consider selling it anytime soon.

Fast-forward 11 days. My client called with bad news. He declared, "You advised against purchasing this car… now can you please tell me about the best way for me to sell it." I was stunned. "Wow! Are you kidding me?" I asked. Sadly, he wasn't.

He explained that after driving her 'dream car' for three days, his wife was not satisfied with its handling and the restricted visibility made it hard to park. I suggested that he contact the dealer where he purchased it — a week and a half earlier — and request to trade it in for another model. This time he should have his wife take it out for a test drive before closing the deal. He agreed he'd do that.

When he called me back 18 hours later, he told me, "I think I'm in the Twilight Zone. Do you know what they offered as a trade-in value for my new vehicle?" I was on the edge of my seat. "Please tell me," I exclaimed. He paused before he belted out, "They offered $78,000!"

A drop of $37,000 in eleven days. Need I say more?

 FUEL FOR THOUGHT

INSURED VALUE VS. MARKET VALUE

In the event of an incident where a vehicle is considered a total loss, an insurance company might offer an amount much lower than market value.

This is important to verify before purchasing. Would you be fine with a payout of only 35 to 40 cents on the dollar? Imagine if you still owed more than that.

- **Sell on Your Terms, Not Under Pressure:** Avoid selling your car under duress in order to receive the best value.

- **Condition and Timing Matter:** For optimal pricing, sell when your vehicle is flawless and demand for it is high. This is typically in spring or summer which is when buyer activity peaks.

- **Life Stages and Market Wisdom:** Select a vehicle with robust resale potential in your location. Look beyond the features. Prioritize practicality and your projected needs.

INFORMATION IN MIRRORS IS MORE EMPOWERING THAN IT MAY APPEAR!

Cracking the Negotiating Code

On a sunny Saturday afternoon, Victoria returned home from brunch with her girlfriend who had excitedly shared the news about her new car purchase. Victoria wasn't really the jealous type, yet she couldn't help but wonder, "Why can't I do that?" After all, her car was starting to get old, and some unexpected repairs had recently put a little damper on their vacation fund.

She felt pressured, an unspoken peer pressure. Yet, deep down, she knew that a brand-new vehicle would likely be out of their budget as she handles the family's finances.

When Christopher came home from work later that afternoon, Victoria immediately ran up to hug and kiss him before saying, "I had such an amazing lunch with my friend today." He knew too well that there was more to the story, so he tentatively asked his wife what made their lunch so delightful. A long discussion followed, when and Victoria, while looking in his eyes, proclaimed, "You deserve a new car, honey." Christopher couldn't help smiling, but their budget was now at risk.

A few days later, the Smiths began shopping for a new car. They had yet to master the art of controlling their emotions and distinguishing needs from wants. Unfortunately, they also lacked an understanding of the rules, tactics and games involved in a car purchase.

Christopher has never been afraid to stand his ground when demanding a better deal and Victoria knows exactly how to put pressure on salesmen who try and charm their way into making a sale. The challenge for them, like most car shoppers, lies in understanding the procedures and games associated with purchasing, trading, or selling a car. Dennis had warned them that falling into 'wanting mode' could mean buying a car they don't really need.

Chapter 3

NEGOTIATING LIKE A WOLF

Welcome to the tricky world of vehicle negotiation. While it may be tempting to jump at the first offer you get, take your time, and thoroughly consider all aspects such as trade-in values for the old vehicle, financing options available, interest rates, plus the cash you have on hand available to spend. Let's get down to business... when it comes to automobile shopping, ask yourself the essential question: What type of vehicle buyer are you?

There are three distinct types of car buyers: those who prioritize the maximum monthly payments; those who are petrified about loan interest and those who care more about the final price of the vehicle. Each approach offers its own set of benefits and drawbacks which should be carefully evaluated before proceeding.

First, you should consider the trade-in value of your current car. How much is it worth in today's market? If there is no vehicle to trade in and you're ready to buy directly, feel free to skip over this step and dive straight into negotiating tactics. I want to help you avoid becoming overwhelmed as we navigate the murky waters of purchasing a vehicle. Knowledge, wit, and an open mind will serve you well during this process.

WHAT IS YOUR USED CAR WORTH?

Knowing the value of your car is important for several reasons. First, it helps set very realistic expectations when dealing with potential buyers. It also provides confidence to negotiate a satisfactory price and avoid settling on a lower offer. More importantly, being aware of its worth enables you to make informed decisions when selling privately or trading it in at a dealership. Here are a few pointers to remember to make sure no one takes advantage of you with an unfairly low offer:

Use Online Valuation Tools

Reputable websites, like Kelly Blue Book (KBB) and Edmunds, provide generic valuation services. They provide estimates based on vehicle make, model year, mileage, and condition. Their findings should always be treated as useful references rather than absolute values.

Research the Market

Conduct extensive market research to identify the range of prices being asked for similar vehicles. It will help you get an understanding of where you stand in terms of value. Use online platforms such as CarFax, Kijiji, and classified ads to collect information on similar makes and models for comparable years, mileage, and conditions.

Consider Local Market Factors

Evaluate local market factors, including location, climate, supply-and-demand dynamics, and regional preferences. Geographical location and climate may have an effect. For example, selling a convertible during winter months could be especially challenging. Keeping such aspects in mind will give a more accurate valuation.

Assess Your Car's Current Condition

Your vehicle's condition plays a pivotal role in its value. Conduct an honest and critical evaluation from top to bottom — including mechanical components like the engine, transmission, brakes, suspension and any recent repairs or maintenance performed. Take special note of cosmetic flaws like faded paint or peeling clear coat which might lower its worth.

Consider Mileage and Age

Mileage and age both play an integral part in valuing used vehicles; higher mileage usually corresponds to wear-and-tear that reduces its worth. Older cars depreciate faster over time than newer models, although certain classic vehicles might hold better value.

Assess Market Demand and Trends

Market demand and trends play a vital role in establishing the value of your used car, including factors like its popularity, fuel efficiency, safety features and any unique characteristics it might have. A great place to begin assessing this is through consumer websites which can provide insight about resale values. Be mindful of changing consumer preferences or technological advances which could alter values for specific models.

Ask a Professional

If you feel uncertain about appraising the value of the car on your own, professional assistance might be required. Certified appraisers or trusted automotive professionals may offer expert opinions and conduct comprehensive inspections that help pinpoint the worth of a vehicle. Their industry experience provides you with peace of mind in making important decisions.

Embrace the Do-Over

Life may throw you a curveball when selling used vehicles. Expected returns don't always match expectations. Instead of saying farewell to a beloved vehicle, why not consider keeping it as an emergency backup ride? Or pass it along as a first car for a friend or family member.

Selling and purchasing cars may feel like daunting tasks, but don't panic. Careful planning and research can make this a satisfying experience. Make sure to trust your instincts while making informed decisions to enjoy successful car transactions.

PERFECTION PURSUIT OR PREOWNED PURCHASE?

Are you wondering: *Will buying a used car be a wise choice?* Now is the time to put urban legends to bed, discover hidden gems, and determine whether that gently worn beauty could be the key to automotive pleasure. Be ready for all possibilities when shopping for your next vehicle. We will cover everything there is to know about selecting between new and pre-owned automobiles, such as the dos and don'ts as well as the pros or cons of each option.

Imagine this: There's a three-year-old Toyota Tacoma available with just over 60,000 miles on it which can be yours for $25,000. But consider that for just $33,000 you could purchase a new model. An $8,000 difference may seem major at first glance, but once you consider every aspect, the difference becomes clear. The new model comes with a full bumper-to-bumper warranty (three years or 36,000 miles) and an extended powertrain warranty (five years or 60,000 miles). That is a better value and more peace of mind, especially when you consider this is usually financed over three years or longer.

INSIDER FILES

YEAR-END LIABILITIES MEAN BARGAINS

When looking for a new vehicle, the last two weeks of December are an ideal time to shop.

Car dealerships operate under consignment from manufacturers. When the new year starts, any unsold vehicles become liabilities. Dealers are motivated to move cars then to avoid penalties that apply each day they remain unsold in the new year. This could mean great deals if you want to buy something around Christmas time.

Down Payment

So, how much down payment is required for a used car, if any? You are required to pay for tax, title, and registration. Any amount put down beyond that is pure profit for the dealer. You may qualify for no money down toward the principal if your credit score is above 700. If your interest rate and credit score are satisfactory and you're unable to afford the cash purchase of the car, consider placing a significant down payment toward your purchase price. This will save both time and money by financing only what remains.

If you're considering leasing a vehicle, take care when placing a deposit. Don't commit more than the first and final month's payments plus any associated costs of starting the lease agreement.

NEGOTIATING TACTICS

Negotiation has been practiced since traders bought and sold cinnamon and spices in ancient Egypt. This is a skill that can be learned, practiced, and improved. Keep a straight face, don't get flustered and don't let car salespeople intimidate you into signing any deal before giving it due consideration. Your 'Pawn Stars' knowledge will come in handy for this.

Let's dive into the exciting field of car sales closing strategies I unveil some secrets of persuasion. This will help you identify steps of negotiation which could be used. These tactics might involve offering you free cappuccinos or complimenting your watch, clothing, or trade-in, as distraction tactics to get you to sign the dotted line without thinking it through. Some of the most effective sales techniques I have witnessed over four decades in auto service and retail sales include the 'Columbo Close,' 'Breaking it Down to Ridiculous Close,' and 'Take Away Close.'

The Columbo Close

Inspired by TV detective Columbo, this closing technique involves the salesperson appearing less knowledgeable or uncertain of an offer. While searching for clarification, they create an atmosphere of trust with their buyer. This approach encourages open dialogue which allows them to identify any objections and address them swiftly.

Example: At first glance, a salesperson may offer to get assistance from their manager about a way to make these numbers work. When approaching the door to leave their office, they pause and ask ridiculous questions like, "You definitely didn't like the red one we looked at, right?"

They might add, "Well, if that was a possibility, I may be able to get you a better price on that unit. But no worries; just give me some time. Let me see what I can do." Now the salesperson has created confusion in the client's price objection and buyers start wondering whether this is really what they should be negotiating.

Breaking It Down to the Ridiculous Close

With this tactic, salespeople break down total costs or monthly payments into smaller, more manageable figures. Comparing costs with everyday items, such as coffee, makes the vehicle's price appear more reasonable. This approach plays on their perception of value as well as priorities.

Example: Salesperson will say, "I know you wanted to be at $350 a month and I'm at $425. We are so close; only off by $75. I see that you're a smoker. Without sounding personal, can I ask how many packs you smoke each day? I only ask because a pack is about $8 and if you say you smoke two a day, that's 5,840 dollars a year. That's basically $486 a month. We only need $75, so if you cut half a pack a day, you can drive this sexy car that you and your wife love so much. Plus, smoking less is better for your health, don't you think?"

The Assumptive Close

With this technique, salespeople confidently assume their buyer has already decided to purchase the car they have in their sights. They use phrases such as "When would you like to pick up your new vehicle?" or, "Which color do you want?" They will guide buyers toward concluding their transaction while reinforcing their decision to do so.

Example: Salesperson says: "I can just see you driving to your cabin with the top down. Man with that wind blowing in your face at 65 mph and the radio blasting... Remind me to show you how to program Spotify® or your favorite streaming platform for your playlists. We'll also connect your phone, so you have easy access to your contacts. Did I tell you that the trunk space is 65 inches wide? We'll load your golf clubs in the back before you leave to make sure they will fit. I'm stoked for you man. Congrats, you deserve it."

Empathy Closing Strategies

Empathy can be used as a powerful persuasion tactic by tapping into the emotions and desires of buyers by actively listening and understanding their needs. Salespeople show empathy using phrases like, "I completely understand how important safety is for you and your family." They establish an emotional bond by empathizing, which increases their odds of closing sales faster.

Example: Salesperson says, "I've been thinking about your lower back issues. That's gotta be tough to deal with. The great thing about this car is that it has three stages of lumbar support, not to mention heated seats. I read an article that explained that heated seats help relax muscles and speed up healing. This will be perfect for you."

The Takeaway Close

This tactic requires a bit of acting from the salesperson and it is performed at a key moment to shift the negotiation into a swift close. After several high-fives, a few jokes, and cups of coffee, the buyer begins to seriously consider a specific car. Suddenly the salesperson reveals, to their biggest surprise, that due to high demand or interest, they may not be able to hold on to this car if they don't move quickly. They may even suggest starting to look at another unit that may better fit the buyer's budget. Some will turn the knife in with a splash of sarcasm, suggesting that this opportunity could slip through their fingers quickly or it wasn't meant to be.

Example: Salesperson says, "I know this is going to sound odd, but I'm looking at my computer and this unit may not be available anymore. Looks like someone may have already put dibs on it but it's not clear if they left a deposit or not. I'm not sure if we can sneak it away from them now, but I hope. I'm crossing my fingers… let me double-check. But don't worry, we can walk the lot to find another unit; we have lots in our inventory. I'm not sure about the color, but we'll find something else that will work." Boom, Hook, Line and Sinker!

Before concluding our exploration into car sales closing tactics, it's essential to recognize that these techniques can be highly effective and inconspicuous. Ethical considerations are not always top of mind for everyone when conducting sales transactions. When you recognize these strategies, it's best to take the high ground and politely walk away.

NEGATIVE EQUITY ARITHMETIC

Before setting foot in a showroom, be certain to know how much you owe on the vehicle you intend to trade in, without this information, you can become lost in a maze of complicated calculations. Dealers will often appear generous by offering the fair market value for your trade-in, but they will add the balance of the loan to the price of the new vehicle you are considering purchasing.

This impromptu arithmetic test may make most people feel like they're trying to find their way through a labyrinth while blindfolded. A friendly explanation kicks off the process, and then the price balloon is inflating. They lure you into a web of games and trap you there.

But what happens if you owe more on the vehicle you want to exchange than what it's worth? This, my friends, is known as being 'Upside Down' or 'Underwater.' As an example, imagine finding out that the car you want to trade in is worth $15,000, yet you still owe $20,000 on it. You're then upside down or underwater by $5,000.

If possible, pay off the loan before exchanging a vehicle. Otherwise, be ready to play a debt rollover game where the dealer will magically work that $5,000 in the pricing of the new car. This will ultimately become an expensive proposition. Interest on the higher-priced vehicle financed over a longer term is often an indecent proposal.

If you are trading in a car with no outstanding balance, keep that information secret until the very last minute. Doing so decreases the likelihood that a dealer would fudge the worth of your trade-in, which would lead you to overpay for your new vehicle. Craft the purchase deal carefully and intelligently before revealing your trade-in. By withholding this information until you have an offer to sign, you will see unfluffed figures about the purchase price. Your genuine trade-in value should then be easy to understand. This approach will help both numbers speak clearly.

Always keep an eye out for fluffed numbers, and make sure you're not dancing to the melody of interest heaped atop interest. The road to ethical automobile purchasing is paved with correct information and strategic disclosures.

Examples of Two Scenarios

The Underhanded Method of Trading Up: Picture yourself strolling into the typical dealership in search of a new Toyota Tacoma. After doing your research and understanding its worth, you have prepared yourself psychologically for sticker shock. You've been really sneaky by hiding your 10-year-old Chevy Impala that you want to trade back home. The sales representative will probably toss exaggerated figures since they think they have a simple deal on their hands.

You can then bargain with them aggressively to get a good price on the vehicle. As you review the final sales contract, you casually mention your trade-in. With this approach, the sales representative won't have an opportunity to rethink the figures and offset the trade-in value in the price of the new vehicle. The goal is to see the full figures in writing before factoring the trade-in value.

Your first goal for holding the trade-in information is to get the best deal for the purchase price, and second one is about receiving top value for the trade-in.

Know Your Numbers and Foil the Fumbles: When trying to trade in your Chevrolet Impala, which you still owe money on, your first step should be to reach out to your bank for details regarding the payoff amount. Walking into any dealership armed with this knowledge allows you to negotiate a better deal and protect yourself against underhanded sales tactics. Using your exact loan balance and a sharp eye for lowball bids or hidden fees can help parry sales tactics used against you.

INSIDER FILES

SUBCONSCIOUS MANIPULATION

When purchasing a vehicle, the questions will subtly shift from needs to specifics, such as color, accessories, and options.

When those questions are presented, buyers are unconsciously getting closer to buying, although they might not realize it. The discussion will then focus on finalizing the selection and the purchase is about to happen. It's now based on emotions instead of needs.

SMOKE AND MIRRORS

Some dealers will use noises and commotions to distract clients and make them feel special. In some cases, they might ask a good-looking staff member to drop in and ask, "Do you need anything, like coffee or water?" Of course, they might flirtingly look directly in the eyes of customers to make them feel in a comfortable and safe environment.

To further impress, or confuse, consumers, the staff member may mention that the dealership just provided another customer with the best bargain ever. Their intent is to prove that the dealership is trustworthy and offers competitive pricing. Friends, this is called ballooning. (Like P. T. Barnum said, 'There's a sucker born every minute.') Just imagine a casino as quiet as a library, devoid of any excitement, fun, or fascinating atmosphere; I venture to guess that few people would even consider playing the slots there. Dealerships use similar smoke and mirrors tactics to provide a 'buying environment.'

Customer service should always remain at the core of sales interactions in a dealership. You shouldn't settle for anything less. Make sure to become your own first line of defense by seeking clarity and remaining alert for shady sales tactics. You can make informed choices by asking questions and remaining aware that decisions rest with you.

 PIT STOP LESSON

SCAM: SCHEMING, CRAFTY, AGGRESSIVE, MALICIOUS

To help you identify suspicious buyers or sellers, here are the five most common warning signs:

1. Cars are priced below current market value.
2. The seller claims to be in the military and is stationed overseas.
3. The posting does not include a phone number.
4. The seller will demand that you use a money or wire transfer service of their choice.
5. A local person will meet to pick up the car, yet payment must be wired to another using a service such as Western Union or Bitcoin.
6. The buyer or seller is only available late at night and is anxious to conclude the transaction swiftly.

FROM AN OIL CHANGE TO A NEW CAR
How did that happen?

Car owners understand their obligations; but sometimes they forget that people could break their trust and take them on unexpected rides.

Imagine the following scenario. You're visiting a dealership for an oil change and feeling confident about your vehicle, until the service advisor presents you with a long list of so-called car needs. This leaves your jaw on the floor but wait... it gets even stranger. Sensing your hesitation to get the work done, the cunning advisor calls in reinforcement from the sales department. An experienced salesman, eager to work his magic on you, begins whispering sweet nothings into your ear. He starts telling you that your car is worth a small fortune and offers you an unbelievable trade-in deal on a new model. Before long, you find yourself wandering the lot, gazing upon shiny new cars as a kid in a candy store. "Oh, you deserve this," the salesperson exclaims, as you nod in agreement. Soon enough, you are driving off into the sunset with your brand-new car, feeling like King Kong. But here's the catch — while you are driving away with excitement, those two deceitful friends are secretly splitting some bonus cash for tricking you into buying a new car. Trust your instincts, and never fall for these devious tricks.

 FUEL FOR THOUGHT

OBD DEVICES CAN BE MANIPULATED
On-board-diagnostic readers (OBD) provide a false sense of confidence as error codes can easily be erased, like a file on a computer. You would never know if it happened. This is why you always need a professional evaluation.

USED CAR SCAMS

Selling or buying cars has never been simpler with websites such as Kijiji, Craigslist, Offer Up, Let It Go and Facebook Marketplace facilitating this process. These sites can be a huge money-saver for both parties. Sellers can expect to make, and buyers can save, more than if they had gone through a third party. Most of these platforms will charge little or no fee to list and they don't add a commission on the transaction.

This is why the Auto category in the classified sections are very active, especially in urban areas. With so much cash being involved in the exchange of vehicles, it was only a matter of time before criminals took notice.

If you decide to purchase a used car privately, be aware of the possible scammers lurking in these marketplaces. You can defend yourself against deceptive sellers or sketchy buyers by doing some research and taking proactive precautions.

Fraudulent postings are more common than you think. The crudest attempts are easy to ignore, but a few schemes are more elaborate. Some scams are operated by experienced con artists with clever answers for everything. Stolen, counterfeit, and bounced checks are costing people their money, cars, or both.

In one common scam, the shady buyer 'accidentally' pays more, by money order or cashier's check, than the asking price and wants the seller to refund the overage. If the seller sends cash back before the money order clears the bank, they are braver than smart. These money orders often turn out to be counterfeit and any amount sent back is forever lost.

Buying and selling cars can be done safely if you take your time and pay attention. Again, don't let your emotions fog your judgment and rush a transaction. Below are a few tactics you can employ confidently for used car transactions.

SECURITY TACTICS FOR TRANSACTIONS

Before meeting private buyers to show your vehicle, it's essential to protect yourself. You should almost think like an FBI agent when you buy or sell a vehicle. It might be a good idea to consider using a temporary phone number that cannot be traced back. Apps like Hushed or Burner provide virtual VoIP numbers which may help stop potential buyers from reaching out indefinitely or at inappropriate times. It can also help to protect your personal details from Google searches.

When meeting potential private buyers, prioritize safety by choosing well-lit places to show your vehicle. Imagine this momentous occasion as an opportunity to unveil your car in all its glory, without concerns for hidden motives creeping behind you.

Always exchange sales proceeds through an established financial institution; this provides extra safeguards. Your bank can verify the buyer's payment methods such as checks or other means and help detect counterfeit bills. Protect your personal information to prevent identity fraud. You can confidently sell your car knowing that you are in control of the process. The experience can be quick and stress-free for both.

With the market for used vehicles on the rise, dealerships and private party sellers may attempt to make quick profits off unsuspecting buyers. Stay on guard against suspicious private sellers meeting at unlit streets to conduct suspicious deals. Conduct due diligence by verifying ownership documents and question anything odd, like requests to meet at strange hours. Trust your instincts when something seems off, employ transparency, and make informed decisions.

KEY TAKEAWAYS

- **Know Your Trade-in Worth:** Awareness of a vehicle's worth enables you to make informed decisions when selling or trading. It helps negotiating and avoid settling on low offers.

- **The Closing Chess Game:** Every move matters in closing deals successfully and avoiding hidden debt traps. Use stealth and strategy when making deals.

- **Be Wary of Showrooms:** Dealerships will divert your focus away from the true cost of purchasing goods or services. Keep an eye out for distractions from extravaganza or theatricality.

- **Financial Fortress:** Due diligence is your defense mechanism against scammers. Take your time and use banking services that shield your transactions from their assault.

INFORMATION IN MIRRORS IS MORE EMPOWERING THAN IT MAY APPEAR!

Queen of the Castle

*S*hopping for a new car was exciting for the Smiths but they reached an unfamiliar crossroad. Should they jump into leasing instead of a standard purchase? Christopher loved the allure of upgrading to something fancier at a lower payment and the possibility of trading it early for another one. The alternative was the usual path of ownership. Many questions swirled through their heads, but Victoria couldn't wrap her mind around the idea. For her, leasing seemed like renting. This didn't feel right as her top pride was in owning her castle.

Christopher liked the idea that leased cars could be changed more frequently. He could already see himself showing a new ride to friends and colleagues every few years and dodging remarks about his old car. Some people at work really enjoyed teasing owners of outdated vehicles. While it was for good fun, the emotions sometimes left a sting.

Dennis warned them, "Here's the catch… Leasing a car with all its bells and whistles may be tempting at first, like fireworks in the night sky. But it is critical to pause and reflect about both advantages and disadvantages. When you peel away layers to fully understand every detail, you can make an informed decision that aligns with your financial goals and personal values."

He explained that the appeal of lower payments and shiny new rides may make leasing tempting. But the fine print might unveil extra costs or restrictions, including mileage constraints and wear-and-tear fees.

Dennis concluded, "Never mind feeling as though the vehicle doesn't truly belong to you. Ownership tells a different tale filled with long-term financial advantages, freedom to customize, and true ownership euphoria. Sure, there may be bumps along that road. Repairs may be needed at some point and it's never fun. But you have time to prepare for them. The decision ultimately lies with you. Choose wisely, for it is your journey that unfolds before you."

Chapter 4

SHOULD I BUY, LEASE OR KEEP MY CAR?

When financing a vehicle, lease options should be taken into serious consideration. While leasing may have historically been used for corporate tax deduction purposes, more individuals are now opting to lease cars.

At minimum, most buyers should have a general understanding of this option if they choose to purchase their next car through a dealership. When entertaining the idea of leasing, certain key points should be evaluated before making such a commitment.

WHY LEASING MAKES SENSE IN SOME SITUATIONS

When considering financing options, it's essential to take both practical and personal factors into consideration. Leasing can be the ideal option for individuals who tend to quickly get over their honeymoon with a car and soon flirt with the idea of trying something new or different. (Especially if it may offer significant tax breaks.)

Leasing a car comes with its own set of challenges, including a strict maintenance schedule. Failure to follow the contract rules could result in unexpected fees when turning it back in. But you never know whether this one could become your permanent ride.

Leasing may provide tax and equity advantages to general consumers; however, you won't gain any equity until after your lease term has ended and the vehicle is returned. Due to all its possible financial impacts, it would be prudent to consult an accountant or tax specialist prior to making a final decision about leasing.

At the conclusion of your purchase loan period, your equity in the car depends on two main elements: its interest rate and how you managed its maintenance after the manufacturer warranty expired. Each decision comes with positives and negatives; an honest assessment requires taking an honest look at expectations, values, and your emotional needs as an individual.

LEASE WISE, WARRANTY FOOLISH
Navigating the Extended Warranty Dilemma

So, you're at the dealership, ready to lease a brand-new car. The salesperson brings up 'The Extended Warranty' and no matter how much preparation you had for this question; it's tempting to you.

Leasing may make more financial sense than a traditional purchase in some situations. But at its core, leasing a car should be treated like a short-term rental fling which should be returned to its prime. Therefore, why should you pay an extended warranty that may range between $2,300 and $4,500 for issues that may happen beyond the term you'll use it for? It's kind of like considering a lifelong commitment with someone after the first date — timing is everything.

If fate compels you to purchase a vehicle at the end of its lease agreement, only then would an extended warranty become an attractive proposition.

Exploring Your Options

If you tend to get bored with your cars every two years and you like them having the newest technology or the most up-to-date safety features, then leasing might give you the freedom to make the periodic upgrades you're looking for without breaking the bank.

Also, when leasing a car, if the residual value is set too low, you can buy the car for less than it's worth at the end of the lease. Moreover, leasing companies must resell their returned cars either directly to a dealer or through an auction. Often, they will negotiate a buyout price that's more favorable to you to avoid that hassle and expense.

The reality is, whether you lease or buy, cars do not serve as financial growth assets. There's no one-size-fits-all answer when it comes to the question of lease vs. buy. It's important to empower yourself to be able to identify some key factors related to cost and your preferences so that you can make the choice that's right for you. The most important thing to understand is that cars lose value over time without offering an immediate financial return. This should be an important consideration for purchasing or leasing. The best answer depends on factors including cost and personal preferences. Therefore, empowering yourself with knowledge is the key element to making the optimal choice for yourself and your situation.

 FUEL FOR THOUGHT

ROOF RACK BAGGAGE
A roof rack reduces fuel economy by 4%. Keep this in mind when shopping for your next vehicle's optional equipment.

A CAR IS NOT AN INVESTMENT

When purchasing a new car, keep in mind that it depreciates by 10% the minute it leaves the lot and, on average, gas-powered cars could see an annual drop in value up to 15% thereafter. (Hybrid and electric are another reality. See Chapter 5 for more details about electric vehicles.)

Contrary to popular perception, car ownership might not always be a wise financial move. Let's talk about why purchasing a vehicle isn't the same as putting money in a piggy bank. Buying items like homes, stocks, or even old, expensive wines typically implies your money will increase over time as their value rises. But what about cars? They're unique in that they provide us with freedom, road trips, and convenience, but don't expect them to make your pocketbook much heavier down the line.

Unlike fine wines which may gain in value with age, new cars depreciate immediately after purchase. Let's consider some of the less obvious costs that accompany car ownership. Aside from the initial purchase and ongoing ownership expenses, such as licensing, storage, parking and insurance, cars require regular servicing, routine maintenance and let's not forget gas. Vehicle ownership quickly becomes costly.

Bear in mind that any money dedicated to your car could quickly dissipate over time without always providing the same returns as other investments. This is why it might be best to abandon any notion that vehicles should be treated as assets.

FUEL FOR THOUGHT

DOWNHILL ASSET

Vehicle values depreciate by up to 15% annually. Specific factors, such as the time of year, the make, model, or updates to the product line design can also directly influence values.

SOMETIMES A CAR IS MORE THAN A CAR

My PhD in 'Car-ology' has given me plenty of experience, and now is the time for me to share some of it with you.

Automobiles are usually considered one of the worst investments you can make. Yet, be mindful that car ownership is more than possessing a large object composed of metal and rubber adorned with badges and mysterious stains. It is an investment, both financially and emotionally, in yourself. Your car is an integral part of who you are and represents freedom. It's creating experiences and memories by transporting you to soccer practice, romantic getaways, and spontaneous road trips.

Your asset requires taking responsibility for its maintenance and safeguarding — something which might help shape you into a more caring individual. So, let's not dismiss those wheeled companions as mere money pits. They are present to serve your transportation needs and improve your life, providing a convenience which couldn't otherwise be achieved.

UNDERSTANDING FINANCIAL FUNDAMENTALS

Let's conduct a detailed audit of essential financial factors before deciding to lease, buy, or keep.

Step 1: Financial Audit. Get involved by employing the Total Cost of Ownership (TCO) formula we discussed in the previous chapter. This tool helps uncover the true cost associated with owning your vehicle, so that informed decisions can be made.

Step 2: Determine Your Reason for Driving. Assess the drivers in your household and ensure their habits match up with their car's capabilities. Are you frequently using a large 4x4 SUV or an overly spacious four-passenger vehicle as your everyday transport just for yourself and some gym gear? Does it have a roof rack or towing package which you never use? The roof rack seems suitable in Vermont or Colorado; yet it might be awkward and expensive on gas in the Arizona desert climate. Take time to reflect upon features and functions that truly suit your lifestyle.

Step 3: Audit Annual Mileage. Take an honest look at how much mileage you drive each year. If it falls between 5,000 and 10,000 miles, it means your new vehicle will be spending more time in a driveway than on the road. Half of its warranty period will pass before reaching 50% of its mileage allowance. What value has this expensive new car given you for its purchase price?

Step 4: Evaluate Insurance Premiums. Before committing to a new car or applying for a loan, speak with your insurer about the coverage costs and options. Can your budget comfortably accommodate the estimated premiums along with the car payments? Are you overstretching yourself financially? Evaluate all potential financial impacts prior to making an informed decision.

INSIDER FILES

STICKER SHOCK

Mileage per Gallon (MPG) stickers in the window of a new car in the showroom are based on a barebones vehicle and the weight of the driver. It does not include such factors as accessories, passengers, and cargo. These may cause a drastic difference from the MPG rating stated.

Well, that wasn't that hard, was it? Congratulations on successfully completing your financial audit. Now equipped with greater knowledge and financial awareness, you are better suited than ever to navigate car ownership with certainty and peace.

Decisions about leasing, buying, or keeping your current vehicle are yours to make and can be revised at any point based on new factors. Understanding financial fundamentals help you make choices which align with your goals and aspirations.

KEY TAKEAWAYS

- **Leasing Prestige:** A lease offers the latest models without long-term commitments. With that in mind, be sure you understand the end-of-term conditions to avoid unexpected costs.

- **Buying Power:** Purchasing might be better for those looking for ownership opportunities with greater equity (despite the immediate depreciation impact).

- **Depreciation Adds Up Over Time:** Consider the long-term financial implications, such as depreciation, maintenance costs, and insurance premiums, when comparing buying and leasing.

- **Financial Literacy is Essential:** A financial audit will provide a thorough understanding of the true cost of owning or leasing.

- **Make Informed Decisions:** Avoid paying for features or capacity you won't use by considering insurance premiums, budget constraints and lifestyle preferences.

INFORMATION IN MIRRORS IS MORE EMPOWERING THAN IT MAY APPEAR!

Electric Avenue

*O*n a quiet Friday night, the Smiths were drinking wine and talking about ways to save the world when Christopher said they should do their part. Victoria felt that there was more to this random statement than met the eye because of the way he had brought it up. She immediately sensed something fishy when he asked Cynthia if she wanted to ride in an electric car.

He eventually admitted that Philip, a co-worker, had recently purchased a "sexy" electric car, and it was "so cool." It was easy for Christopher to catch that bug. With a big smirk, Victoria had her moment to call out her hubby with a "Well, well, well. Looks like you got hit by high-voltage and the cat's now out of the bag."

The Smiths had been married for more than a decade and had worked hard to give their daughter Cynthia a good life. Like many parents, they sometimes wondered about the future their kids were facing. Christopher convinced himself that electric vehicles would save the environment for the next generation. Of course, this was easier than admitting his attraction for the newest and shiniest things.

Victoria knew her husband well enough to understand when he was acting on a whim. His emotional wants occasionally got ahead of their practical needs. She kept sipping on her wine and gently explained that their current car was fine and that they didn't have to buy a new one just to keep up with the Joneses or, in this case, the Philips.

While he didn't like Victoria's advice, he had to admit to himself that it made sense. He quietly poured another glass and changed the topic rather than admitting that she was right.

Christopher cared about his family and didn't want to put their finances in danger. He really thought that electric cars might be better for the environment but accepted that they weren't right for their family at this time. It also wasn't the best idea to try to keep up with his co-workers, since their lives were so different.

Chapter 5

SHOULD I DRIVE ELECTRIC?

Electric Ave was the song Eddy Grant sang in 1982 and a lovely tune it was. Though the 80s seems like such a long time ago, it aligns with today's direction, or should I say push, from governments and the auto industry. Their vision is to stave off earth's looming climate crisis with electric vehicles.

The reality though is that there are many factors to take into consideration when looking at electric cars, other than saving on fuel consumption. Sure, it's great to save on gas money and sneaking by all other single passenger car drivers as you drive in the high-occupancy vehicle (HOV) lane feels exhilarating. Trusting the auto pilot to drive you home as you check your emails or Facetime grandma is a dream finally accessible. But let's not forget about the real carbon footprint that manufacturing electric cars has. Some facts may come as a surprise, but knowing this will give you a brief break from the clamorous trappings of marketing and cost-cutting grandeur.

The average size of an EV battery is about the same as three 24-pack cases of beer. And contrary to gas-powered vehicles, these batteries contain lithium and cobalt. Most buyers forget that 60% of the precious metals for these batteries is mined in the People's Republic of Congo by families, including children as young as six. Never mind their age or how many hours they work each day. It's the conditions which are concerning. Most don't even have basic protective equipment such as gloves and face masks, which is heartbreaking.

To reach their destination on other continents, the minerals are shipped and transported by carbon-emitting boats and trucks, just like oil. This is somewhat ironic.

NAVIGATING CHOICES FOR A
GREENER FUTURE

Mining often leads to the destruction of local ecosystems by the release of wastewater and other unusable ores onto the environment. In many countries, workers are forced to work and live in bad conditions because their wages are very low. Amnesty International has documented cases of children and adults mining cobalt in small man-made tunnels where they are exposed to dangerous gases emitted during the procurement of these rare minerals. This should make us pause for a second and consider our moral obligations.

Many materials come from hostile or uncontrollable regions, such as China, Mongolia, Congo, and Bolivia, which makes the supply unpredictable.

An electric car battery requires about 8 to 10 kilograms of lithium to power itself. While it might not seem like much, some details will leave your jaw dropping. Mining one metric ton of this mineral requires an astonishing 500,000 gallons of water. That's a lot and a bit of a contradiction considering it's for green vehicles. At a glance, it feels like the problem is pushed in someone else's backyard, far away.

Governments and cities in America are so concerned about water that laws are implemented about usage, such as overwatering grass. This is not only impacting regular U.S. citizens but also several businesses, like golf courses, especially in desert cities with scarce water resources.

OK, with this new perspective about the impact of mining and transporting minerals, let's close our eyes and imagine a perfect world where batteries are manufactured in an environmentally and socially beneficial manner.

The main purpose of electric batteries is to hold and provide power, so we'll shift our attention to their charging capacity. This is similar to the fuel tank volume, or how much mileage the car can do before a top up. The average electric car battery will lose roughly 10% of its charging power within the first three years and roughly 3% to 5% each year after that. So, hypothetically, by the fifth year, your electric battery will be operating at around 75% of its original charging capacity. Oh, wow! How much did you say that electric car costs again?

PIT STOP LESSON

SOME EV PARTS MIGHT BE HARD TO FIND

It is common to hear stories of people waiting over two years to receive their electric car. Sadly, if they get into an accident, they may have to wait an extra year for parts to drive their car again.

We once had a Toyota Prius Hybrid sitting in the garage for 6 ½ months while waiting for parts. The client was driving a rental the whole time. Can you imagine what that bill looked like?

Extra delays could exceed the rental car coverage provided by insurance companies. This isn't an issue for gas vehicles as most parts are readily available within 15 days.

THE TRUE BENEFITS OF DRIVING ELECTRIC

Owning an electric car can feel like winning an eco-friendly lottery. You're driving a clean and quiet machine, while simultaneously saving cash and time by leaving gas stations behind. Charging at home overnight is made effortless while you sleep or eat. Not to mention all those savings for your wallet as no cash will go toward gas or oil changes.

But let's flip the coin for a second and consider this reality: Your electric car could quickly feel obsolete as soon as new models with the latest bells and whistles hit the market. And just like phones and laptops, replacing batteries and other major components could cost your bank account dearly.

While now might seem like the time for green glory, just remember in a few years' time you may find yourself asking, "What was the worth of this car?" Being at the forefront can come with its share of drawbacks; being a trendsetter on wheels comes with consequences and requirements that must be considered and accepted before purchasing.

Watts That Cost?

Charging is a central aspect of EVs, so let's compare some numbers, shall we? A full charge will usually provide around 180 to 240 miles of autonomy. To keep things simple, the average EV vehicle will cost around $30 to be fully charged. This will usually provide around 180 to 240 miles of autonomy.

The cost to charge an electric car at a public station depends on several factors. For the sake of argument, let's just ballpark those numbers. The average U.S. cost per kWh is between $0.40 and $0.70 cents and most vehicles will do three to four miles for every kWh.

The time to recharge will also vary based on the type of station used (home or public). The slowest equipment, Level 1, provides charging through a common residential 120 volts AC outlet. These chargers can take 40 to 50 hours to charge an empty EV battery. A fast-charging station on direct current (DC) could take 20 minutes to one hour. In both cases, a full charge will cost about $30.

Let's break it down these numbers to the ridiculous. It costs about *17 cents* to drive one mile in an average gas-powered vehicle versus roughly *five cents* for an electric vehicle. If we compare both, the gas vehicle will essentially cost the owner **$29 more** than the EV to drive 240 miles. This might seem like a significant difference; yet it can also be quite relative.

Just for a moment, let's try and understand what people are really chasing. What does that $29 saving represent in the bigger picture? Most people spend an average of $27 a week for Starbucks coffee without having a second thought about it. It's not life-changing savings.

With these numbers in mind, let's analyze the purchase price. On average, the upfront cost for an electric vehicle is roughly $12,000 more than a gas one. (According to Kelley Blue Book.) That represents 36 payments of $333/month. If your main incentive for an EV is to save on gas costs, you'll need to do a LOT of mileage to make up for this overhead. Better get a calculator to compare your options. (If you're wondering what to do with that extra cash? Perhaps start a Starbucks fund. It would cover most people's coffee addiction for 37 years, without factoring interest...)

Speed Is Relative

The cooling system for some EV's batteries will make it challenging to drive long distances as their cooling system will slow charging speed to protect cells. As an example, a fast charge on a Nissan Leaf may average 45 minutes while the car is cold, yet the same charge, while the battery is warm, could require up to 50% more time. And it might only get to an 80% charge.

Wait time at charging stations can also be challenging as some people will go eat while their car is plugged in. If you find it frustrating to wait after a couple of cars at the pumps taking a few minutes each, imagine a similar lineup with cars requiring 30, 45 or 60 minutes each, with owners casually eating, shopping while you bite your fingernails.

Remember that charging stations aren't standardized. Depending on your make and model, you may not be able to recharge at every location.

What About E-Waste?

Consider the disposal of electric batteries once they fail. We know they can be recycled or reused, and they have the capacity to fuel many things from electric bicycles to elevators. Some myths about EV batteries ending up in landfills persist, even though the minerals and energy left inside them is far too valuable to waste.

Be aware that it's hard to find evidence of recycling plants for electric batteries. Specific information, like physical street addresses or location of plants that disassemble them to recycle all those precious metals to put them to good use is sparse.

In the end, I'm sure we can all agree. There is nothing wrong with electric vehicles and no one is flat out saying, "Don't purchase one," or, "It's a bad idea." There are positive and negative aspects about everything, and we have seen valuable outcomes of owning and driving electric vehicles. Yet we can't pretend there's no flip side to the story.

INSIDER FILES

ZAPPING EV RESALE VALUES ONE VOLT AT A TIME

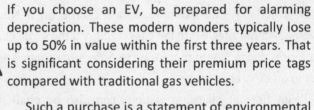

If you choose an EV, be prepared for alarming depreciation. These modern wonders typically lose up to 50% in value within the first three years. That is significant considering their premium price tags compared with traditional gas vehicles.

Such a purchase is a statement of environmental responsibility. But keep in mind there could be a considerable loss on the resale value.

CLIMATE PITFALLS OF EV BATTERIES

Electric vehicles are widely praised for their environmental friendliness and innovation, yet it's important to assess how they perform under extreme weather conditions. EV batteries are particularly sensitive to temperature changes and may suffer diminished efficiency and range under cold or hot climates. Cold temperatures slow down chemical reactions inside the battery which reduces their range. Simultaneously, they face increased demand for heating purposes. On the other hand, extreme heat may speed battery degradation while facing a greater demand for keeping the vehicle cool.

One way of mitigating range loss during cold weather driving conditions is 'preconditioning' your car while still plugged in. It warms the battery before starting your journey. But this requires some foresight as well as having an accessible charging spot nearby.

Like with any piece of specialized equipment, keeping batteries healthy under extreme climates might require special consideration, be it through garage storage solutions, regular checkups or just more often griping about the climate. These factors must be carefully considered for people living in areas with harsh winters or scorching summers. Here are important aspects to know.

Shrinking Stamina Syndrome: Batteries, like people, prefer comfortable conditions over extreme ones. In cold weather, chemical reactions in batteries slow down, thus reducing the available energy to power your car resulting in a significant decrease of range. This could represent a drop of up to 40% in some instances.

Toasty Tax: Temperatures drops usually means an increased reliance on the heater. Unlike gasoline cars, which rely on engine waste heat to warm the cabin, electric vehicles must use battery power. This will further diminish their range. Imagine being caught out on a snowy evening with zero range left when heat is most needed...

Cool Comfort Guzzler: Just as heaters deplete batteries during cold spells, air conditioners eat away energy reserves in hotter environments.

The Internal Charging Siesta: Just as phone batteries take more time to charge in cold conditions, EV batteries also charge at slower rates in freezing weather.

Sun-Kissed Battery Blues: Excessive heat can be devastating to lithium-ion batteries. Prolonged exposure to high temperatures accelerates their aging process and shortens both their capacity and lifespan — like sunbathing too much can-do long-term harm if left too long exposed.

The Big Freeze Fiasco: Just as heaters deplete batteries during cold spells, air conditioners eat away at energy reserves in hotter environments. This means the AC is using more power to stay cool, thus decreasing driving range and potentially reducing dependability.

Thermal Temperature Tantrums: High temperatures can place batteries at risk of overheating. While modern EVs have cooling systems that may help counter this effect, extreme conditions require these systems to work overtime which will require more power and thus reduce performance.

Vintage Model Meltdowns: Older EVs tend to feature less sophisticated thermal management systems. This will make them more susceptible to weather fluctuations. A second-hand buyer in Minnesota or Arizona would likely face unique environmental conditions and may need extra consideration before purchasing a pre-owned EV.

When Lithium Burns, Run!

The toxic and carcinogenic risks posed by lithium battery fires present the biggest hazard associated with ownership of electric vehicles. Car fires are obviously a major safety issue, but a fire in an electric car is a particularly dangerous risk to occupants and people nearby.

Lithium reacts with the atmosphere and produces carcinogenic fumes, including pure fluorine gas which is highly toxic if inhaled. Exposure to such fumes may lead to deadly illnesses in humans as well as animals. This is a concern to anyone within breathing distance of an electric vehicle on fire. Being a bystander next to a burning electric vehicle is like watching BBQ fire next to a propane tank. It's no time for voyeurism. Run and stay away.

The Grand Finale of Facts

Electric vehicles may be impressive technological achievements, yet they still come with some temperamental issues due to Mother Nature. Technology continues to advance, and these issues should eventually be taken care of. But, for now, though, they should be taken into consideration as you attempt to balance eco-friendliness with the realities of our imperfect world. Choose wisely and pack an emergency blanket just in case.

WILL YOUR EV BECOME A PAPERWEIGHT?

OK, so you've bought an electric car. Now what? Your high-tech EV was great just a few short years ago but, thanks to advanced technologies, it no longer shines as it used to. Today, a better and newer version has appeared right before your eyes. Now that your hopes have turned into electric fears, you're doing your very best to try and avoid getting stuck with a large paper weight in your driveway.

What you should recognize and, most importantly, understand is that you cannot make blanket statements like, "I bought and drive an electric vehicle, so I'm saving the planet" or "I'm saving more money with my EV." Same thing with, "I'm doing my part to save the human race." These are all fluffy, feel-good self-empowerment beliefs that are just not 100% true.

The unspoken emotion that consumers have when purchasing an electric car is often a false sense of relevance. Most owners are proud to mention that they own such a vehicle, yet they fail to realize that the core of their purchasing decision was mostly based on the promise of saving money and the environment.

For many, an electric vehicle (EV) is considered like a trip into the future in a sleek, technologically advanced vehicle that travels softly, almost magically. Sadly, the financial aspect will bring people back to reality in a drastic way. That depreciating shock is greater with electric vehicles as they tend to lose value at an alarming rate. Buying the most cutting-edge technology is exciting, but as soon as you drive off, a newer and improved model appears on the market. Most EV buyers didn't realize that their electric snazzy techno-chariot would turn from futuristic whizz kid to yesterday's slowpoke in the blink of an LED.

Many of my professional clients jumped on the electric car bandwagon; but, as they felt the 'not so normal' financial strain and inconvenience of keeping them charged, they sank back into the more familiar and comfortable seat of gasoline-powered automobiles.

Friends, I hate to break it to you, but as soon as the novelty wears off, your shiny new electric car will feel like a laptop on wheels. Don't go chasing the electric dream blindly. Keep in mind that progress in the technological realm is a race in which no one can afford to lose ground. In this fast lane of electronic wonders, may your journeys go smoothly, and your decisions be wiser.

Note that the president of Toyota has already announced that the end of electric vehicles is on the horizon. It's too early to say if this is just marketing talk, but they might be on to something with their advancements on ammonia engines.

ELECTRIFYING DIVERSIONS: WHAT COMES AFTER EV?

At a time when electric vehicles are promoted as the holy grail and more people are venturing into EV ownership, Toyota is asserting that there are more avenues leading to a greener world. They chose to focus development on other types of technologies to offer more options for their customers.

Their partnership with the GAC Group of China led to a notable achievement. They've developed and introduced an impressive ammonia-powered engine, proving that there may be multiple viable solutions for powering automobiles. Ammonia is a good option as it is readily available, inexpensive, and has a lower environmental impact.

In a fascinating turn of events, Toyota's new engine not only threatens the very existence of EVs but also hints to the possibility of future vehicles being fueled by a wide range of unconventional sources of energy. Time will only tell as we discover this future together.

KEY TAKEAWAYS

- **Shifting Carbon Footprint:** Electric vehicles (EVs) offer reduced emissions during operation, yet their production presents ethical and environmental concerns. These include such facts as the use of child labor for mineral mining operations and the excessive quantities of water needed for lithium extraction. The electric vehicles might be shifting the carbon footprint rather than improving it.

- **Depreciating Returns:** With advances in EV technology, current models may quickly become outdated, jeopardizing their resale value, and negating short-term fuel savings due to higher initial investments. Plus, battery degradation may decrease efficiency — further adding costs over time — and increase mineral extraction requirements.

- **Greener Alternative on the Horizon:** While EVs remain trendy, other emerging technologies, like Toyota's ammonia-fueled engines, suggest they may not be our sole path toward a sustainable automotive future. Diversifying in green technology may offer more environmentally conscious and socially responsible choices.

INFORMATION IN MIRRORS IS MORE EMPOWERING THAN IT MAY APPEAR!

Mileage Guru

*T*he Smiths are infamous critics of rising fuel costs who quickly cast blame and point fingers. This is an ongoing heated topic for them, like an evil spirit lurking beneath their car's hood.

Christopher is easily provoked and often fueled by emotion when seeing gas prices move upward, yet he won't blink an eye for his $7.00 cup of caramel-whipped coffee that costs more per gallon than fuel. Meanwhile Victoria noticed that her grocery bill has steadily increased and couldn't believe that her 5 oz bottle of Tabasco hot sauce now costs an outrageous $3.99. Same thing for that coffee creamer. Once an everyday indulgence, it now fetches $4.69 for a 32 oz bottle.

When reviewing the last credit card statement, Victoria noticed that Christopher had spent a lot on the fuel gizmo that was supposed to save them money. She immediately called Dennis to get his opinion on this device. He explained that there's no magic device you can install in your ignition or fuel system that will do any miracles.

Dennis also shocked them with the fact that 32 ounces is only 1/4 gallon. Their perceptions changed slightly and the price of gas at the pump took on a new perspective. The affordability and value became evident, yet they continued adopting new habits. The Smiths are still processing this newly acquired knowledge while embarking together on an endeavor to unlock the secrets of fuel efficiency. Their intent is to combat the ever-increasing prices by gaining an awareness of all factors impacting fuel consumption — from proper tire inflation and vehicle maintenance to smooth acceleration and gentle braking. Their route planning still needs work as it's not the most efficient yet. While it brings heated discussions, they still enjoy the journey and experience.

While fuel prices will always fluctuate depending on economic cycles, they try not to fret too much about it. They believe their fresh outlook as mileage gurus will outwit rising tides as their fuel-efficient lifestyle will make each gallon go further.

Chapter 6

UNDERSTANDING FUEL ECONOMY

When the weather changes to delightful temps, it's hard to resist hopping in the car for a trip. But the steady increase in gas prices seems to hit the brakes on this impulse to travel. It's no surprise that people keep looking for ways to increase their fuel economy.

Are you driving from gas station to gas station looking to save on your next tank of fuel? You cannot control the price of gas, but you can often maximize your mileage with proper maintenance and better driving habits.

Filling up a gas tank can be one of the most expensive aspects of car ownership, so you'll want to do everything you can to stretch your money and your gas mileage.

 **FUEL FOR THOUGHT**

THROWING MONEY BY THE WINDOW
Driving with open windows can slash fuel economy by up to 32%.

As gas prices rise, it's necessary to reconsider fuel consumption. Fortunately, a few small changes can make a big difference. Some simple tips can help. For example, everyone should know that using air conditioning or heating can significantly affect gas mileage. Other factors, such as aerodynamics, the weight of the car, and the type of terrain can decrease fuel efficiency in ways you might not have expected.

With basic planning, a household with two automobiles might easily save the equivalent of a car payment each year. Businesses with a fleet of vehicles can save even more by following a few simple tips.

PIT STOP LESSON

GAS TANK TIP

When you need to fill up a rental or borrowed car, you can easily determine where the gas tank is without getting out.

A quick way to do that is by looking at the gas icon on the dashboard. You will find an arrow pointing left or right. This indicates the side where the fuel intake is located.

Some vehicles will display a fuel pump to indicate where it is.

GASOLINE WISDOM

Car owners should understand that they are in control of how much fuel they buy and use. Once empowered with this information, the dynamics of car ownership will change completely.

The purpose of a car is not to buy gas. It is solely for transportation. However, most require fuel to do so. By changing a few habits, you can get immediate relief at the gas pump and become the master of your gasoline destiny.

Lose Some Weight

No, not you. (Well, it doesn't hurt trying…) Do you use your vehicle as storage by keeping all your belongings in your trunk or heavy items inside your vehicle as storage? Put your vehicle on a diet by getting things out. Getting rid of any excess weight in the trunk, as well as extra stuff on the back seat, is a great idea. The lighter the load on your car, the more you'll save on gas. Excess weight makes your vehicle less

74

aerodynamic, so it causes a mileage drag. For every 100 pounds added to the load on the car, you're reducing your fuel efficiency by a full percentage point. It's time to become an automotive personal trainer and help your car lose some weight.

Slow Down, Be Sensible, and Observe the Speed Limit

We're all in a hurry and often cycle between aggressive speeding, braking, and accelerating again, 'Stop and Go,' in short distances can burn up to 10% more fuel. This is why paying more attention to avoid forceful stops and jackrabbit starts are two habits that increase fuel economy. Look ahead and concentrate on the road. Decelerate as soon as you notice lights and stop signs. The smoother the ride, the greater the savings.

Using cruise control helps to reduce frequent acceleration and deceleration. Try using it whenever possible, especially on the highway. It can help reduce fuel consumption by up to seven percent. It's also a great tool to help you follow speed limits and save on speeding tickets (just because you're distracted, of course!)

Get Organized and Avoid Making Several Short Trips

Multiple short trips in your car might seem convenient, but they're weakening your precious gasoline budget. Imagine making multiple quick stops for errands before driving back home quickly only to unload and rush off again to pick up children from school — sound familiar? Well, guess what: you're probably burning more fuel than necessary. Here's one effective strategy to save some hard-earned dollars: plan out your weekly routine so most errands can be accomplished in one swift trip. Make sure to turn off the engine when parking at school or store. Sitting and idling is slurping up your gas faster, so plan your shopping trips, school pickups and outings carefully. And whenever possible, avoid peak traffic hours — flexibility goes a long way toward saving fuel. Take advantage of any company policies which permit flexible work hours by consolidating errands. You will soon be on your way to fuel-saving success.

Map Your Ride

Do you take the same route every day because your favorite coffee shop or restaurant is on your way? You should try mapping your route and see if there is a simpler or faster way to get there. By removing just one or two left turns from your route, you can often avoid several red lights. Right turns usually don't require waiting at red lights. It makes a difference in the long run. Mapping your routine could help you save up to 19% on your overall trip. An effective way to be a fuel-saving champion is to use your GPS as it knows much more than you — sorry to burst your bubble. It will guide your route zigzagging through neighborhoods and alley ways to bypass any roadblocks or construction that may slow your ride time. I personally enjoy the WAZE app as it also includes community feedback about cars stuck or other road hazards (not to mention where the 'popos' are hiding! ☺)

🏁 PIT STOP LESSON 🏁

SPEED IMPACTS YOUR WALLET IN MANY WAYS

The ideal speed for maximum fuel economy is between 40 mph and 55 mph. Once your car travels faster than 60 miles per hour, your fuel economy begins to decline.

Schedule Routine Checkups

A well-kept vehicle is always more efficient. Following your car manufacturer's recommendations for changing oil, replacing filters, and topping off fluids impacts fuel consumption. Using the proper fuel grade helps prevent engine deposits, which affect efficiency. Visit your trusted repair facility and get on a preventive service plan to keep your vehicle in tip-top shape.

Change Your Engine Air Filter

By changing your air filter every 15,000 miles, or as recommended by your car manufacturer, you can improve your fuel mileage by as much as 10%. This simple procedure will keep particles from damaging the inside of your engine and helps it run more efficiently.

Keep Tires Properly Inflated

When tire pressure drops, so does fuel economy. According to the U.S. Environmental Protection Agency (EPA), proper tire inflation can improve gas efficiency by as much as 3.3 percent.

Make it a habit to frequently check all four tires. This is best done in the morning — when they're cold — and add air as needed. You can find your vehicle's suggested pressure on a label in the driver's door jam or in the owner's handbook. If you want someone to check and fill them, many retailers — including Discount Tires and Costco — offer free tire pressure service.

Properly inflated tires are safer and last longer. (See Chapter 15 for more details about tire care.)

Roll With the Windows Up

Although it may not appear to have an impact on your car's fuel economy, leaving windows rolled down can diminish efficiency. This is especially true when the car is driven at higher speeds. Wind adds resistance, noise, and drag, which requires more energy. If you enjoy driving with the windows open to feel the fresh air on your face, the sunroof is a better option as it won't increase fuel consumption.

Stop Idling Your Car and Wasting Gas

Most owners think that starting and stopping their vehicle repeatedly is wasting fuel. This is false. A vehicle idling without moving is using the most amount of fuel.

Many people also like to turn up the air conditioning or heat for a few minutes before their morning commute. Yes, cars get hot during the summer months or cold in the winter, but operating the heater or AC when idling causes your gas gauge to drop at a faster rate.

Remember that for every two minutes of idle time, a car burns the same amount of fuel as if it was driven for one mile. Consider that next time you're waiting in line at a coffee shop or at a fast-food restaurant drive-through; they can really hit your wallet hard.

Turning off your vehicle and walking in is a much cheaper alternative. It's also better for the waist and might make you rethink those donuts or hash browns you're about to get.

 FUEL FOR THOUGHT

THE REAL PRICE OF DRIVE-THROUGHS
Your morning coffee might be more expensive than you think. Every two minutes of idle time burns the same amount of fuel as driving one mile.

Fill Up at the Right Time

When it's hot outside, removing the cap on the gas tank allows gasoline fumes to escape more quickly. To save fuel and reduce pollution, it is preferable to refuel when it's cooler, like early morning or late evening.

Understand Seasonal Fuel Blends

It's important to realize there are two blends of fuel and understand their relationship to weather patterns.

Winter-blend gas boasts a higher Reid Vapor Pressure (RVP) to enhance engine performance in cold temperatures by permitting easier evaporation. Summer blends feature lower RVP levels to limit excessive evaporation when temperatures climb higher. However, summer blends often face the misconception of being more expensive or ineffective due to being reformulated from their winter predecessors.

Reformulated summer blends may cost two or four cents more to refine due to lower butane content; but don't let this fool you. These minimal differences won't translate to reduced efficiency. Both winter and summer blends offer similar fuel economy.

Being aware of fuel blends may alleviate unfounded fears and prevent unnecessary repairs being offered by some repair shops. Winter and summer blends have different purposes that optimize engine performance depending on climate conditions.

At the change of season, many clients visit the shop with concerns that their vehicle might be having sudden issues with fuel economy. I keep reminding people that fuel consumption might be off when the seasons change as their vehicle might be running on gas in the middle of a fuel transition. Don't panic, it is just adjusting to the different blend.

 PIT STOP LESSON

NO MAGIC PILL FOR FUEL ECONOMY

We have heard everything about secret additives promising to work miracles on gas mileage.

Here's a little secret — you can save cash by ditching those additives and octane boosters. The real key to fuel-efficiency lies with proper driving practices, habits, and vehicle maintenance rather than magical potions peddled on the internet.

Evaluate Alternatives

Going green might help you save money in the long run. Hybrids or electric vehicles usually cost more than standard automobiles, but they can help reduce or eliminate trips to the gas station. Make sure to do your homework and know what to expect, such as the cost of installing a charging port in your home, the availability of nearby charging stations and, most importantly, the distance you can drive before needing to recharge. Extreme cold weather may also impact battery performance. (See Chapter 5 for more details about electric vehicles.)

There are many other options to consider, such as taxis, Uber, public transportation, carpooling, or car sharing apps, such as Turo.

THE POWER OF BEING "TANK FULL"

Did you know that running low on fuel can be more than just an inconvenience? Life can get crazy busy, and finding time to fill up becomes a feat worthy of an Olympic medal. But hold your horses, neglecting fueling up won't save money — it may lead to costly repair bills or an unpleasant date with a tow truck.

Now, I understand. Seeing gas prices increase can be alarming; but don't despair my savvy drivers. There is an easier and smarter way of saving money than playing the "How far we can drive on fumes" challenge.

Proactive Fueling

Embrace the power of filling your tank up before it sputters and fizzles out completely. Yes, life can become hectic quickly and we may sometimes forget our thirst for fuel in a sea of family and work tasks. We've all experienced moments where we waited for that "20 miles remaining" indicator before heading toward the nearest pump. But those warnings are approximate. Tanks sometimes run dry when least expected, so put on your responsible car owner's hat. No more excuses for driving on fumes. While ignorance may put you in harm's way, knowledge will lead to smoother drives and safer journeys. So, fill 'er up. Proactive fueling is key to an enjoyable driving experience. Stop waiting for a miracle price drop on gas. While surprise reductions or pricing errors might happen, it's just like the Loch Ness Monster. We've all heard about it, but there's no definitive proof that it exists, and it's unlikely that you'll ever see it.

The Mechanical Risks

Most people know how important gasoline is to power an engine, but they might fail to realize that it also functions as a cooling system for the electric fuel pump. In today's modern cars, this pump sits in the middle of the gas tank where it is cooled by gasoline. A near-empty tank could cause the fuel pump to suck in air and overheat, causing increased wear and premature pump failure.

Commonly running the vehicle with an empty tank could potentially lead to repairs costing hundreds or even thousands in parts and labor. Gunk and debris from the bottom of the fuel tank are more likely to get caught in various components of the vehicle. Sediment in your tank can also foul the fuel filter. If the fuel filter doesn't catch them, you run the risk of clogging your fuel injectors. This is less of an issue today as modern cars use heavy-duty plastic fuel tanks, but in older vehicles with metal fuel tanks, rust particles can be a danger. Either way, you get the idea that filling up is always a good idea.

In cold climate states, there is a common concern with running low on fuel once the mercury dips below freezing. That's because the condensation that builds up in the tank when it's low has a greater chance to get sucked into the fuel lines and freeze. When this frozen water blocks the flow of fuel to the engine, this means your vehicle won't start, but worse than that, the lines themselves may become damaged by the expansion and contraction of the freezing water.

INSIDER FILES

SEASONAL GAS BLUES

Summer fuel typically features lower Reid Vapor Pressure (RVP) to delay evaporation during warmer weather months. Meanwhile, RVP levels rise in the winter to allow better combustion.

This knowledge will enable car owners to recognize a slight difference in the way their engine functions at the change of season. Their vehicle may not require a tune-up or maintenance after it adapts to the new gas.

Winter mileage vs. summer, now you know.

Fuel Mileage Concerns

Some will argue that a lighter tank will give the car more fuel efficiency. Yes, we've covered the weight factor before, but there's a caveat. It's true, a lighter load requires less gasoline, but the weight of a full tank is not significant. If you're commuting long distances stopping every hour to add fuel won't really save much. But if you're mostly driving short distances, like 500 miles per month or less, than a half tank might make sense for better fuel economy, while keeping your fuel pump protected.

 **FUEL FOR THOUGHT**

DID YOU KNOW?

WEIGHTING GAS

A gallon of gasoline weighs roughly 6.3 lb, so the total weight of a full tank is usually under 250 lbs. While this might seem important, it is preferable to driving with a nearly empty tank.

Personal Safety Concerns

Make sure to understand that running out of fuel while driving in traffic is a super dangerous situation. This is not to mention the personal risks from the elements during extreme temperatures of summer or winter. When an engine stalls, brakes and power steering can be lost, so running out of fuel at highway speeds can be hazardous. When considering the risks of becoming stranded and putting yourself or family in danger, you realize that delaying fill ups is never worth it.

- **Maximize Fuel Efficiency:** Regular service visits, selecting an efficient fuel grade, and maintaining properly inflated tires can significantly enhance mileage and extend tire lifespan.

- **Reduce Drag and Waste:** Removing extra weight and using AC, instead of driving with the windows down, will help save fuel by lowering drag. Decreasing idle time will also limit unnecessary fuel burn.

- **Drive Smarter:** Adhere to speed limits, use cruise control, and employ smooth driving techniques to save up to 10% in fuel expenses.

- **Plan Ahead:** Consolidate trips. Use the GPS for efficient routing. Refueling during cooler hours will also save on costs.

- **Don't Run on Fumes:** Running low on fuel poses safety risks and can result in mechanical damage. Keep a full tank to ensure longevity and uninterrupted performance.

INFORMATION IN MIRRORS IS MORE EMPOWERING THAN IT MAY APPEAR!

Insurance Woes

When Victoria first told Christopher that she wanted to live in a gated community, he initially teased her by saying that her taste for champagne didn't really fit their beer budget. Yet, they set their sight on this dream and eventually made it happen. After the move, their insurance crept up significantly. They assumed the increase was tied to the new neighborhood since people had more expensive properties and vehicles. While that logic made sense in their mind, when they dropped by for an oil change, Dennis encouraged them to investigate this and possibly consider changing insurer.

When they called a new insurance company to get lower prices, the agent confirmed that the area they moved into was one factor, yet he noticed right away that the Smiths had a low credit score due to ID fraud. This was a significant issue, although the candy apple red color of Christopher's car didn't help.

The Smiths didn't know that so many factors impacted the cost of their insurance. Their biggest surprise was learning that their insurance increased by close to 50% because Cynthia turned 15. "Ouch! That was an expensive birthday," Victoria thought. The agent explained that once teenagers are of driving age, car insurance policies can result in a significant increase in rates, ranging from 50% to 100%.

On a positive note, he added that after Cynthia establishes her good driving record, they can anticipate a reduction in premiums. This might only happen when she enters her 20s, so they would have to be patient.

The Smiths realized that it was a good exercise to get familiar with all aspects of their comprehensive coverage; not just paying their premiums. Although little can be done about changing some aspects, they saw that fixing the identity error to increase their credit rating was a low-hanging fruit. "Knowledge is power." Christopher said.

Chapter 7

UNDERSTANDING CAR INSURANCE

S hopping for car insurance can be frustrating, yet understanding basic facts about the industry might help you make better decisions and get the most when needed. For example, knowing your driving record can help avoid high estimates based on incorrect assertions that you are a high-risk driver.

An easy place to start when evaluating car insurance options is by getting quotes online. If you're worried that lower rates mean less coverage or poor service, you'll be happy to know it's not the case. There are plenty of insurance companies that offer affordable premiums, well-rounded coverage, and excellent customer service.

The basics of car insurance can be difficult to grasp. Understanding the lesser-known intricacies involved with the guidelines, policies, and procedures of today's insurance providers could be a complex journey.

When it comes to car insurance, you pay one amount, your best buddy pays another, and your neighbor also pays a different rate. What's going on? Let's try to shed some light on this.

THE AUTO INSURANCE MATRIX

Back in the day, insurance companies evaluated a short list of factors when calculating premiums. Today, that list has grown to include a confusing labyrinth of criteria, causing insurance rates to differ dramatically between providers.

To clear things up, it is important to take a closer look at factors that affect premiums — some of them even provide additional cost-cutting tips.

Brand Loyalty Can Cost You

If your mindset about automobile insurance is "I'm covered, so I don't need to look into this," think again. It's a good idea to occasionally re-evaluate your policy. Just like TV, Internet and cell phone services, insurance companies might change their policy and use different key factors to calculate premiums. Those might not always be to your advantage.

How Is Your Policy Written and What's Your Deductible?

The monthly cost of an insurance policy for a vehicle is greatly dependent on options selected for the coverage and the deductible. Here are the general options:

Want lower monthly payments? Opt for a higher deductible. Taking on more responsibility in case of an accident may mean extra savings.

Looking for additional peace of mind and higher coverage levels? A lower deductible might provide an added level of assurance — though your monthly premium might increase slightly.

So, there it is — the influence of deductible choices is shaping your insurance cost. Finding that perfect balance between coverage and budget allows you to ride safely and confidently.

Be Well Informed and Well Covered

It's a good idea to periodically review your policy with your insurance agent and eliminate any coverage you don't need. Evaluate whether you have, and need, comprehensive coverage on an older vehicle, rental reimbursement, or emergency roadside service. This is a good approach to saving money. Your agent should advise you and, most importantly, educate you. Keep in mind that while they represent the insurance company as an agent, they are not the policymakers. They usually have little time or interest in explaining the details, so they often tell you to read your policy. Unfortunately, the verbiage is often so convoluted that most people kind of skim through their contracts and get lost in confusion. Make sure to list specific questions or points you don't understand and ask your agent to provide more details. They should know or find those answers for you.

How Sexy Is Your Car?

What you drive is a huge factor affecting your premiums. Car insurance companies frequently develop safety ratings by evaluating industry statistics and gathering a huge amount of data from customer claims. They may use this information to offer discounts to clients who drive 'safer' vehicles. The opposite can also be true.

- Some insurers increase premiums for cars more susceptible to damage, theft or causing injuries to occupants. They usually lower rates for cars that fare better than the norm on those measures.
- Driving vehicles highly rated in terms of driver and passenger protection could mean greater savings on insurance.
- The color of the car can also influence premiums. Some colors are more targeted by thieves (and police officers for speeding). Think about this before buying a candy-apple red car.

It's good to do some research before going down to the showroom. Is the car that has piqued your interest well rated in terms of safety? Is this model frequently stolen? Knowing the answers to a few simple questions can help you keep premiums down.

Do You Live in Your Car or Just Love to Drive?

How often you use your car and how much mileage you drive each year will also influence premiums. People who drive for business or long-distance commuting usually pay more than those who drive less. No matter how cautious you are behind the wheel, the reality is that the more miles you drive in a year, the more likely you are to be involved in a collision. Keep the following points in mind when your driving habits change.

- Shorter commutes to work or lowering your annual vehicle mileage may reduce your premiums.
- Consider joining a car or van pool, riding your bike, or taking public transportation to work to reduce your driving time.
- Ask your insurance company whether you can get a discount if you drive less.
- Usage-based auto insurance companies may save you money when you drive less by applying in-car technology.

What's Your Zip?

Where you live is a factor influencing your premium. Urban drivers, on average, pay more for auto insurance than those who live in small towns or rural locations. This is due to greater incidences of vandalism, theft, and crashes.

Do You Have Any Priors?

Accident-prone drivers pay more than those who have been accident-free for several years. Unfortunately, your driving record doesn't just disappear. Don't become complacent if you haven't had an accident in a long time. Maintain your safe driving habits by remaining vigilant. Some insurance providers may offer discounts, such as accident-free savings if you have been insured for three years without any incident.

Even if you can't magically change your driving record, having an accident on your record might serve as a useful reminder to always drive cautiously and carefully. The impact of previous collisions on your premiums will diminish with time.

Did You Stop Payments?

If you think that switching car insurance companies is as easy as stopping payments, think again. Sure, your policy will get canceled if you stop paying, but your existing insurance company could report you to the credit bureaus for nonpayment, damaging your credit score in the process. What's more, your insurance history will reflect a termination, which may cause other providers to decline your application or charge you higher premiums in the future.

If you decide to change providers, be sure to complete the necessary cancellation process with the current one and time it right by starting your new policy on the date the old policy ends.

INSIDER FILES

SAVING MONEY WITH LITTLE SNITCH

Many insurance ads promise something like, "Be a good driver, and we'll give you a break on your premiums." The only catch is that they will install a tracking device in your car. Be aware that this will monitor your every move. This little snitch doesn't bat an eye and records everything, from fast accelerations to sudden stops.

This might be a concern since the last thing most people think about when upset or angry is driving safely. The device stores and relays all information, regardless of the circumstances. If the insurer determines that you are not a safe driver, the agreement that was supposed to save you money might backfire and cost you more.

How High Do You Score?

Credit seems to be at the core of everything relating to money. Did you know that maintaining good credit might help you save money on your car insurance premiums? That's right. Believe it or not, your credit may impact your rates since providers can use credit data to forecast future claims. They have found that certain credit characteristics for an individual are useful to predict how likely it is that they will have an insurance claim.

These characteristics are not the same ones used by banks to measure lending risk, but rather, insurers may use credit-based insurance scores in conjunction with other variables to assess the likelihood of claims being submitted. These variables may include age, driving record, claims history, place of residence, the type of car and the average miles driven, among others.

As a general best practice, it is advisable to do what you can to improve your credit. Be sure to monitor your credit report on a regular basis and contact the credit bureaus to clear up any errors.

You Look So Young... Are You Married?

It sounds silly, but yes, your age, sex and marital status do make a difference. Drivers under the age of 25, particularly single males, are statistically involved in more collisions. In most states, insurance rates reflect this reality. You might also be eligible for discounts if you're a student, especially if you're on the honor roll.

Are You a Couch Driver?

A growing number of people now work from home, where their commute consists of dodging Legos or cats on their way from the bedroom to the office. This lifestyle could prove more beneficial financially than they imagine.

If you are in such a situation, call your car insurance agent right now to discuss downshifting premiums. When the total mileage driven is dropping by thousands of miles each month, it might be wise to switch from 'full coverage' to 'part coverage.'

🏁 PIT STOP LESSON 🏁

INSURANCE DISCOUNT FOR GOOD STUDENTS

Most vehicle insurance companies will offer discounts to student drivers who maintain good grades.

Ask your insurance agent to see if they have such a discount policy.

Are You Insurable?

Your insurance company can terminate your policy, or non-renew, at any time if you violate one or more of their guidelines during your policy period. Things such as failing to pay your premium on time, losing your driver's license due to a suspension or revocation, submitting too many at-fault claims, or misrepresenting your driving history or past insurance claims could all be reasons for termination or non-renewal.

Your carrier must notify you in writing about such decisions within a specific time frame legally required by your state. The insurance company is required by law to tell you why. If you aren't provided with one, you must send your insurer a written request. You may have legal recourse through your state's department of insurance if you believe you've been unfairly treated.

INSIDER FILES

UNHITCHED HAVOC

Full coverage might sound comforting, but the details can often prove otherwise. When towing is involved, it can become increasingly complex. For example, the coverage might not apply if a trailer detaches from the towing vehicle. It could be wise to add towing coverage to your standard policy.

Imagine this: While towing your beloved boat to the lake, disaster strikes. Suddenly your trailer breaks loose from your vehicle and causes havoc among other cars on the road. Panic ensues until your eventually tell yourself, "It's a good thing I have full insurance coverage on this baby!" Unfortunately, you might be in for another bad surprise.

CREATIVE WAYS TO PROTECT YOUR CAR

Auto insurance serves as financial protection in the event of an accident. However, there is an interesting new twist in specific situations where you are not present when your car is broken into or vandalized. Or what about things like a storm surge that happened naturally? In cases like these, knowing your homeowner's policy is crucial.

Unleash Your Home's Superpowers

Your home policy might cover damage to your automobile caused by natural disasters. Think about it as a 'Big Brother' policy, which can also be able to help in the event of vandalism.

There are a lot of potential mishaps that may occur while your car is in the driveway, and your homeowner's insurance may cover some or all of them. From theft and broken windows to fallen trees and ice falling.

A good rule of thumb to follow when comparing insurance policies is to look for one that strikes a good balance between price and coverage.

The home policy should cover a vehicle in the garage for incidents such as flooding and fire. Just ensure the coverage is sufficient if you have a vintage or collectors' vehicle.

The savings might be substantial, compared to buying standalone home coverage.

Also make sure to remind yourself that commercial properties such as supermarkets and malls should also have coverage in case something happens to your vehicle while on their premises. In that eventuality, try submitting all claims to their business policy before your own.

BEST KEPT SECRETS OF INSURANCE COVERAGE

Consumers are often too focused on the dollar amount of their insurance coverage, and they don't really understand what they're getting for that price. You would never purchase a pizza solely based on price, without knowing which toppings come with it, would you?

Now comes the challenging part: Everyone should read through their policy to discover exactly what coverage they have. This may seem like an insurmountable obstacle course, like navigating through an underground maze without lights, especially if your policy was put together many years ago. But don't panic; it's never too late to audit your coverage and make any necessary modifications so you can drive with peace of mind.

 PIT STOP LESSON

IS YOUR TOWING INSURED?

If your vehicle needs a tow, make sure the towing company is insured and bonded. Why does it matter? If something goes wrong while the vehicle is being towed (pulled, or on a flatbed,) the company's insurance should cover it. Otherwise, this could turn into a nightmare for both parties and add major claims to your policy record.

Get the Full Scoop on Goodies from Your Insurance

Did you know that some insurance policies include comprehensive car rental coverage? Yes, in case of an accident or emergency repairs on your vehicle, some insurance may cover your rental car.

Most comprehensive plans offer complete protection whether you're driving your own sports car or taking a road trip in mom's minivan. It does not matter who owns what. Your policy might have you covered.

Are Your Claims Properly Reported?

If your car repairs are reported under your collision coverage, instead of comprehensive coverage, your car will then show on future CarFax reports, thus impacting resale value. This is a major concern if you are leasing as the dealership will run this report when you return the vehicle and charge you or use this to convince you into purchasing the lease contract out. You will also be at risk of increased premium for having a collision reported in your driving record. Discuss this with your insurance agent ahead to make sure you understand your coverage. Remember that their job is to educate you, not to sell you.

Is It Your Fault? It Might Not Matter...

Many clients are surprised to learn that they are covered, even if something happened following their own mistake. Always ask your insurer if something is covered. You might happily discover that your comprehensive full coverage policy covers major things, such as

- using the wrong gas in your car
- hitting your house while backing up
- breaking your side mirror at a drive-through
- driving over something that punctures your engine or transmission, even if you now need a replacement.

INSIDER FILES

YOUR MISTAKES MIGHT BE COVERED

Most car owners might not realize that some types of repairs might be covered by their insurance. For example, if you're at fault for putting the wrong fuel in your car, or damaging your engine, transmission, or major components after running over something on the road, your comprehensive insurance should cover it. This is not dependent on whose fault it is, even if no police or witnesses were involved.

Here is another fascinating tidbit: certain policies offer coverage when traveling, whether it's a spontaneous road trip or if you're embarking on a well-planned vacation. This coverage usually includes optional extras, like hotel rooms and related expenses.

When renting a car, your credit cards may offer unexpected solutions if you're involved in a collision by covering your deductible costs as well. Check with your card issuer first to see if they offer this benefit before dipping into your savings to cover something yourself.

Don't be shy calling your insurance provider to ask questions and start making them work for you so you can benefit from those high premiums.

- **Keep Your Agent's Number Handy:** Inform your provider if there have been any lifestyle changes in your household, such as marriage or remote work. This could cause your premiums to change.

- **Ask Questions:** Clarify your policy's cryptic lingo with your agent to ensure you're well insured and well informed. Ask, even if you did a gaffe, like using the wrong gas. Many errors could be forgiven under your policy. (It's okay to be human.)

- **Harness Hidden Coverage:** Your homeowner's insurance can extend its protective arm to cover both natural and human-caused mishaps. If you rent a car with your credit card, it might provide coverage for unexpected events.

INFORMATION IN MIRRORS IS MORE EMPOWERING THAN IT MAY APPEAR!

HEREIN LIES THE HEART OF OWNERSHIP

As we approach the end of this road trip through car ownership, let us remember that, when owning a car, it is wiser to keep emotions under control than succumb to temptation. Don't get seduced by sleek machines with powerful engines; remember the wise side of steering wheels too.

Cars should not serve as status symbols or driveway decorations. They're partners we should depend on to fulfill our practical needs and ambitions. Look for one that complements your lifestyle while meeting all your requirements.

Herein lies the heart of car ownership: not what but how. That is correct; real magic lies not in brand or horsepower alone but how one manages their vehicle on public roadways with consideration for fellow drivers, pedestrians, and safety in mind.

As you venture forth into the vast realm of car ownership, I offer you this inspiring advice: Choose Wisely, Own Responsibly and Drive Safely. ***It's not what you drive, it's how you drive!***

Lap One: Conquered!
Take a bow.

You're cleared for
the next round
of learning!

Section 2

MAINTENANCE

"Cars wear out, empowerment stays!"
—Shahe Koulloukian

Unplanned Driving Lessons

*C*hristopher and Victoria have been remiss by falling into the typical car consumer habits. It was easy for them to take their cars for granted and forget the importance of responsible car ownership. Victoria has always been a loving and caring mom, but she failed to see that vehicles require constant monitoring and care just like children. When something is neglected, bad things can happen.

The Smiths tended to make a big deal out of minor issues, especially cosmetic stuff. After all, appearances matter. Yet they both failed to notice and keep track of issues which might require more attention, like squeaking noises, or rattles.

By not sharing such issues with their repair shop, problems that could be handled with inexpensive work might turn into something more costly. Christopher thought he was clever with his macho male approach, but he was shooting himself in the foot when telling his mechanic, "Do me a favor, keep the repairs under a thousand." Now that he's doing business with Dennis, he learned that it is a major "No—No" to give a maximum budget for repairs. Dennis explained that by doing so, unscrupulous shops will feel that they have carte blanche to charge for any work under that threshold. Even if the vehicle only needs minor service, some shops will do things not yet required within the budget requested.

While Dennis tries his best to keep repair costs low, the Smiths are likely to spend more on repairs that would have been a quick fix a few months earlier. They are learning to distinguish between car repairs that need attention for safety, and issues that don't directly impact safety, like dings and dents.

Christopher thanked his trusted mechanic and remembered his grandmother's words from when she used to watch over him as a kid: "My dearest Christopher, I would rather you cry for five minutes now because I corrected you than have me cry forever because I ignored the opportunity to correct you."

Chapter 8

EMPOWERING OWNERSHIP

I t's important to remember that purchasing a car is only the beginning of an ongoing relationship which creates responsibilities. While it might seem easy at first when you're choosing your vehicle, there are many aspects to owning a car. The long list of things to consider ranges from maintenance and repairs to insurance and registration. Keeping a car running smoothly is a long-term commitment. It demands serious attention and effort to keep it running in tip-top shape.

WHAT IT MEANS TO OWN AND MAINTAIN A CAR

Car owners must manage numerous things, starting from the moment they finish negotiating their purchase before they even hit the road. It can be exhausting to always have your hand in your pocket to pay for things. However, there are ways to make car ownership easier.

It's key for car owners to remember that the complexities of vehicle repair have similarities with healthcare. This is a reality that most people might not fully appreciate. To keep an automobile in good shape and avoid costly repairs, you must understand the fundamentals and importance of using skilled professionals for routine maintenance.

Owning a vehicle is a source of pride and it has become a way of life for many people. A car is often one of the most significant purchases a person can make, and it becomes the second-safest place after their home.

Vehicle owners should empower themselves by recognizing their duties and responsibilities. Worrying about social acceptance might lead to purchases motivated by convenience and vanity. Whether you're a first-time buyer or seasoned car owner, remember that having a vehicle provides more than just transportation. It's an essential element of your life that you must maintain, much like your family's health. Regular maintenance and attention will keep your car dependable and long-lasting.

🏁 PIT STOP LESSON 🏁

I SEE, I HEAR, I FEEL, I SMELL...

Listening, seeing, touching, and smelling are allies when it comes to protecting both your car and wallet from costly repairs. They can help you detect signals such as leaks, vibrations, weird sounds or burning scents.

This way you will be able to take action before things get worse and even more repairs become necessary.

DEFINING YOUR MAINTENANCE DUTIES

Good news: Taking care of a car is simpler than most people think. It all comes down to developing the habit of caring for the vehicle and avoiding excuses, such as "Not Having Enough Time."

Three Steps to Responsible Car "Parenting"

Step 1: Start by learning about the simple fundamentals. You'll be surprised how much you can discover by reading your owner's manual. Yes, that dusty book you keep pushing out of the way in your glove box. (I have peppered this throughout the book, and I will keep doing so until it sinks in.)

Step 2: Find a repair shop driven by a willingness to educate. They should be happy to explain what your car needs immediately and mention things that you can do later. Don't listen passively; ask questions and seek to understand what you are being told.

Step 3: Take these valuable maintenance tips below and put them to good use. Trust me, it's not as boring as your high school textbook.

Plus, you might impress your mechanic with your newfound knowledge. So, let's get cracking, shall we?

Maintenance Tips

Do Not Procrastinate. The most expensive car maintenance mistake you can make is letting the little things slide when busy. Become aware of the signs you get from your car by observing for oil or liquid leaks. Touch it to assess the type of fluid. Smell the odors to identify what they are. Call your repair shop to share this information and ask what may happen if you ignore those signs.

Keep Service and Repair Records in Your Car. Hold on to all receipts, invoices, and recommendations from your auto shop. These will come in handy if you're advised that repairs are needed. Before agreeing to them, you should refer to your file and check to see if you have already had that work done as those repairs might still be under warranty. Receipts serve as a great tool to showcase the value of your vehicle when you plan to sell it. It is a great way to prove how well you took care of it and thus get top dollar for it.

Just don't leave this folder of receipts easily accessible in case of a break-in. I suggest keeping it under the spare tire as thieves don't usually check there. (See Chapter 22 for more suggestions about keeping your information secure.)

Pay Attention. Warning lights could indicate engine problems, brake failure, overheating or malfunctions. It's your vehicle's way of communicating that it needs help. Sure, your favorite song is on and you're singing like the next runner-up for American Idol, but make sure you're not missing important messages or unusual sounds.

Start a Relationship Now. Don't wait until you have a breakdown to find a repair shop, if you don't have one yet. Start the relationship with a simple service, like an oil change, to evaluate the new facility and see if they communicate with you openly and honestly. Make sure you tell the whole story about your vehicle. The more information you give them, the better (and likely cheaper) the diagnosis will be. And, most importantly, don't feel intimidated. Always feel free to ask questions about your vehicle's overall health.

Dot the I's and Cross the T's. Getting an affordable estimate is one thing, but what about the quality of the parts and warranty? It's easy to be reeled in by a cheap estimate, but make sure to ask if the parts are new or used, and if it is original equipment from the manufacturer (OEM) or aftermarket. Inquire about the warranty on the repairs to understand if it covers both parts and labor. If there is no warranty on the work or parts, take some time to consider if the savings are worth it. The better informed you are the better positioned you are for an open dialogue and a trusting relationship.

Get Empowered with Expert Resources

Car owners hold more power than they realize. (I don't mean this in a literal sense as mechanics lift heavy stuff all day long... just saying!) Prior to visiting a repair shop with your vehicle, it would be prudent to familiarize yourself with online automotive resources. Many sites and forums provide insight into your vehicle, such as common issues, recalls and even estimated resale potential. However, don't rely solely on these sources; use them as steps on the journey toward empowered ownership. By taking control and planning intelligently, you could become the best car parent ever. Your budget will thank you. Refer to the website list in the Resources section at the end of the book.

VROOM OR GLOOM?

When considering repairs on their vehicle, people often prioritize cost as the primary factor and that is completely understandable, but it could be an expensive decision. It is important to inquire about the quality of parts being used and their warranties as cheaper parts could fail and require more expensive work not covered.

The Parts and Promises of Auto Repair

Independent repair shops and some dealerships may use aftermarket auto parts instead of original manufacturer parts (OEM). Don't get me wrong, purchasing aftermarket parts can save you money. But when paying for OEM components make certain you're not receiving aftermarket ones instead. Before making decisions about parts, always inquire about their warranties. Asking the right questions will help you assess their worth accurately.

INSIDER FILES

HOW TO SAVE ON WIPER BLADES

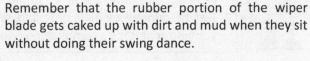

Remember that the rubber portion of the wiper blade gets caked up with dirt and mud when they sit without doing their swing dance.

If you simply wipe down the rubber blades occasionally with a baby wipe and rub a little Vaseline, to keep them soft and pliable, they will keep performing longer. YUP, it is really that simple.

It's Okay to Do It Yourself — Correctly!

You may not be a mechanic; however, you can take simple maintenance repairs yourself. That may include replacing the engine air filter, the wiper blades, your battery, or even the cabin filter. And believe it or not, you can learn this directly from your mechanic. An honest repair shop will show you how to do some of these tasks if you ask. I teach my customers about easy DIY tasks all the time.

Some work, such as brake pads getting low, can be held off in some situations. When ignored for too long, the cost could increase significantly. This is why you should evaluate repairs based on your specific situation.

For example, replacing brake pads when they still have 20% of life remaining can often wait if the vehicle is mostly driven around town for short distances. But if it's about to be used for a long-distance trip, it may be better to change the pads now before the rotors get damaged and increase the total repair bill.

 FUEL FOR THOUGHT

WELCOMING ENQUIRIES

A professional mechanic should welcome and encourage inquiries. They are often willing to educate customers about essential repairs or maintenance needed to keep them and their vehicles safe. There are no stupid questions. Just be mindful of their time and schedule an appointment if it's a complicated issue.

LEARN, FIX, DRIVE, AND SMILE

Following regularly scheduled maintenance recommendations has never been more important. Any missed checkup can cause irreparable harm to its performance. Missed appointments means depriving your beloved ride of essential care it needs for optimal functioning.

Skipping Regular Maintenance

Now more than ever, modern cars boast sophisticated technologies and intricate systems that require frequent attention for optimal performance and economy. Routine maintenance helps detect minor problems before they escalate to major expenses; this also keeps warranties valid. Do not underestimate the significance of setting aside regular maintenance visits to your repair shop.

Consistency is key when it comes to car maintenance. Regular oil changes are an essential step contributing to your car's lifespan and reliability. They're recommended every 3, 5 or 10 months depending on vehicle mileage.

It is also wise to have oil/fluid levels checked periodically between oil changes. Check tire pressure too and adjust as needed since it drops over time.

What to Do: Get to know your vehicle's maintenance requirements. Start with the service interval schedule in the owner's manual or on the manufacturer's website. Keep track of any work done, and don't skip anything.

Overlooking Wear and Tear

Tire wear, while often hidden in plain sight, could represent a fatal oversight. Everything wears out over time, including brakes, tires, light bulbs, engine, belts, hoses, transmission, and internal parts. Some wear is obvious, like a blown light bulb or squealing brakes, but not all. Regular inspections help keep you on top of issues before they cause collateral damage or a crash.

What to Do: Get to know your car. Ask your repair shop to give you some tips to stay on top of things. If you're not inclined to do these things yourself, it might be a good idea to drop into the shop on a regular basis to have the basics inspected. Consider doing this monthly or before any trips. Taking care of issues as soon as possible will prevent them from spiraling into more costly repairs.

Ignoring Recall Notices

Never ignore safety recall notices as they could save your life. Automakers and suppliers spend billions of dollars on research, engineering, and development, but defects can still occur. If a manufacturing issue is serious enough, particularly concerning safety, they'll announce a safety recall to repair or replace the defect. Ignoring those recalls could put you and those around you in danger.

What to Do: Check with the National Highway Traffic Safety Administration (NHTS) or with your dealership to inquire about any recalls for your vehicle. If something is applicable, have the repairs completed as soon as possible. When you call for your appointment, ask if the parts are in stock. There is nothing worse than dropping off your vehicle only to find out at the end of the day that you must come back. Make sure the dealership has your current address in order to receive safety recall notices by mail.

PIT STOP LESSON

WHAT IF THIS WAS YOUR MOM'S CAR?

If you have some doubts when told that repairs are required on your car, simply ask your mechanic or service advisor what they would do if it was their own mom's car. This might affect their answer.

Ignoring Warning Lights and Messages

Since your vehicle can't talk, it uses warning lights to provide information about its status. When a light comes on, it means something is wrong. Many cars will notify you about issues with tire and oil pressure and brakes. The check engine light might be the only indication that your car may be in failure mode or unsafe for the road. Driving with warning lights might lead to higher refueling costs, excessive emissions, vehicle damage, or a crash. Addressing those issues quickly will save you money and keep you safe.

What to Do: If a warning light comes on, have it checked by a professional for proper diagnosis and repair. If you can't get in to see your repair shop right away, it is OK to visit a parts store to have your code read, but you need a true diagnosis by a professional mechanic, not a parts salesperson.

Saving on Auto Repair

If you think experts are expensive, wait until you work with amateurs. Sure, everyone wants to save money, but cheap parts or the least expensive mechanic may not be the best approach in the long run. Genuine parts are usually more expensive, but they're made specifically for your vehicle. Aftermarket parts might require adjustments to fit, and they may not work as well as the originals. Yet in some instances, they might be better, so it's a good idea to consult with a trusted mechanic. Competent auto repair shops may charge more, but their training and experience will easily justify the price.

What to Do: Pay for the best parts and service that you can afford. It doesn't have to be the most expensive option, but something that will ensure reliable repairs. Focus more on what warranty comes with the parts and repairs versus the bottom line. There is nothing worse than saving $50 or $100 on repairs with a limited warranty that ends up costing more to redo the work.

Relying on Google Diagnosis

Anyone with a scanning tool can read diagnostic trouble codes from a check engine light, but not everyone can diagnose them. There is a big difference! Real diagnosis and repair require training, experience, and diagnostic tools, not a browser. It's not a good idea to simply replace a sensor because Google said, "It's a sensor code."

What to Do: Educate yourself and follow the manual. If it's beyond your expertise, don't waste your time and money throwing parts at the problem. Get a professional diagnosis.

Self-Diagnosis

No mechanic will take responsibility for someone else's diagnosis, not even from your uncle's Bob's neighbor, Jim, who worked on cars his whole life. Today's auto repair technicians spend a significant part of their time learning about auto repair strategies, auto diagnostic methods, and the use of special tools. Telling them what to do is like explaining to a doctor that you've self-diagnosed a health problem. It is wasting everyone's time.

What to Do: Let the mechanic diagnose the problem and make the repair — that's what they're trained for. If you tell them to replace something and it doesn't work, whose fault, is it?

Unclear Explanations

Miscommunication with your mechanic leads to wasted time, money, and broken trust. You drive your car every day. Your mechanic may only see it once every few months. Since they deal with up to a dozen cars every day, they might need a quick update on what's happening with yours. Vague concerns won't give them a clear direction on where to focus their attention, and what they address might not be what you're concerned about.

What to Do: Be clear and precise. Instead of saying you hear "a sound," note when and where it happens, on what kind of road, how fast you're driving, how frequently it happens, and what it sounds like. If the car is "lacking power," it's good to provide additional details, like when was the last time you refueled, in what circumstances it acts up, even the temperature and the weather. Also, if you or a friend attempted some Do It Yourself (DIY) repairs, be sure to confess. It will only cost you more in the end if you withhold such important information.

KEY TAKEAWAYS

- **Responsible Car Parenting:** Keep in mind that your car is more than simply transportation. Ensure it receives regular maintenance through periodic check-ins and record keeping so you can enjoy its fullest life span.

- **Preventive Care Trumps Reactive Despair:** Take an active part in caring for your vehicle by approaching maintenance and repairs with as much care as you would give healthcare.

- **Focus On Quality Over Price:** Although low-cost options might initially appear attractive, investing in quality components and diagnostic services could save money over time. A well-maintained car with documented service records ensures a safe ride and demonstrates your dedication to both quality work and parts to potential buyers.

INFORMATION IN MIRRORS IS MORE EMPOWERING THAN IT MAY APPEAR!

Mysterious Lights

C hristopher walked in the house screaming, "That car's going to cost us lots of money, again!" Victoria wondered what happened this time. He explained that the engine light had turned on. "That's the most expensive thing to fix," he said.

She asked, "Are you sure? Those pesky dashboard warning lights seem to come on and off randomly. I don't understand their meaning half the time." The Smiths had quarreled over lights before but never really attempted to understand them. "Let me call Dennis before we blow the engine. We really can't afford a new one," she said.

Dennis praised them for being extra cautious about this and asked if they still had their bible. "Bible?" Victoria replied, thinking it was another joke. "No, I mean your Owner's Manual," he said before adding, "It's probably in your glove box with gum stuck on it."

At these critical moments, the Smiths were quick to assume the worst, but Dennis had a feeling it wasn't major as he had recently worked on the car. When he asked Christopher if anything had happened that day. He replied, "No, I went to work, stopped for gas on the way back, and noticed the light when I parked in the driveway."

Dennis said, with a chuckle, "Find that book and look at the meaning for that warning light. Illumination might follow..." before adding, "and check to see if your gas cap is screwed tightly."

To his surprise, Christopher noticed that he had failed to put back the cap after fueling. It was still clipped to the trap door. "That's it!" Dennis said. "That light alerted you that something was wrong. Yes, some lights deserve immediate consideration as they could indicate potential danger or imminent damage, but most serve only as gentle reminders or signals that something requires further examination."

He concluded by reminding them to "Flick through your car bible and become acquainted with each light's meaning. It's not Morse code. I'm just glad you didn't go to a shady shop nearby that could have capitalized on your fear... Go enjoy that drink, now!"

Chapter 9

WARNING LIGHTS

A s a responsible car owner, you must be proactive in maintaining and repairing your vehicle. Even with the best care, unexpected challenges can arise, leaving you feeling helpless. However, by educating yourself you can make informed decisions and minimize your concerns.

OK, so your holiday shopping is starting and you're driving to your favorite mall. You're gleaming while sipping on your peppermint mocha-chino double latte fusion frappe-lino as you're ahead with your holiday preparations this year. You even hung up all the lights already. Then you suddenly notice that your dashboard lights are chiming and flashing, just like your decoration lights back home.

What's happening? Is the vehicle warning you of impending doom, or is it just a gentle reminder that it's due for maintenance? Should you pull over immediately, or can you keep driving? Is it something you can address yourself, or do you need to hire a professional?

Once you've been driving for years, it's easy to forget the importance of indicator lights, or what they could mean. Or perhaps it's a new vehicle and you didn't realize that various makes or models display icons or symbols differently.

Sure, the dashboard indicator lights are not as exciting as holiday lights, but they are essential to the overall function of your vehicle and its performance. While repairs can be pricey, disregarding those warning lights can cause even more expensive damage to your car. More importantly, you could be endangering both yourself and others on the road. So, if you see a warning light on your dashboard, don't ignore it.

You can be a responsible car owner by simply learning about your vehicle's needs and, most importantly, your safety. A good place to start is by skimming through your car's owners' manual, AKA the vehicle manufacturer's bible. Stop worrying, you don't have to read the whole thing in one sitting. You can simply go to the index guide and look up warning lights…WOW, there it is!

CRACKING THE LEXICON OF WARNING LIGHTS

You might want to sit back and continue sipping your yummy drink as I share some quick references on what these warning lights mean and what you should do about them.

Check Engine Light

This 'malfunction indicator lamp' is a signal from the computer system letting you know that something is wrong with the engine, and it needs your attention. It is the most misunderstood indicator on your dashboard, as it could mean several things. It may turn out to be a very simple problem with an easy fix. Or it could be warning you about a serious issue which could potentially damage your engine or the transmission; in extreme cases it could impact both.

For example, minor issues could be as simple as a faulty gas cap or a loose vacuum hose. It could also mean something more serious, such as a misfiring engine due to a faulty injector or ignition system. In many cases, it means that you should consider visiting your repair facility soon to get it checked.

What to Do: It's important not to panic when the Check Engine Light comes on while you're driving. Remain calm and notice if the car is handling differently. Is it making a different sound? Is it overheating? Or is it running rough, feeling like it's about to stall? If so, then consider stopping immediately and having it towed to your repair facility.

However, if everything is normal, you can probably keep driving, while remaining cautious and alert. Get the issue looked at sooner than later to make sure it doesn't spiral into more serious and costly problems.

If the Check Engine light is blinking or turning from yellow to red, that typically signifies a more severe issue. When this happens, it is recommended that you pull over and have the vehicle towed to a mechanic for a diagnostic. To confirm the issue, you should get it checked by an experienced auto repair shop as soon as possible.

ABS Light

The anti-lock braking system (ABS) prevents skidding on wet or icy surfaces by keeping the tires in contact with the road when braking. When this indicator turns on, your brakes will still function, but the ABS might not engage if you need to make an emergency stop.

What to Do: Have a technician diagnose the problem in the near future. If both the ABS and the brake lights are on at the same time, pull over immediately; it's no longer safe to drive.

Battery Charge Warning

The battery powers everything electrical in a vehicle, from the headlights to the taillights. When this indicator light comes on, it means something in the recharging system failed. It could be a corroded battery cable, a problem with the alternator, or an issue with the voltage regulator. If the battery doesn't get recharged, you might not be able to start your engine at a future stop.

What to Do: Shut off as many electrical accessories as you can, such as the stereo, air conditioner, or heater. You should visit the auto mechanic soon to determine the exact problem.

Oil Pressure Warning

This light could indicate that your car is low on oil, that your oil pump or pressure gauge is faulty, or that something is seriously wrong with the engine.

What to Do: Pull over immediately and turn off your engine. If the oil doesn't need to be topped off, take the car to an auto mechanic as soon as possible.

Tire Pressure Monitoring System (TPMS)

The TPMS light might indicate that at least one of your tires is under inflated. If the light turns back off automatically, it could be in response to a change in temperature outside.

What to Do: Check the pressure on all tires. The recommended pressure level should be listed on a sticker on the driver's doorjamb. Add air to any tire as needed. If the tires are OK and you still have a warning, check your spare, as it might also have a sensor.

Engine Temperature Warning

A faulty cooling system triggers this light. It is letting you know that your engine is overheating. This could be due to a coolant leak from a broken hose.

What to Do: Pull over and turn your heater on to help reduce engine overheating and let it completely cool down. By turning on your heater, you're forcing the hot overheated antifreeze to flow out of the engine and into the heater core. This allows the engine block to quickly cool down. Make sure to add coolant to help control the integrity of the engine block until you have it towed to your repair facility. Attempting to drive it before the problem is solved may cause serious damage. Towing it will cost less than damaging your engine.

Brake Warning Light

This alert could mean that your parking brake is on, your brake fluid is low, a brake light bulb needs to be replaced, or in certain cars it means there's a problem with your anti-lock braking system. (Some cars don't have a separate ABS light.)

What to Do: First, check your parking brake to see if it is enabled, and your brake lights to make sure they work properly when pressing the brake pedal. If the warning light stays on, take your car to an auto mechanic to determine if your brake fluid needs to be refilled or flushed, or if your brakes need repair.

 FUEL FOR THOUGHT

DIAGNOSTICS REQUIRE EXPERIENCE

While local parts stores may offer to read your engine light error codes for FREE, that does not constitute a diagnosis. Their plug-in tool simply displays engine light codes. The vehicle has over 30,000 parts and many components work together. The code doesn't always tell you exactly what the problem is. It could indicate the general area of the malfunction, but further diagnosis is often required. Full diagnosis requires skill, experience, special scanners, and guidance by knowledgeable hands.

KEY TAKEAWAYS

- **Dashboard Dilemma Explained:** Just as you wouldn't ignore flashing lights approaching you on the road, don't dismiss your car's dashboard warnings. They are there for your safety.

- **Understanding Warning Lights:** Dashboard lights could indicate anything from maintenance nudges to urgent system breakdown. Your vehicle's handbook is a reference to understand them.

- **Critical Lights, Critical Action:** The check engine light isn't simply an advisory; it signals the need for help. This would include such things as leaky gas caps or an engine misfire. While ABS and oil pressure warnings might seem harmless enough at first glance, they require immediate attention to make sure vital safety systems, such as brakes and engine lubrication systems, are functioning as intended.

INFORMATION IN MIRRORS IS MORE EMPOWERING THAN IT MAY APPEAR!

When a Deal Is Not a Deal

Victoria knew that her car was due for an oil change but procrastinated for a few weeks as she was too busy. When she drove by a new quick lube offering a free car wash with every oil change, she thought it was a perfect opportunity to get it done and have a much-needed shine for her wheels. Unfortunately, she was duped into unnecessary repairs while the car was on the lift. The sign read, "$15.00 Oil Change — Come in for the best deal," yet her final bill had an extra digit.

When she got back home, Christopher couldn't believe what had happened. "Why didn't you go see Dennis?" he asked. She explained that she wasn't near and didn't think it was worth bugging him for a $15 job; "And he doesn't have a car wash," she thought. Victoria was usually quick to throw phrases like, "You wasted money again!" However, this time she was at the receiving end of such comments from her husband. He said that quick lube shops were notorious for scams using low pricing, free washes, or coupons to get people in the door and then finding expensive issues that require immediate repairs. Now she felt worse as she began doubting if all that work was necessary.

The Smiths had started reclaiming some "car" powers by reading their owner's manual, and being proactive but they still didn't have a full grasp of every maintenance aspect. Victoria got lured by the deal and then surrendered to the work suggested since a part of her felt guilty for waiting so long to get an oil change. Christopher could swear all night long about the questionable approach or the work done, yet she accepted the responsibility for enabling these individuals to take advantage of her. Never again, she thought.

Christopher told his wife that jumping between different shops is not a good way to build a continuing relationship. When you call Dennis, "My Mechanic…" it should be because you have a long-term relationship. "No cheating allowed, right?"

Chapter 10

FINDING AN HONEST MECHANIC

In the United States, there are around one million automobile mechanics, including those who work in independent repair shops, dealerships, and body shops. These experts spend lengthy shifts diagnosing, repairing, and preventing automobile problems. Individuals choose to work as mechanics for a variety of reasons, such as growing up in a family of mechanics, having a passion for taking things apart and putting them back together, or simply falling into the field. They usually have one trait in common: their original interest in the trade itself, rather than the opportunity for financial benefit.

Consumers may feel vulnerable due to their lack of knowledge about vehicle maintenance. This could make them fearful of being taken advantage of by technicians. It is necessary to differentiate between mechanics and technicians to better understand what they do.

Mechanics typically repair automobiles and have limited diagnostic skills. Technicians identify problems using computers and scanners and have evolved beyond the mechanics' function. They have a wealth of experience diagnosing and repairing various parts of a vehicle. Some consumers prioritize budget and price over safety, while others are unaware of auto repair fundamentals. As a result, mechanics and vehicle owners often have a bumpy relationship.

To overcome such issues, owners must educate themselves about their vehicles and keep mechanics accountable for providing quality and honest service.

This entails adopting proactive measures such as understanding the basics of vehicle maintenance and organizing all service records and receipts. Keeping track of spending and being aware of the cost of repairs can help you make educated choices about fixing a car or buying a new one. While delaying critical repairs or maintenance may save you money in the short term, it undermines the car's safety and may result in higher costs down the line.

If your engine light comes on while you're driving, you may feel panicked and hurry to find out what to do. But here's a little-known fact: your panic may end up costing you more money. The first step in preventing surprises is to be prepared. Having a relationship with an auto repair shop is priceless as they will answer your call and you'll get an honest answer from someone you trust. Calling or visiting any business for the sake of convenience can be dangerous, especially in an emergency.

Customers must recognize that hopping from one shop to another in search of lower-cost repairs is hurting their wallets more than they realize. When you call a repair shop for a quote over the phone, they understand that they must offer you a low price to entice you to come see them. That is a strategy many use to get you in.

You want a shop that will ask why you need a specific repair and, more importantly, who recommended you that you need it. The shop you want is open for business because they take joy in repairing problems rather than selling you on the need to get expensive repairs. The shop offering great prices isn't always a bad thing but examine the value you're getting for what you've been quoted. You need to ask the right questions. Check to see if there is a warranty on certain repairs, know the type of parts used, and who will be working on your vehicle. Most auto mechanics are trustworthy and hardworking, but some are not. The auto repair industry is still riddled with incompetence and fraud, so finding a shop you trust can be difficult. This is why you must find one before running into urgent issues. You must be patient and accept that a relationship will not happen on your first visit.

The cluttered, filthy garage with old parts on the floor, dim lighting and mechanics wiping their hands with oil-soaked towels are a thing of the past. Those mechanics have been replaced by a new breed of individuals that have been trained in electrical theory, mechanical and computer systems, and are now known as technicians. They usually work in well-kept, well-equipped repair shops.

REPAIR SHOP BEHAVIOR INSIGHTS

When visiting a shop for the first time, be watchful. Look around. Clutter, fluids on the floor, disorganization, dirty lavatories, and shabby equipment are clues to a badly managed business, which may indicate poor workmanship. You must maintain an open line of communication with your car technicians. Are they paying attention to you? If they keep interrupting you or dismissing your reasoning, walk away. Here are a few behaviors to watch for.

How Non-Verbal Clues Might Increase Repair Costs

Make yourself comfortable and enjoy the synthetic leatherette of your car's interior for an interesting lesson which could potentially save you thousands of dollars.

Let's face it, auto repair shops can often feel like the gambling tables of the mechanical world. And the house almost always wins—right? The simple truth is that car technicians will analyze everything about you, from the minute you drive in, and will memorize your non-verbal clues and history like an open book. They may then use this information against you.

Exhibit A: Expensive upgrades. Your high-end stereo system may increase your repair bill. When a service advisor notices an expensive sound system, they take this as an indicator that you love to spend money on your baby. They know you need it to render Queen's 'Bohemian Rhapsody' with the full sound reproduction and attention it deserves. It's an indicator that you're more likely to fix anything they suggest. They know it, you know it, Freddy Mercury knows it!

Exhibit B: Baby seat. Repair shops know that parents will take extended measures to protect their family. They will mention security concerns when suggesting replacing brake pads or other repairs to push that button. The same goes with anecdotes about children or family stickers in the back window. These clues will be used to cause fear with statements such as, "Your car requires repair; it's a safety issue for you and your children." Ultimately, most repairs are worthwhile in the end, yet this tactic may shorten the repair schedule and cost more in the long run. As an example, brake pads with 30% remaining on them might be good for a while, if you don't plan long-distance trips.

Exhibit C: Expired registration. Expired plates, damaged body or paint and tape on windows convey that a car owner has little money or interest in their vehicle. It's subtlety saying, "Don't even try me... I'm broke." Owners in this situation can expect a high estimate designed to scare them off as it might not be worthwhile for them to work on the car. They anticipate that the owner might turn down most repairs suggested due to costs. Ask around if you feel the estimates are unrealistic so you don't overspend on repairs.

Awareness is the key here. Realize that every aspect of you and your car sends signals, and it's not always supporting your best interests. Listen carefully to the language used by salespeople to prevent getting in financial trouble. With auto repairs, either you take charge or just follow along for an expensive ride.

THE CONSUMER SIDE OF REPAIR SHOP COUNTERS

Congratulations on finding a mechanic! But now comes the hard part — creating a trusting relationship. I will now outline car ownership guidelines for consumers beginning this collaboration.

So, how do you talk about strange noises, leaks, warning lights, or other issues on behalf of your car? You can start by being proactive and learning the basics of your vehicle and how it works. When your vehicle is at the repair shop for maintenance or repairs, you want to make sure it's receiving quality and honest service.

Organize your service records and keep them in a folder. This will be helpful to see if you have already done similar repairs and if they are under warranty.

Now, let's check some facts. It's your car and you're responsible for it. If you complain and say things such as, "I don't know much about cars," I'm telling you that "It's your fault" if you get taken advantage of. For most consumers, the budget is the bottom line, but it might not always dictate the most sensible decisions. The average age of vehicles currently on the road is at an all-time high of 11 years. Cost-conscious consumers are choosing to keep their existing cars and trucks running rather than trade them in for new models. This means that many drivers are postponing needed repairs or maintenance as a money-saving measure. Unfortunately, delaying service not only represents false savings, but it can also compromise a car's safety.

There Are No Rules; It's Your Car and Your Safety

Knowing your car will help you understand what you can hold off on and what you must do to stay safe for the time being. It also gives you the power to know what's the worst that can happen if you ignore certain repairs. This control is the key to staying safe.

Now let's talk about dollars. It's unfortunate, but you often have no choice but to repair your vehicle when it comes right down to it. The best way to save money over the life of a vehicle is to choose a high-quality, full-service repair shop and allow them to know you and your budget.

Don't be shy about asking them if they can tell you more about specific repairs or maintenance issues. If they laugh or shrug it off, then you are in the wrong place. You want a repair shop that runs their business based on honesty, not the bottom line. Team up with them and let them know that you would like a game plan to keep your car safe on the road. This will do two things; it will allow you to have peace of mind and it will let the repair shop know that you are depending on them. This responsibility is what they are in business for. You can see them like a doctor who is responsible for helping keep you healthy and alive, without milking your wallet or insurance company.

It is important to understand that making the decision to bring a car in for service is only half the battle. To get the most out of your maintenance and repair dollars, you need to know how to deal with an automotive technician. The goal is to have a long-lasting relationship with a repair shop based on open and honest dialogue and that starts with you. Share everything. Do not lie out of fear of incurring more repairs or facing judgment. Instead, provide an honest account such as, "My neighbor attempted to repair it," or "I tried to do it myself after watching an online tutorial."

After being in the auto business for over 40 years, I could write another book on the unspoken truth about bad customers. Some shady actors make it their job to try and cheat auto repair shops by putting the blame on them and ruining their reputation.

Of course, we can't forget the stigma of crooked mechanics; it's very real. But who can we blame for this unfortunate reality? Consumers often allowed these things to happen by not being diligent and not knowing the basics. No one is saying that you need to become a mechanic, but having a general understanding of your basic auto repair needs will help you win in most situations.

THE LANGUAGE OF AUTO REPAIR

It's time for confessions... Simply put, there are things you should always share with your mechanic. On the other hand, there are forbidden things you should never talk about. Don't worry, this is no Fight Club.

Here are a few hush-hush secrets and whispered suggestions to master the love language of cars and ensure you're heard and understood.

The Dos

Do Get Regular Oil Changes. A great way to keep your car running at its greatest (and longest) potential is by taking it in for regular oil changes. Typically, vehicles with conventional oil will require an oil change every 3,000 miles or 3 months, whichever comes first. The range for synthetic oil is every 5,000 miles up to 10,000 miles. By having regular oil changes, you will be increasing your car's engine life and keeping your powertrain warranty in compliance.

Do Set Realistic Expectations. You might bring your vehicle in for routine maintenance only to be told that unexpected repairs need to be performed. Understand that mechanics have the longevity of your vehicle in mind, so they might recommend fixing certain things now to prevent further damage from occurring down the road. These should actually save you money in the long run. If they suggest more repairs, ask, "How busy are you? Can it be done on the same day?" Make sure you communicate properly to let them know about your time constraints and set realistic expectations.

Do Stay Close to Your Phone. The time required for your auto repair sometimes depends on whether you can be reached. If you decide to leave the shop, make sure they have your phone number in the event they need to discuss parts, service or timeline based on their findings. You'll also be notified as soon as your vehicle is ready, or not… There's nothing worse than expecting the vehicle to be ready on the same day, and not knowing it won't be possible because you failed to answer a call from the shop to confirm something.

Do Communicate Clearly. The saying goes, "I LOVE MY CAR." But one thing nobody loves is getting their wallets hit by hefty car repair bills. Now, imagine how much that would sting if your bills were higher based solely on your gender. For women, this is often the unfortunate reality — the stereotype that women know less about cars makes it easier for unscrupulous repair shops to take advantage of them. But this unfair practice can be changed through empowerment.

No one should feel intimidated by car repairs or pay inflated prices. When consumers have no idea how something works, they are dependent on the repair shop to inform them. If your repair shop lacks integrity, you're ripe for a rip-off. It's important to learn how to communicate with repair shops, so they don't take advantage of you.

No matter your gender, never call a repair shop and say, "I know nothing about cars. What is this supposed to cost me?" Unknowingly, such a statement might set you up for a hefty bill. There are many reputable shops with professionals making an honest living, but a few bad apples will try to cheat car owners if they feel they can get away with it.

The Don'ts

Don't Wait for a Breakdown to Consult. You want to start building a trusting relationship way before an emergency happens. Start with a simple oil change to get to know the shop and see how they operate. Ask to meet the owner to introduce yourself and share that you are looking to start a relationship to help keep your car maintained properly.

Don't Choose a Shop Because They're the Cheapest Option. Of course, saving money is optimal in all spending situations, but choosing an auto mechanic simply because they are cheap could cost you more in the long run. When you select an auto mechanic, you want to look at their credentials rather than their prices. You'll thank yourself later. Besides, repair shops that shout, "We have the lowest prices," are often set up for bait-and-switch. You want a shop that stands firm about the quality of work and the warranty they provide.

Don't Ever Ignore Service Lights. If any light on your dashboard turns on, never ignore it. These lights are sensor-specific, therefore, if one of them turns on, you know it's time to have it looked at. Ignoring these lights may cause long-term damage to your vehicle. Not to mention, you could be putting yourself at risk when driving. If a light turns on, it's time to take it to an auto mechanic. (See Chapter 9 for more details about warning lights.)

Don't Rely on DIY Solutions for Automotive Repairs. Regardless of whether your car is new or old, you should never perform DIY repairs unless you know and understand what you are about to do. It's empowering to be able to do some basic repairs, like changing air filters, wiper blades and even fan belts. But with newer technology, it's not always that simple. Watching videos on YouTube might help if you are mechanically inclined and have an idea of what needs to be done. But keep in mind that most of these videos are edited down to a fraction of the actual time it took to do the work. Just make sure you understand what you are getting into. If you make a mistake, it will cost you more as the repair shop will have to correct what you did wrong and then start over. Although automotive repairs can seem pricey, you'll be receiving high-quality work with a warranty rather than a faulty 'quick fix.'

Don't Constantly Check in When Your Vehicle Is Being Repaired. Avoid hovering around the mechanic as they perform auto repairs. This can prevent them from focusing on the task and it puts you in harm's way. Instead, consider staying in the waiting room, renting a vehicle, or asking for a courtesy ride back home or to work.

Don't Bring in a Cluttered Car. You never know which areas of your car the mechanic may need to access. If the interior of the vehicle is a mess, take a few minutes to clean it up. That way, the professional can efficiently and systematically work on the vehicle and do the best job possible.

Don't Forget to Ask About the Warranty. Prior to allowing a repair to be done, make sure you ask,

- **"What is the warranty?"**
- **"Does it cover both parts and labor?"**

Sometimes there is a good reason for low-price repairs, and you might only find out why when you need the same repairs again. Learn to ASK those questions and ASK AGAIN. This will prevent you from dealing with extra costs and losing more time if the repairs or parts fail.

BEFORE SAYING "I DO" TO YOUR MECHANIC

Before getting on one knee and whispering, "Will you be my mechanic?" let's review six simple commandments that will ensure an unbreakable match made in automotive heaven.

Do Your Research

You should have a solid idea of what to expect before you even set foot in a repair shop. Find out how long they have been in business and whether they offer a warranty on their work. Get an idea of their reputation by asking around. You want value over price, so don't be led by lowball pricing. The cheapest quote isn't necessarily the best one.

Communicate Clearly

When speaking with a mechanic about your vehicle's issues, make sure that all necessary details are shared such as lights or strange smells that you noticed; any unusual behaviors like lights coming on unexpectedly. Take note of times and temperatures along with any additional observations they could use as clues for diagnosis. Get an outline of exactly what steps will be taken to resolve your situation and clearly state your understanding of how that will happen. The more specific the information you have about what to expect, the quicker the repairs can be performed.

Get It in Writing

Before you agree to any service, make sure your estimate is in writing. Ask for the final price, including tax and shop fees.

Keep Track of Your Car's Suggested Services

Dig out the maintenance book that came with your vehicle. It might be shoved deep into your glove compartment or buried under fast food and parking receipts. Check to see when your car will need certain services, like spark plug replacements or oil changes. You can then ensure that mechanics perform those services only when necessary. If they attempt to perform something prematurely, ask for a detailed explanation before deciding whether to allow it.

FUEL FOR THOUGHT

Take a picture of the maintenance schedule page in your vehicle's manual and keep it in a note or folder on your phone for quick access. If you ever wonder if maintenance might soon be required, you'll have the information handy.

Understand the Three Different Repair Types

The first type is **recommended repair work** for something that's visibly starting to leak, fail or is broken. It's important to catch this before it gets worse. The second is **maintenance** that is suggested by the manufacturer at certain mileage intervals. This helps you do your part to keep the vehicle in tip-top shape and most importantly keep your factory warranty in force if you still are under its timeline. The third type is **preventive repairs.** By agreeing to preventive work, you could be saving major bucks on more serious problems later.

Sometimes It's Just Expensive. There's really no way around the fact that repair costs can be expensive. Required parts and labor can cost a pretty penny, even for normal scheduled maintenance. You may not be excited about paying for 12 hours of labor, but a mechanic who takes the time to perform a thorough, quality service is worth the price. The best advice is always to "Ask and tell; don't get pushed around." Trust your instincts. Car owners who tell repair shops that they've done their research about the facility, who aren't afraid to ask for explanations, and who understand the difference between necessary repairs and what can wait are less likely to being taken advantage of. And that's definitely something to love.

The Forbidden Phrase

Never, ever, tell a repair shop to keep repairs under a certain dollar amount. Saying, "Please keep my bill under $700 because that's all I can afford now." Is a big mistake. Such a statement might give that repair shop permission to charge up to that amount, whether you needed those repairs or not.

FROM THE GARAGE SIDE OF THE COUNTER

Let's peek into the garage side of the counter to understand how shops function and charge for work. This information isn't designed to call out or criticize auto repair business owners. Rather, it provides you with a glimpse of their operations so you can better assess your spending power and know when and why to approve repairs.

Many consumers have had the unsettling sensation of overspending for repairs, despite not understanding why, at least once. Your concern may not entirely rest with the shop; most mechanics work at a flat rate rather than charging per hour. There are references in the trade providing estimates for how long typical repairs should take. If you pay for a three-hour job that could have been completed in 30 minutes by an experienced technician, those three hours will still be charged. It might not seem fair, but it's similar to an emergency room visit. You could easily be charged $13,000 for a two-night stay in a hospital with tests that come back negative — only to be sent home with nothing but Tylenol. While nothing can change the process involved here, you can ensure fair treatment by empowering yourself.

It starts by asking questions to understand if there is a real safety concern or if fear is being used as a sales tactic to push some work on your car. Please don't become a graduate of 'Google University' and challenge the repair facility about everything you read online. Stick to the basics and ask questions in order to learn. Ask to see and handle the parts which are being replaced and, most importantly, find out how these repairs affect your driving and safety. The right questions will stop the selling process and turn on the learning experience.

 FUEL FOR THOUGHT

EXIT FEAR LEFT

If fear is being used as a tactic to push some work on your vehicle, remember this: **The bigger the fear the bigger the lie.**

REV UP LOYALTY: A LOVE AFFAIR WITH SHOPS

The world of car repair shops can seem wild. Consumer loyalty may feel like a deceptive road sign that changes with the wind. Owners are sometimes known to be price-obsessed, always asking, "How much will this repair cost?" Even if they pay an agreed-on amount, they may switch to a competitor the next time they have a similar need if they feel they can get a better deal elsewhere.

Don't misunderstand me; I do see the point. You need to keep a close eye on your finances. However, keep in mind that the owner of the shop wants more than a one-night stand with you. So, here's the secret sauce. The key to a lasting relationship between car owners and repair shops is open and honest dialogue. Mix that with a big dollop of empathy and you have the answer. Instead of focusing on what's wrong and how much it costs, let's talk, like, really talk.

Fixing a vehicle will cost money. You're putting your faith in the judgment of the repair shop's staff about what must be done immediately and what can wait. Friends, this is a group effort. Car owners should accept that repairs can have their quirks, like faulty parts or minor hiccups. Let's get this engine of mutual understanding and communication going in our relationships.

Owners of auto repair shops have a responsibility to step up for their customers and provide guidance and education. The aim is to create a long-lasting bond via this alchemy of understanding and conversation.

I wish you and your mechanic a long and happy relationship based on mutual understanding and teamwork. Celebrate each anniversary of your first appointment by taking pictures of your car, like a proud parent, and try to catch the twinkle in its headlight.

UNDERSTANDING SHOP MENTALITY

Let's examine some behaviors and the unspoken questions or opinions about dealing with auto mechanics. What may seem irrelevant today could cost your wallet in some way later. Let's explore some of these eccentric interactions with repair shops (and consumers).

Managing Your Expectations

Your car might not be 100% perfect when you pick it up. They will fix what you request, but some issues may still not be resolved. You could be disappointed when paying your bill as some gremlins may still be lingering.

You're Not Allowed in the Garage, Ever

You've probably heard the advice about asking to see defective parts to guarantee they're not simply making up extra work, but in some cases, this request may be denied as it would require a trip beyond the "Do Not Enter" sign. This is standard practice as the repair shop does not want the liability if you trip or fall. It might be understandable, yet if the repair shop is adamant that you can't be in the back and yet won't offer a quick picture or video from a cell phone, then you need to get out of that shop ASAP.

Technology makes it so easy today to share pictures or videos. You could ask for a video call with your technician so they can show and explain what is going on without putting you in 'harm's way.' At the same time, it wouldn't be a bad idea to ask for a quick tour of the repair facility, even from a distance. This is a good way to see how clean the repair shop is, and it will give you an indication of how much pride they take in the quality of their work. In my four decades in the industry, I have always worked in a clean and safe environment. Like most colleagues, I am passionate about what I do, and I want to keep doing it safely.

They Don't Always Perform Every Little Task

Cars brought in for maintenance are supposed to undergo a litany of small adjustments and inspections. Do you know what it means when repair shops boast statements like 39, 64 or 85-point inspection? What are they looking at? It sounds very important or tedious, but the truth is that it takes no more than five minutes to look at most of these things with a good flashlight. Make sure to read the fine print about what is included in your maintenance services, like lubricating hinges and doors, tightening front and rear suspension or cleaning and adjusting your brakes.

Here's the truth. Most new vehicles cannot be lubricated and if you have disc brakes, there's nothing to adjust. Make sure to read your owner's manual for more information or, better yet, put your trusted repair shop to work and ask them to tell you what can be lubricated, cleaned, or adjusted on your vehicle. Take notes and keep them handy. If you find yourself at a new repair shop that does not know your car, you will be ready to stop the new sales pitch in its tracks.

Would Your Car Pass the Gramma Test?

Let's flip the tables for a moment. Cars are a huge part of our lives, and we use them so much that they can often resemble a mobile living room. Some are full of decorative accents, music and, occasionally, spilled coffee over electronic components and, in the wort case, evidence that someone didn't sneeze in their elbow or didn't bother getting a tissue.

We often find seats sprinkled with fast-food wrappers, empty chip bags and soda cans, which create a lovely bacteria pool for a mechanic to work in. You certainly don't have to detail your car before you bring it in but taking a few minutes to tidy it up and give a quick wipe down will be much appreciated.

Ask yourself if driving Granny in your messy car would make you blush near and far. Would she scowl at the stinky feet scent and frown at the crumbs under her dress?

Remember that if the technician needs to get into your glove box, back seat, or trunk for repairs, it would be a good idea to clear out all your treasures. If they need to spend 20 minutes emptying your vehicle and another 20 minutes putting it all back, would you cringe at the extra cost of labor added to your bill?

It's OK to Make Silly Noises. They are Expected.

Cars make all kinds of odd sounds, especially older vehicles with higher mileage. Before you go down the deep rabbit hole of identifying that annoying concern, check out your car sounds. The first step is to take pens and sunglasses from door panel side pockets and remove loose trash from the glove box or center console. Make sure your spare tire is secure or the jack, lug wrench or tools did not come loose. If you still have a noise, bring it to the shop and have fun trying to replicate that noise for the technician; we love hearing that. After you get it out of your system, we might go for a drive to confirm your performance. Always take the technician with you on the road to point out the noise. What you might call a buzzing might be a squealing, and what you call a rattle might be a hum. Nothing is worse for a technician than hearing four different noises and wondering which one you're worrying about.

Keep your knowledge improving by asking if the noise is dangerous or just a nuisance. You want to make sure you're not throwing money at a noise that is not a safety concern and soon find a more threatening sound requiring more important repairs.

The Whole Story: Summarizing Shop Dynamics

So, why do clients end up overpaying and then complaining about it? While mechanics might have a reputation for deception, guess what, it's not always their fault. Yes, consumers are often enabling this by raising their hands in the air and claiming, "I'm not a mechanic," or "I don't have time to learn this stuff," or "Just do whatever it needs." People use other excuses that pertain to patience and convenience. They don't mind paying $6 to $8 for a coffee each day, yet they will quickly scream, "I've been ripped off!" or "It's not fair!" when it comes to necessary auto repairs. The truth is that they have often allowed this to happen by ignoring their ownership responsibilities. You don't need to be a mechanic or know all the proper verbiage. However, it's important to be responsible enough to question things that don't make sense or sound untrue. That cooperation can only happen when you have taken the time to get to know your car and build an open relationship with your repair shop.

KEY TAKEAWAYS

- **Look for Clues:** When visiting a shop, notice clutter; fluids on the floor, disorganization, dirty lavatories, and shabby equipment. These may indicate a poorly managed business, which may result in poor workmanship.

- **Set the Table:** Discuss your expectations about the work to be performed, the timing, and any warranty questions in order to prevent surprises. Stay close to your phone in case they need to discuss parts, service or timeline based on their findings.

- **Don't Choose the Cheapest Shop:** Cheap options may cost more in the long run. Consider credentials and reviews rather than just prices. Also compare warranties for a clear picture.

- **The Gramma Test:** Clear out all stuff from your car before service. If the technician needs to get into your glove box, back seat, or trunk for repairs, extra labor might be billed for emptying your vehicle and putting stuff all back.

INFORMATION IN MIRRORS IS MORE EMPOWERING THAN IT MAY APPEAR!

Driving With Peace of Mind

*V*ictoria's dad always repeated, "Honesty Is King." This is what she remembered and thought about every time she met with Dennis, their trusted mechanic. She appreciated how he explained things so she could fully understand the repairs suggested. She placed safety first and learned to ask, "Is it safe if we don't fix it?"

This was quite an improvement over Christopher's usual and nonchalant approach which consisted of asking, "How much will this cost me?" While they both felt that their questions were legitimate concerns, the Smiths frequently felt insecure asking them.

They both know that asking questions is essential when you're a car owner. They learned to ask, "Please explain what I will be paying for?" and "Can you tell me why it failed?" but it was still outside their comfort zone. Focusing on their bottom line helped. The alternative was feeding the shop's bottom line and they only wanted to go that route if absolutely necessary.

Christopher used to compare going to the mechanic as going to the hospital. No matter the circumstances, he's now understanding that it doesn't have to be this way, even when terrible news about expensive repairs is announced. Victoria promised herself that she would never be intimidated into making impulsive repairs out of fear again. She often repeated, "Fool me once, shame on you; fool me twice, shame on me," as her mantra. She recognized that it was imperative that they do their research and question everything.

It helps that they now have a better understanding about repair shop practices, fees, pricing of components, and warranty on parts and repairs. Knowing these basics and asking about alternatives helps them make more informed decisions. No coughing necessary!

Chapter 11

THE NUTS AND BOLTS
OF A REPAIR SHOP

K nowledge can help you develop trust with your auto repair shop. It's important to go beyond just paying for the repairs. You want to also get an understanding of the business practices involved. Taking a more comprehensive look at how auto repair shops operate their business will allow you to make informed decisions and stay clear of potential risks. While you cannot change the past, you can empower yourself by learning how to take better care of your car. Even if you feel that dealing with auto repair shops is nerve-wracking, know it doesn't have to be that way. Building confidence and trust can be enhanced by arming yourself with knowledge and asking questions.

As a car owner, you need to put value and safety before savings. Developing a relationship with a single repair shop might help you gain confidence and knowledge about your car. Devotion to a particular shop will allow them to have a complete history of what has been done and determine what may need to be repaired in the future.

Imagine yourself singing along to your favorite song as you go down the highway when suddenly a dashboard warning light flashes, indicating that your car is overheating. You can't help but panic. Why? Well, it's because you are aware that it is unsafe to drive when a car is overheating. You're now frantically searching for a safe place to pull over. In the shop, you're then told that your brakes need to be replaced. The mechanic also claims that you have multiple significant oil leaks, need to change your air filter, and have blown shocks. You unavoidably feel uncertain about whether these repairs are necessary. As you hand over more money than you expected to continue your journey, the little voice inside tells you that they might be taking advantage of you. Auto repair doesn't have to be such a bad experience.

Start by asking questions without being afraid. And practice requesting explanations in layperson's terms. You'll feel more assured the next time you visit your repair shop. The biggest error you can make is to chase the price. So, avoid doing it. Discounts come and go, but knowledge lasts a lifetime.

Any car owner understands that the focus should be on safety, regardless of cost. The secret to achieving this is to stick by the shop that you've established rapport with. This loyalty helps them understand your car better than you do. Hopping from shop to shop trying to find a deal could leave you vulnerable to being taken advantage of. They won't have a full history of what has been done or what you have been postponing.

THE TRUTH ABOUT AUTO REPAIR SHOPS

With over four decades in the auto industry, I have seen a lot of changes in the business. But as much as cars have changed, my commitment to one solid set of principles — honesty and integrity — has stayed the same. In a world where auto mechanics are often viewed as untrustworthy crooks, ready to swindle their customers into unnecessary repairs, I have made it my mission to build a foundation of trust with all my customers. I want every client to feel confident that they're getting only what they need. The key is to find an auto repair business that is strongly connected to their mechanics and open to teaching their customers the fundamentals. They should also educate their employees about being committed to solving problems, rather than selling. A mechanic can tell you that the clunking sound you hear means your car needs thousands of dollars' worth of repairs. But how can you tell whether the problem was diagnosed correctly, and if that price is fair?

WHAT HAPPENS BEHIND GARAGE DOORS

I'm very excited to share some insights about the inner workings of the auto industry and guide you toward becoming a better car owner. You can put your best interests first without compromising quality service or breaking the bank. It's time to make sure you're getting the most bang for your buck.

Unveiling the Hidden World of Auto Repair

Behind every garage door lies a secretive world. I want to provide you with an opportunity to witness how repair shops operate; their billing methods, whom they hire and how they run their business. Most importantly, we'll explore their inner workings by uncovering some of their practices, such as written estimates, labor charges and scare tactics that keep them functioning effectively.

You'll now step inside an industry filled with grease-stained overalls, well-used toolboxes, and an endless pursuit of automotive excellence.

Basic Flat Rate Billing

There's a history behind the development of the flat-rate system, but we don't need to go into that, unless you need a nap. Simply put, repair shops have an hourly labor rate that is matched to billable labor hours based on the automotive industry's labor guide. Your first line of defense when dealing with repairs is to ask for itemized estimates for parts and for labor. This will help you understand what you're actually paying for and gauge what makes sense and what doesn't. When you don't understand the estimates, ask for detailed explanations. If they decline or dismiss your questions, walk away.

Communication Versus Explanation

The more details you share with your mechanic, the less it will cost you. Try not being vague by saying, "I don't know, it just sounds funny." Or "I have no idea; I'm not a mechanic." These statements are no-no's. Try to identify as much as you can about your vehicle's problems so you can relay that information. Make sure to take note, when it acts up, of details like it's only happening when going uphill or while braking. Repair shops do not have a magic thing-a-ma-jig to plug into the car which tells them everything. The repair shop must start by using the process of elimination and go through the vehicle's systems until they find what's failing. But, if you go past the "I'm not sure," and honestly share the details you have, the technicians will get closer to the source and diagnose the problem quicker. It will then be cheaper as they won't be chasing their tails and charging you for it.

Audit the Repair Facility

Sure, some shops have big signs; a clean-looking parking lot and a great website, but who's running it? Ask if it's an owner-operated facility. It's OK to ask how long their technicians have been working there. If they have four or five employees but the longest-standing employee has been there less than a year, it's a clue that something is not right for a shop that's been operating for over 10 years. If they have a service manager, a shop manager and foreman, then it usually means you have three people to go through before you get a clear answer. Make your concerns known by speaking to those making decisions. Ensure your complaints are taken seriously, even if this means speaking directly with the owner or general manager.

The technician is the person working on your vehicle, relaying information to the shop owner, manager, or service advisor. The important thing is to make sure that both the technicians and the owner or manager are on the same page.

A Test Drive or a Joy Ride?

Occasionally, some technicians could be tempted to take your vehicle out for a joy ride. For some a 'road test' might include getting lunch or even picking up their kids from school. If the car is staying in the shop overnight, they might even take it home to impress their friends and family. A simple solution to be aware of that behavior is to take note of the mileage when you drop off the vehicle and recheck it when you pick it up. If it's up by two or three miles that's OK. They may have needed to test-drive the vehicle before and after the repairs.

If this is a concern for you, adding a hidden GPS tracker, like an Air Tag or Tile, would give you back control and increase the security of your vehicle. Their secret trips won't remain so secretive anymore.

They Will Use Scare Tactics

"You shouldn't drive this car." This is one of the scare tactic statements thrown around like popcorn at the fair. Be aware that shady shops will commonly use words like, **Fire**, **Car Accident**, and **Death**, to prey on clients. They understand that fear will make people more concerned about the safety needs of their family and will make them more likely to proceed with the repairs suggested. They subtly coerce customers into spending money right away. It is one of the most popular ways that repair shops use to make quick money; lots of money. You must be alert and question the consequences if you decide to wait. Perhaps it will be perfectly safe to use the vehicle for a short period of time for a daily commute. As a seasoned auto industry professional, I cannot emphasize this enough. "Take responsibility" as a car owner. Don't let fear force you to spend money if you don't have to and hold yourself accountable if you do spend it. While legitimate repairs might be required, be wary of a laundry list of ridiculous issues with dire warnings of impending danger. You know your vehicle better than anyone, so take a step back and assess the situation. Take note of the warning signs and smoke before it becomes a blazing fire.

DRIVING ON THE ROAD OF INTEGRITY

At a time when people tend to question car maintenance and repairs, finding an honest service center that values integrity as much as you do is key. Aim for open communication, competitive prices, and superior service using the following suggestions.

Customer Service

The way your auto repair facility treats you says a lot. You should be greeted promptly with a smile and a friendly attitude upon arrival. An auto shop that leaves you wandering on your own for five minutes, before even saying hello, may not be too eager to gain your business.

Quality of work is important, but their attitude toward customers is equally so. You should never feel like you're bothering your auto shop with questions. Their job is to explain. You shouldn't be made to feel inferior because of what you don't know about how cars work.

Details: Of course, you want to hear that someone can fix your engine problem, but don't you also want to know why it needs to be fixed? A good auto repair facility will make you feel comfortable by explaining the 'why' in every situation. We encourage you to ask as many questions as you can; this is your time, there's no reason to feel rushed. You need to be educated so you know you're making the right choices.

Honesty: Mechanics are often portrayed as dishonest but it's only a few bad apples that metaphorically 'spoil the bunch.' A good auto repair shop will listen, allow you to engage, and address your concerns. They will only suggest other services if their professional opinion deems it necessary for your safety. Additionally, an honest mechanic will offer a fair price. Sure, the competition is big, but a good repair shop should provide you with solutions, not sell you additional problems. A shop that's in the business of up-selling will stand out as feeling pushy and aggressive. Open, direct communication is the best foundation for an honest service relationship.

Trust: The only way an auto repair shop can be trusted is by earning it every day and for every customer, PERIOD. This is accomplished by standing behind what they say and by believing in their word. It all boils down to one simple fact: "It's not what they say or what they do, but how they make you feel that matters the most." Distinguishing the good from the bad can be tricky, this we can all agree on.

Asking for Referrals

Online reviews are OK, but wouldn't you like to hear, "We have been using them for years. They are great. Make sure to tell them, I sent you…" straight from Aunt Mary, Uncle Frank, or your best buddy Joe? If you ignore this step, you're gambling. Be patient and diligent by asking for references. Remember, if an auto shop's service and quality of work result in a positive experience, people tell their friends, families, and co-workers. Make sure to ask around.

Please Don't Mind Waiting

If a repair shop can't fit you into its schedule immediately, you may be inclined to go elsewhere because you're impatient. This might not be the best approach. The right repair facility is usually worth waiting for. A bit of a wait is actually a good sign as it typically means that the shop is not only servicing a lot of customers, but it is also taking time to ensure quality and educate clients.

Watch for the Fright Factor

If a mechanic says something like, "I wouldn't drive this car another mile," or employs other scare tactics to discourage you from leaving, you should probably do just that, leave.

Be honest. Yes, truthfulness is important for an auto mechanic, but it's also important for the customer. It may be a bit embarrassing to admit that you've been slacking on routine maintenance, or that you recently had your car worked on at a different shop, but the more 'back story' your mechanic knows, the better off you'll be. Hiding symptoms may result in additional diagnosis (which cost money) or worse, incomplete, or improper repair. Your mechanic can't read your mind, so the more information you can share, the better.

Add-Ons Aren't Always Necessary

If you take your vehicle in for an oil leak and the shop starts pushing engine flushes or transmission additives without asking you about your maintenance history, head to the door. Fluid services should be performed according to the vehicle manufacturer's maintenance schedule, not because they have a coupon for the week. Taking your vehicle to a new mechanic for repairs is an exercise in trust and communication. It isn't always easy to tell the good from the bad, but when your auto shop is up front about your repairs and empowers you with knowledge, you've found a keeper. I have made it my mission to educate my customers, one car repair at a time.

- **Empowerment Through Education:** Dealing with a reputable business will help you reduce costs, stress, and provide for your safety.

- **Loyalty Pays:** As you build a relationship with a shop, you will avoid fear-based upsells, ensure quality repairs, and make more informed choices.

- **Navigating Auto Integrity:** Look for a service facility where integrity guides every aspect of their service; expect welcoming greetings, honest processes, and genuine advice without sales pitches.

INFORMATION IN MIRRORS IS MORE EMPOWERING THAN IT MAY APPEAR!

Sensible Repairs

*C*hristopher liked to think he could do anything. With his best friend Google and its sidekick YouTube in his pocket, it was sometimes true. After watching a few car videos one night, he started to think that they might be able to save some money if he began to take on some car maintenance tasks himself. It seemed quite simple according to a few popular video channels. While Victoria believed in her man and knew he was determined enough to tackle challenging projects, she had a few concerns. She quickly dismissed those thoughts when considering that the money saved might enable them to do a special night out.

After spending an afternoon working on replacing a rear brake light, Christopher was quite happy with the result, yet the next day they began noticing a strange squeaking noise when closing the trunk. He didn't really care about this, but it was a concern for his wife.

Later that week, Victoria decided to stop and see Dennis to ask his opinion. He quickly noticed that the stop light cover wasn't clipped properly, so the screw that Christopher had put back wasn't holding tightly into the frame. "A rookie mistake," Dennis said. She was happy that she took the time to drop in as it was a 30-second fix. Left as is, the part might have cracked from the vibration and cost $155 to replace.

When she shared the good news with her hubby, he didn't see it the same way. He was frustrated that she went behind his back to double-check his work. It was a hit for his ego, but he quickly swallowed the pill. Victoria knew firsthand the power of being honest and humble. She had realized that by concealing previous DIY repair on home projects, it only created more confusion for contractors hired to finish the job. She saw it the same way with car repairs. By being open about everything that has been attempted, money was saved. It ensured that work remained focused on real issues rather than billing unnecessary diagnostic fees or labor services. Victoria trusted that communication was key in any relationship, including repair jobs.

Chapter 12

AUTO REPAIR SINS, RACKETS, AND SCAMS

C ar owners must take responsibility for their part in the auto repair process. It's easy to point fingers, but you must ensure to provide your repair facility with the whole picture and trust that they are doing their best to diagnose and resolve problems. Similarly, repair shops must be honest in their business practices, resisting the urge to cut corners, overcharge for services, or offer unnecessary fixes. It's time to break the cycle of hypocrisy and collaborate to have a relationship built on trust.

THE COSTLY LITTLE WHITE LIES

Oh, the unpleasant aspects of car repairs. Getting taken advantage of can make us so angry that we can't help but think horrible things, which may force us to kneel at confession or speak with our priest or rabbi sooner than we'd like! Do you know anyone who enjoys the feeling of being taken advantage of or being overcharged for services not required? Don't even get me started on the 'joy' of being treated as if you don't know anything about basic car maintenance.

On the other hand, customers often have their own faults, some attributable to that little thing known as the internet. Though it's great for watching funny cat videos (admit it), it isn't always the most dependable source of technical information. It's easy to look up a cold symptom and become sure that you're dealing with a dangerous disease. You might find it impossible to determine what's true and what's not, especially if you're not an expert. The same is true when it comes to diagnosing automotive problems. Customers call or come in all the

157

time, afraid that something is wrong with their vehicle because of a certain noise or smell. This fear is often fueled by their part-time studies at 'Google University.' They walk into the shop with comments like, "I'm concerned because I read on the internet that my car may blow up." Here's some sound advice for all those Google graduates. Remember, the internet did not generate the information; it simply relays what it was told, and that is not necessarily correct. Despite their best efforts, humans make mistakes and provide incorrect information, sometimes leading to panic. Recognizing that there is a problem at the source is the first step toward solving it.

It's totally fine to do some research on the internet to get a sense of what you're dealing with, but don't allow it to determine the outcome of what's going on with your automobile. You'll need open conversation with your repair shop for this. The better you can communicate to a mechanic what you believe is wrong, the easier it will be for them to diagnose and fix the problem.

A good step is to make a list of the problems you're having ahead of time, including specific sounds, sensations, odors, or leaks, as well as when and how frequently they occur. What happened right before the automobile broke down? Did it work the day before it wouldn't start? These are important things to relay before the repairs begin.

Of course, many issues might be avoided entirely with a few preventive maintenance procedures. Oil changes, tire pressure checks, and periodic inspections are like going to the doctor on a regular basis. The doctors keep your overall health in check and greatly increase the chances of finding something bad before it becomes a huge issue. This may all sound very complicated, but I do have wonderful news for you. I am not your priest. Thus, I will not bestow seven Hail Marys for your thoughts, nor will I tell you to repent. I will not chase you down on Yom Kippur for your Liturgy. Not to worry, there are solutions for all your auto-repair problems.

Simply put, ask questions. It is not advisable to take broad or convoluted explanations at face value. If a diagnosis sounds absurd, trust your instincts and get a second opinion. This can be turned into opportunities to gain more car ownership clarity. You can become a more confident car owner by learning from these experiences.

DECODING COMMON MAINTENANCE SINS

As we dive deeper into the vibrant world of automotive shops and their unique challenges, we will uncover and address situations which affect both shops and customers. I hope to shed some light on this dynamic relationship by discussing some of the unspoken sins associated with auto repair. It's time to KNEEL AND WEEP.

Sin 1: Failure to Listen. It's important that repair shops listen to what you have to say. After all, you drive the car every day, so you're the best source of details about its status. You may not explain it properly, but your information helps with their diagnosis.

Sin 2: Not Being Available. Sure, the repair shops get busy, and so do you. If a shop cannot give you the courtesy of calling you back promptly, it is a sign that they are not organized, or they don't have the manpower to handle the workload. They should at least take your call, even if it's just to ask, "Can I call you back?"

Sin 3: Under Performing. As a customer, you want three things. Speedy service, quality service and, most importantly, service you can trust. We know that the world is not perfect. However, a quality repair shop can at least provide two out of the three. Which one would you be willing to forgo?

Sin 4: Assuming That You Understand All the Lingo. Sure, the 'doohickey' and the muffler bearing need to be replaced, but what does that mean? Have them break down the explanation about how the failed parts work is more valuable than giving technical names that feel straight out of a Star Wars movie.

Sin 5: Getting Mad at the Customer. There is absolutely no excuse for that. You are there for a reason and anger has no room in the conversation, especially if it's because you simply cannot understand their explanations. When asking questions, the truth usually comes out.

Sin 6: Lying. While this may seem obvious, you would be surprised at how many businesses overpromise and under deliver. There is nothing worse than being told that your car is going to be done on the same day, only to find out they meant the same day... next week.

Sin 7: Lack of Manners. One of the worst things a repair shop can do is disrespect their clients because of gender, age, or lack of auto repair knowledge. You want to be treated with respect and be given clear explanations.

Sin 8: The Internet Made Me Do It. Don't even think about Googling your car's maintenance needs, friends. No, no, no! The only true source of information is the owner's manual, straight from the manufacturer. Who needs the internet when you can just flip through that dusty old book instead and get wisdom from the 'original source'?

But hey, at least there's hope for finding that mechanic who's technologically advanced, yet still upholds old-fashioned values of trust and transparency. But fear not, with the right combination of trust and basic car knowledge, you can experience the joys of honest car repair. No Googling Required!

MASTERING AUTO SERVICE OFFERINGS

Understanding auto repairs and requirements beyond oil changes, tires, brakes, and tune-ups can be daunting to most car owners. Some mechanics use complex language to push unneeded repairs through to meet their bottom line. This is why I suggest unearthing the truth behind mechanic shop lingo.

Remember you are the boss. Seek clarification, without feeling intimidated, by asking why repairs for issues you hadn't noticed are now being suggested. Fear-based tactics are often used to inflate repair bills. There are no bad questions. Here are a few statements to watch out for.

Enhanced Brake Package

This is all about selling you pricier brakes under the guise of enhancing safety. Learn to discern whether your current brakes truly need an upgrade for improved control.

Suspension Precision Tune

This is a tactic employed when selling suspension repairs with promises of smoother rides. Discover exactly what's involved and if a tune-up on that system is really necessary.

Transmission Optimization

Transmission service offers will promise gentler shifting between gears for smoother rides. This is rarely an issue, so inquire about the details specific to your car to assess whether you need such services.

Premium Oil Change

It means a very expensive oil change. Understand that your vehicle originally came equipped with the right oil. The manufacturer has used and suggested the best for the health of that engine. Ask questions and get clarity about any claims to enhance performance before considering this upgrade.

Cooling System Overhaul

Most newer vehicles come with extended coolant that does not require servicing until 100,000 miles. Unravel the allure of such a cooling system overhaul service by learning its true meaning for your vehicle. It will help determine why they are suggesting this extensive service.

Electrical System Analysis

Understand the meaning of an electrical system analysis, as this could incur considerable labor expense. What is the significant electrical issue requiring such an analysis? Arm yourself with knowledge to make smart decisions regarding maintaining your vehicle's electrical system in good shape.

Air Conditioning Restoration

Understand how preparing yourself for potentially costly air conditioning repairs will save time and money by learning whether your AC truly requires restoration.

OUTSMARTING AUTO REPAIR RACKETS

Automobile maintenance requires expert help due to safety and technology regulations. Auto repair facilities may unfortunately appear chaotic, at least initially. Not to worry. With a little patience and determination, you can easily find solutions that put YOU back in control. Investigating repair shops may seem time-consuming, but it will pay off in your wallet.

It's about time you exercise your control over that shop. Blaming the vehicle or the mechanic will never fix an issue. Many people find it easier to point fingers at individuals rather than the circumstances. They always come up with reasons why someone ought to have acted in a different way. Wait before speaking and lay out all the facts before making decisions. Some things are less complex than they first appear to be. We can avoid needless anger and arrive at more effective answers by adopting a non-confrontational approach.

When you start looking for a new mechanic, you must pause and ask yourself, "What was wrong with the other shop?" Please make sure you give yourself the HONEST answer.

INSIDER FILES

NON-VERBAL COMMUNICATION SAYS A LOT

Some shops may speculate about how much a customer might spend on repairs, based on various clues. Before they even say anything, the staff might have made assumptions about the repairs to offer.

Baby seats, fancy stereo systems, or expired license plates are the first clues used to quickly qualify a client as a spender or a looker.

Everything you say, or don't, can be used against you. Make sure to ask important questions about what is suggested, and what is not.

SNEAKY REPAIR SHOP SALES TACTICS

It's important to be aware that shady auto repair shops may employ devious service advisors and use questionable sales tactics. Some just know how to push your buttons to make you take specific actions.

Be wary if you are a female dropping off a car with child seats. Service advisors may use fear tactics against you by mentioning the safety of your child. If they're not sure if you have kids, they might use language such as, "Well, if this issue goes unaddressed, you could end up crashing and causing serious injuries. Safety first, right?"

Gentlemen, You're not immune. They know just what to say to boost your ego. "Mr. Johnson, your car looks great. Your taste is impeccable," they will exclaim with admiration before giving helpful tips like, "You should tune up that engine for increased horsepower. It will be perfect when driving yourself to epic golf games."

But here's the deal, ignore the sweet talk and stick to your guns. Stay true to your intentions when bringing in your car. Don't allow fancy words and smooth talk thrown around to derail you from what's best for you. Always remember that knowledge is your greatest weapon.

Understand your car, and its needs, and don't fall for misleading tactics from dealerships or third-party franchise repair shops.

One of the things they look for includes expired license plates. If they notice that, they will assume that you might be short on cash and try to scare you away as it's not worth it to waste time on small repairs.

Some shops will sweet-talk potential customers by promising that their car will be purring like new in no time, such as, "Oh Mr. Johnson, your automobile is stunning. With only minor tuning it will purr like a cat on a warm windowsill." This language is intended to capture interest and convince them to proceed with the work suggested. Service advisors often use every trick available to secure that sale, including playing on fears while simultaneously building ego.

They may tell you to "Think of the children" or "Visualize increased horsepower." Don't succumb to flattery or intimidation tactics. Remain true to your objectives and understand the requirements of your vehicle.

WINDSHIELD REPAIR AND REPLACEMENT SCAMS

Cracked windshields are an all too familiar sight, and most car owners will experience them from time to time. You're on the road, feeling in control, enjoying the wind in your hair, until you notice that a small crack on your windshield is growing like a web of spiders. Even though it might seem harmless, driving with this crack leaves you at the mercy of fate and puts your safety and others in danger. It is best to fix this as soon as possible as it will ensure a clear view and stop the crack from spreading. When caught early, you will save money on future repairs, and get peace of mind while you're on the road.

Unfortunately, scammers take advantage of people when they are most vulnerable. That's why it's easy to fall prey to their traps. Scams appear to be ubiquitous these days. We all like to believe we have this unspoken superpower to tell if someone is attempting to con us. The reality is usually quite different, especially for things we don't deal with every day. The key is to understand that scammers aren't always directly after your money. Some are targeting your auto insurance provider through windshield repair scams, but it could still end up hurting your wallet in the long run.

If you are ever approached at the gas station, car wash, or at home by someone who promises to fix your windshield for free, it could be a scam. While this is most popular in Arizona and Florida (two states without deductibles for windshield breakage), it can occur anywhere.

Recognizing auto glass scams from the start can help you stop fraudulent activity in its tracks. Here are some empowering tips to help you avoid being taken advantage of in a potentially fraudulent windshield deal.

It's Free and You'll Get Cash Back...

Some questionable auto glass businesses may be pushy and offer incentives, like free vehicle washes, movie tickets, or gift cards. They may even promise to reimburse your deductible with cash rebates. These firms aren't attempting to keep you safe by mending a windshield chip and they're not giving you a good deal out of charity. Instead, they're usually attempting to defraud your insurance provider. Be sure to ask questions to protect yourself. **Nothing is free!**

Undamaged Windshield Replacement

Keep an eye out for auto glass shops that wish to replace a windshield that isn't broken or one that has minimal glass damage. They may be attempting to benefit from your policy by filing a claim with your auto insurance provider for frivolous repairs. This is insurance fraud, and everyone suffers as a result. Firms usually pass on the expense to all policy holders in the form of higher premiums. Reputable companies will first try to repair a windshield that has minimal damage instead of instantly providing a 'free' replacement. In addition, rather than making an insurance claim, paying for a windshield repair out of pocket can be a considerably more economical choice.

Sneaky; Sneaky!

There are many sneaky repair shops that feed on windshield scams. If you're asked to sign any windshield repair papers by a technician, make sure you read the fine print before putting the pen to paper. If you don't, you risk signing away certain insurance benefits to a shady shop that isn't looking out for your best interests. An unscrupulous shop may inflate your claim or sue your insurance company in your name to profit from your policy. The telltale tease for you is to just sign after they tell you, "It's totally free."

What are the risks? Don't fall for a good deal from an auto glass firm that might not be around next year. Using amateurs or a questionable repair company could lead to problems such as

- **Leaking Windshield:** Untrustworthy repair shops may lack the necessary training, equipment, or materials to complete quality work. This could produce air or water leaks, and cause damage to your car, including electrical system problems.

- **Recalibrating Not Being Performed:** Many modern vehicles have windshields with electronic sensors or displays. Some of these systems, such as side-view mirror turn cameras, require advanced safety system recalibration (also known as ADAS). Some repair shops may fail to provide this important service after a windshield replacement, putting your safety at risk. Until the recalibration is complete, features like autonomous emergency braking and forward-collision warning may not work properly.

- **Loss of Insurance Coverage**: Some profit-driven businesses may file multiple claims with your insurer in a short period of time. This could result in the cancellation of your insurance coverage.

- **Higher Insurance Premiums**: It's possible that filing an unnecessary claim by a repair company will raise your premiums. All policyholders suffer premium hikes because of such losses.

- **Getting Caught Committing Fraud**: If the worst happens, you could face insurance fraud charges. Remember that the business you picked made false insurance claims in your name. You signed for it. **They won't tell you that when pushing you to sign.**

All That's Left Is to Fight Back

Every year, insurance fraud costs Americans at least $90 billion. If you believe you've been duped, the Coalition Against Insurance Fraud (CAIF) recommends filing a complaint with your state's insurance department. They also advise taking the following precautions:

- Hire the services of a reputable auto glass repair firm. Your insurance agent can help you find the information you need. You may also make an online appointment with a car glass shop that works with your insurance provider.
- Make sure the repair firm you choose offers a warranty on windshield repairs and replacements.
- Examine your bill for any overcharges. You may have been duped if you need a small chip repair and a shop bills your insurance company for a total windshield replacement.

KEY TAKEAWAYS

- **Trust and Transparency are Possible:** Seek an environment of mutual respect with a repair business. Every inquiry should be an opportunity to clarify things, free from jargon and upselling.

- **Auto Service Navigation:** Insist on clear explanations and justifications for each service recommended. Distinguish necessity from upsell by becoming an informed client who questions claims of 'enhanced' or 'premium' services.

- **Sidestep Fear and Flattery:** Avoid doing business with repair shops employing fear tactics or exaggerated praise to sell unnecessary services.

- **Shield Against Windshield Scams:** Be wary of 'free' windshield repair offers and high-pressure sales methods. Only use trustworthy service providers to make repairs when necessary and be careful to read before you sign.

INFORMATION IN MIRRORS IS MORE EMPOWERING THAN IT MAY APPEAR!

D.I.Y. Superhero

Christopher Smith often reiterated the wisdom passed down by his father by reminding himself about the importance of taking charge and watching out for ourselves. Many times, he had heard the line, "If you want it done right, do it yourself."

He still wanted to prove that he was competent to handle basic tasks on his own vehicle. Unfortunately for him, Victoria now had some doubts about his abilities, so she ignored mentioning that she had a malfunctioning headlight on her car. It was just another minor inconvenience that she would handle later. That was until she got pulled over while racing to her daughter Cynthia's violin recital.

As soon as Christopher noticed the ticket on the counter, he questioned why she had never mentioned it. He felt that she intended to go straight to Dennis before asking him to take a stab at it.

A heated discussion ensued when she saw him heading toward her car to replace the bulb. Victoria said she should have taken the car in sooner to get a new light bulb. Christopher's ego got tested again, yet he remained calm and stated that it was an easy fix, and he already owned the right tools to do the job.

This time he was right. He got it fixed in no time and was proud that he could demonstrate to his wife the value of being an ambitious and conscientious DIY car owner. By taking some time to do this, they saved both money and the hassle of getting to the shop. When he proudly told Victoria that it was fixed, he sarcastically mentioned that she would have saved a ticket if she had been straightforward with him about the problem. She replied, "What do you mean ticket? It was a warning, so thanks to you, I'll drop by the station tomorrow and everything will be fine." They had a drink to celebrate Christopher's skills and the extra money saved.

Chapter 13

THE VERY BASICS OF CAR MAINTENANCE

Mastering your car's maintenance by unleashing your inner auto aficionado is something I always encourage. Now hear my roar, fellow car owners, because I'm about to reveal some secrets about becoming an effective caretaker of your four-wheeled companions. It's time to fasten your seatbelts because many aspects of car care lie within your grasp.

THE HOLY TRINITY: AIR FILTERS, OIL, AND BRAKES

It's time to gain a general understanding of some vital elements that can make all the difference. So, let's shed some light on all these simple yet important car care essentials, starting with the holy grail of air, oil, and brakes.

Clean Air Matters

Vehicles have several different filters, and they all need to be changed within certain mileage intervals recommended by the manufacturer. Your car has two air filters, one for the engine and a cabin filter for climate control. It's very simple to learn how to remove and inspect air filters. They generally need to be replaced every 15,000 to 25,000 miles, or about once a year, depending on how many miles you drive.

Knowing Your Engine Oil Type

An oil change is the most common type of routine maintenance and it's vital to keeping your vehicle running smoothly. We've all heard about vehicles going in for oil changes and being offered, 'the better oil.'

Don't fall for that line. Whatever oil came in the engine the day it was sold is the best one for your vehicle. Simply consult your owner's manual to find out what grade and viscosity are advised for your vehicle.

Understanding Your Brakes

Brakes are important, that's a no-brainer, but knowing when to take them in for service can be a little convoluted. The great rule of thumb is if you hear them squeaking for more than a day or two, you should get them checked. Sometimes brakes will squeak if they've been sitting for a while, after a long trip, or after lots of rain. Humidity, snow or even a car wash might explain the noise. Unless the vehicle has a stopping issue or it's making grinding noises, it's usually not necessary to go in immediately. Noises often go away after driving for a bit. In case of doubt, it's better to be safe and sensible by having them checked, especially if the noise is persistent.

INSIDER FILES

BE A HEADLIGHT HERO

No specialized knowledge or complex tools are needed to adjust headlights. Anyone can follow a straightforward step-by-step guide to ensure their lights are shining accurately and effectively.

Keep your lights pointing straight ahead to maintain optimal visibility on the road and stay safe.

For help tackling this simple yet essential task, download my Headlight Hero guide in the bonus section. https://carconfidential.net/ccbonus

HEADLIGHT ALIGNMENT

As you will see, no pun intended, headlights are important for night driving. But daytime running lights help other drivers notice you, especially if they are distracted. What most people don't realize is that headlights can be adjusted to aim higher or lower. This simple information can be a major safety issue.

Illuminating the Importance of Proper Alignment

Working headlights are important, this we all know, but those bulbs aren't doing any good if they're not correctly aimed at the road. Headlights can become misaligned over time due to bumps, rough roads, or constant vibration. This could then lead to reduced visibility, which can be a problem when driving at night. That reality is something many owners don't know, forget or downright neglect. Think about this. When you're traveling at 60 miles per hour, you have mere seconds to avoid a collision if something darts into the road. Misaligned lights can reduce reaction time to zero.

All it requires are some minor adjustments. While this task is relatively simple and often tedious to perfect, every car model varies and may require special consideration. With some practice and patience, you could learn how to perform this task within minutes in your own driveway. Don't fret, though... **I got you covered.**

Divided We Light: From Headlights to Taillights

Your lights are your safety lifelines. Headlights allow you to see at night and in low-visibility conditions. Taillights indicate your car's presence to drivers approaching from behind. If any of these lights are not working, it might be dangerous for you to drive at night or in inclement weather. You must check them regularly to make sure they work properly as most vehicles do not have sensors to indicate when they are out. Aside from safety concerns, you may get a ticket for driving with a light out, which should be reason enough to make it a priority.

While you're on this, it might be a good idea to clean them. Working bulbs are one thing, but visibility is the goal. Dust, ice, and sand will dim those lights, so it's a good idea to wash them frequently, such as when filling up the tank.

THE BATTERY CONUNDRUM

It's important to always be aware of your car's battery because it is a crucial component that powers your vehicle and accessories. When faulty or dead, it can leave you stranded and unable to start your car. In extreme weather, this is a major concern as without a properly functioning battery, you may not be able to use heat or AC.

Regular maintenance, such as checking the charge level, cleaning the terminals, and replacing it, when necessary, can help ensure that your car's battery is in good working condition to help prevent unexpected breakdowns.

Another proactive step to take is to audit how often your vehicle is driven. Many snowbirds only use their cars for part of the year. While they spend a few months away, their vehicle just sits until their return. Some residents are older and retired and their vehicle spends more time in the driveway or garage than it's driven. Fear not, my snowbird friends, there is some good news. You can head over to your trusted repair shop and have them install a switch designed to preserve battery life until you return from your half-year escapades. A better idea might be to purchase a battery tender to keep cells alive when not in use.

Yes, batteries have warranties, and it might be possible to replace them, but you only get one free replacement from the original purchase date. This may not be relevant in every part of the country but in extreme climate states like Arizona, Texas, or Nevada, you'll be lucky to get more than two years on a new battery. Extreme heat boils the internal acid and evaporates it, thus killing the battery faster. Most four-season states have very few issues with premature replacement.

Know Your Type

There are different types of batteries and they come with specific sizes and specs for each vehicle. The key is to never purchase one without knowing what your car requires. Make sure to buy the type that was designed for your vehicle, instead of following a salesman's pitch about the 'Better Battery.' The best one is the original that was in the car when it was brand new. Do a little fact-finding to identify what you currently have and store that info in your glove box. You want to be ready to make the most sensible purchase and not the most exciting one. Recognizing the types of batteries for gas-powered vehicles is not difficult.

- **Lead-Acid Battery:** This is the most traditional type of car battery and is still widely used. It is made up of lead and sulfuric acid. They are relatively inexpensive. However, they have a limited lifespan and require regular maintenance, including topping them up with distilled water.

- **Absorbed Glass Mat (AGM) Battery:** This type has a longer lifespan and requires less maintenance. AGM batteries are sealed, making them leakproof and vibration resistant. They can also handle a higher rate of discharge. This means they hold steady over a longer lifespan; this is why they are usually more expensive than lead-acid ones.

- **Gel Battery:** Those are similar to AGM batteries, but they use a gel-like electrolyte instead of liquid, making them spill-proof and vibration-resistant. They are more expensive than lead-acid batteries but require less maintenance.

- **Lithium-Ion Battery:** Lithium-ion batteries are becoming more common in modern cars, especially electric and hybrid vehicles. They are lightweight, have a longer lifespan, and are highly efficient. However, they are also more expensive than other battery types.

Battery Health

Find the purchase receipt to verify the replacement warranty and then store it safely in your glove box. While batteries have a general five-year standard warranty, most of them last between two and three years in extreme-climate states. If you work from home and don't drive your car much, get into the habit of starting your vehicle at least twice a week and let it run for 10–15 minutes to keep the battery alive.

OK, now that we've covered different types of batteries, let's seek to understand how to maximize their longevity. As temperatures swing between bone-chilling cold and blistering heat, the effects of the weather could cause havoc with most battery's health. An offsite worker driving their trusty ride only once or twice each week for work purposes might imagine having a healthy battery. This infrequent usage takes its toll. The lack of charge from the alternator while running leaves it weak. This is also compounded with extreme weather. Again, behold the incredible battery tender. It is your ultimate secret tool that slowly provides a rapid pulse of low voltage keeping those cells alive and raring to start when you need them. Just plug it in like a lamp, pop the clips to the battery cables and forget about it.

 FUEL FOR THOUGHT

A battery tender or trickle charger is a small device that provides tiny pulses of very low voltage to keep the cells alive when the battery doesn't get much use. This tool will save a battery which is not in use for several months. Look for a smart tender that automatically turns off to avoid overcharging the battery.

ODORS SPEAK LOUDER THAN ENGINES

Your trusty air freshener can work wonders, but sometimes, unusual odors slip through the cracks. Don't ignore them; just follow your nose. It's a fancy diagnostic tool.

Here's a quick list of what those funky smells might mean:

- **Burning Carpet:** That whiff might mean your brakes are in a bit of a pickle. Don't play chicken — have them checked pronto.

- **Rotten Eggs:** Nope, it's not Uncle Bill's famous breakfast. It's a troubled engine, possibly due to a cranky catalytic converter clogging or failing. Time for a checkup.
- **Sweet Syrup:** If you're not at your favorite diner having pancakes, it means trouble. A cooling system issue, overheating or a sneaky coolant leak, might be lurking.
- **Burning Rubber:** This might smell like a nostalgic sign of rippling speed, but it may be indicating trouble. It could mean your drive belts and or hoses are throwing a fit.
- **Hot Oil:** No gourmet cooking or poolside tanning here. This means oil's leaking from your engine, steering, or transmission. Time to intervene.
- **That Old Gym Locker:** We all remember it, yes, we do! But when your car reeks like you're back in the locker room, it's really mildew having a party in your AC vents. Clogged climate control condensation tubes or dirty filters might be the culprits.

Be your car's bestie. Even if the odor vanishes like a magic trick, it's probably playing hide and seek. You know your car best. Don't ignore these signals. Get it checked before trouble makes itself at home. Avoid costly repairs and embrace the sweet scent of peace of mind.

 **FUEL FOR THOUGHT**

ROOT CAUSE

Car problems are usually found between the steering wheel and the driver's seat. 😊

KEY TAKEAWAYS

- **Self-Maintenance Mastery:** Harness the power of DIY by regularly checking and replacing air filters, choosing appropriate engine oil levels, and monitoring brake condition. By understanding these fundamentals, you are more likely to extend its lifespan and dependability.

- **Illumination and Power Conservation:** Proper headlight alignment and taillight performance are safety beacons. Be vigilant regarding the health of your car's battery as it keeps all electrical systems functioning optimally when temperatures drop or after long periods of inactivity. It's about more than just starting up your automobile.

- **Sensory Diagnostics:** Trust your instincts. Unusual odors could be early warning signals for issues ranging from brake trouble to electrical system breakdowns. Being mindful of any unusual smells could save repairs and money down the road.

INFORMATION IN MIRRORS IS MORE EMPOWERING THAN IT MAY APPEAR!

Lovestruck by Shine

*T*he Smiths enjoy cleaning their vehicles together and always smile seeing the attention they attract when driving their shiny rides. Christopher feels powerful at the wheel, while Victoria is proud and will never complain about the extra attention.

Mr. and Mrs. Smith had never considered all the costs involved with maintaining that showroom appearance until they heard Dennis mention that the pursuit of shiny cars comes at a price. They initially thought that he meant financial, which they knew as they always factored the cleaning products in their budget. Yet he explained that there was a flip side to clean cars and that was news to them.

Dennis shared that many owners are drawn by the gleam and shine, but this might have unintended repercussions that go far beyond its shiny surfaces. The Smiths were puzzled and wondered if he meant extreme cases of OCD personalities who might be considered as being addicted to clean cars, like compulsive gamblers. That was until he clarified that cars could show side effects resulting from their owner's passion for shiny surfaces. Now that got their attention.

"Polishing products and chemicals, much like medications, may produce potentially adverse side effects. While your car might look amazing at first glance, drawing envy from many, it has a downside." Dennis said. He added that, over time, these seemingly benign chemicals could wreak havoc with both paintwork and interior surfaces. Victoria was stunned, but Christopher quickly replied, "We should be fine, we only use top brand products."

Dennis laughed and said, "The brands you trust might not be ideal as some use harsh chemicals. Fear not, my friends, there's a middle ground where beauty and value coexist harmoniously. I can teach you how to maintain a gorgeous exterior without jeopardizing the long-term health or integrity of the vehicle."

Chapter 14

THE TRADE-OFFS TO
SHINE SMART

C ar owners all want their cars to look new; but most fail to consider the long-term effects of their cleaning decisions. As soon as you drive away from a car wash, the sheer satisfaction you feel viewing your freshly polished vehicle can be astounding. Shining tires and sparkling dashboards may feel great, but are you aware of the flip side? Arm yourself with knowledge to avoid unnecessary expenses and the premature aging of your vehicle. Be wise, do your research.

  FUEL FOR THOUGHT

A ROLLING STONES GATHERS NO MOSS

 Did you know that driving can reduce tire cracking and dry rot? Using your automobile serves more than one purpose, it also helps the health of the tires. Even though those gleaming wheels look amazing, leaving them idle can cause premature aging. Keep the car moving to stay free from tire issues.

CAR CLEANING FACTS YOU NEED TO KNOW

Car owners must understand why their vehicle gleams. Tire dressings boasting eye-catching sheen may contain petroleum-based compounds which can lead to problems down the line. Oil-based treatments may give your dashboard more than a pretty glow; harsh sunlight and heat may transform it into something unrecognizable, leaving more than a pleasing sheen behind.

While it may feel good to admire a freshly polished car, its shine quickly wears off once on the road — sometimes within hours. While treating your car every now and then may provide temporary respite from stress, the benefits are only temporary.

Most car fans eventually face an age-old conundrum: should their tires and dashboard reflect like starlight, or should they tone it down a notch? This question is often raised among vehicle aficionados worldwide. The good news is that you can have a shiny car without damaging the paint, fabric, or tires.

SECRETS BEHIND EFFECTIVE DETAILING

Shiny tires may provide satisfaction, but do they really justify the trade-offs? As knowledgeable car owners, it's time for us to abandon the "Let It Shine" attitude and consider other viable approaches. While some gleam is welcome, compromising tire and dashboard health should never be done. Make informed decisions that benefit you and your vehicle. Here are key points to help your car shine, without causing side effects.

Know What's Making It Shine

Before applying any tire dressing, familiarize yourself with its ingredients and its potential side effects. Petroleum-based dressings, such as aerosols, can lead to tire browning and cracking over time.

Carefully Consider Shiny Tires

Gleaming tires may look amazing at first, but their appeal quickly diminishes after driving. Before investing in tire polishing services or opting for the shine look, carefully evaluate costs. Continual application causes tire damage over time.

The Dashboard Dilemma

Car interior cleaning is important. Be aware that using oil-based shine solutions could wreak havoc with its fabric. For optimal results, use water-based products instead.

Quick and Easy Cleaning Tips

To easily get rid of those pesky white flecks on your dashboard, try using baby wipes followed by a microfiber cloth to clean it off safely and quickly.

Petroleum-Based versus Water-Based

Petroleum-based dressings contain dangerous chemicals and flammables that may create an unsafe baking effect, often leading to early dry rot. Water-based tire dressings are safer and will always lead to longer-lasting results.

Silicon-Based Dressings

While silicon can provide excellent wheel protection, it should always be removed prior to washing. For an eco-friendly solution, select water-based silicon compounds. These alternatives don't contain petroleum-derived ingredients.

Brown Tire Mysteries

Brown tires are often the result of trapped dirt and anti-ozonate substances. By regularly cleaning and scrubbing these areas of tire tread, the brown hue may be eliminated altogether.

Repellant Dressings for Dirty Areas

Solvent and silicon-based products may attract dirt and brake dust, so water-based dressings that repel them may be best in dusty locations.

BIDDING FAREWELL TO DROPLET DRAMA

Are you tired of seeing your ride looking like something from an epic battle royale after every wash or tears of water droplets leaking onto its paint after an initial bath session? So it is time, fellow car owners and neat freaks, to roll up the sleeves and plunge your toes into vehicular vanity. Put down those sponges and buckle up those aprons.

Power Points of Pristine Drying Perfection

After an intense lap of automotive aquatics, you'll need to spin those towels for a perfect drying session. Here are a few drying suggestions.

Drying Off with the Sun: While the sun may seem to provide brilliant illumination and warmth, its harsh rays do not mix well with your damp car. That's a big No, No! Sun drying can destroy its flawless appearance by producing freckles and sunspots across its surface that will eventually harm your clear coat. This could make your paint look blistered. Shade is your best friend for drying.

Microfiber Mastery: For optimal results, opt for a microfiber towel with waffle patterns — these towels have amazing moisture wicking abilities. Old T-shirts from your closet could potentially leave scratches or swirl marks on your paint job. So, leave them for your next football game and take precautions if you use them for other purposes.

Preparing Your Tools: Get organized by stockpiling all your drying towels, chamois, step stools and possibly forced air dryers. Invest in an excellent dust mop today for maximum shine. Keeping everything tidy is key to making the job easier and more enjoyable.

Accurate Drying Techniques: Use long, graceful strokes from roof to chassis to dry your car, as you would when showering. Wring out that towel after each stroke and replace it if it has seen better days. Don't do laps around your ride when drying; concentrate on one section at a time and don't rush. Drying your car is like giving it the spa treatment.

Top to Bottom Law of Succession: Start from the roof and work your way downward to prevent water tears at the top from marring your newly dried surfaces. Do it on leg day, you'll get your squats in at the same time.

Frequency — What the Evidence Suggests: Cleaning your vehicle once every week may not be sinful, but failing to do it correctly would be sacrilege. Regular washing and dusting between washes are the keys to an immaculate-looking automobile.

The Dirty Side of Automated Car Washes

If you choose to use an automated car wash more than twice a week, because you're a VIP member, you might be causing more problems than you think, like those squeaky brakes you're complaining about.

All brakes cause micro dusting, that's part of their normal wear. When you pull into an auto car wash, that soapy cold water automatically crystallizes those dust particles that end up getting caught between your brake pads and rotors. This is why your brakes are now making enough noise to compete with the next-door neighbor's cat in waking up the cul-de-sac when you leave early in the morning.

What can you do? You might not like the answer but getting it hand-washed is a better option to preserve the paint and clear coat. It's the best way to prevent those auto wash jets from spraying directly into your wheels. Yes, I know. You're thinking the car wash is convenient. But visiting your repair shop to correct problems created by it isn't convenient either.

INSIDER FILES

THE SUN-SCAM SERENADE

Some dealers will suggest a paint-protective coating, often referred to as the **Arizona Sun Protection**, for your new vehicle. They claim it will protect your investment from almost everything (although I'm not certain about alien laser beams.)

Spending an extra $500 dollars may seem like a good idea at the time of your new car purchase. Before agreeing to this upsell, carefully consider that sun protective coating simply involves adding a bottle of solution to the predelivery wash.

Remember that most car manufacturers already include paint protection as part of their warranty.

- **Aesthetic vs. Integrity:** Maintaining immaculate tires and dashboards could result in damage from the chemicals.

- **Automated Car Wash Caution:** While automated vehicle washes can be convenient, they could also shorten the lifetime of your braking system by creating dust particle crystallization. This results in noise and wear on brake pads and discs.

- **Detailing Product Wisdom:** Petroleum-based products used for detailing that may hasten wear and cause damage requiring expensive repairs down the line.

INFORMATION IN MIRRORS IS MORE EMPOWERING THAN IT MAY APPEAR!

Treading Lightly

Christopher and Victoria enjoy making automotive decisions together, although they don't always see things the same way.

Victoria never fully understood her husband's undying thirst for flashy wheels. She knew that he was an audacious soul and appreciated his bold spirit, yet failed to see how they could justify spending money on expensive mag wheels. He exclaimed that "wheels can improve driving experiences dramatically while giving an exhilarating sense of confidence." She wondered how valid this information was as it sounded like marketing to her ears.

Victoria was at the other end of the tire spectrum. Her main concern was safety and price. She wanted to hear about tread, durability, warranty, and peace of mind on unpredictable roads. The priority is her family's safety as well as that of those around her. Her goal is to always invest in reliable tires.

Once again, they needed Dennis as a guide, although he sometimes felt like a referee. He told them, "Flashy doesn't always translate to quality or performance. You need to strike a balance between style and substance when selecting tires. The aesthetic appeal should not eclipse their functionality and durability." Christopher scratched his head while absorbing this.

Dennis added, "Safety and warranty are commendable. However, an overly cautious approach could result in paying too much for your needs. Therefore, we need to find an acceptable middle ground. We can have safety, at the right price, without compromising other factors, like performance and comfort."

The Smiths felt like they had just heard Yoda speak. They had to let that sink in as they couldn't figure out which one had won the debate. On this note, they left to begin exploring their options.

Chapter 15

TIRE SECRETS

Yes, we all get excited when it's time to load up the vehicle and head out to see loved ones. We also know that the smart thing to do before hitting the road is to have a repair facility inspect all the basics. This will include belts, hose, battery, and brakes. But we seldom remember to have the tires inspected. Tires are one of the most important safety components of your vehicle, especially on a trip. The last thing you need is a blowout keeping you stuck at the side of the road with a car full of family and luggage.

Your trusted 'car friend' might check your tires with a dime and claim that you'll be fine. But it might be time to visit your local tire store if your tires seem to scream, "Replace me!" Shopping for new ones shouldn't be a daunting experience, especially if you do some homework.

For example, do you know which option will suit you best? It's important to be aware so you don't just nod in agreement to a sales pitch. Tire specialists are also experts at selling. If you don't prepare, you're more likely to be taken for a ride.

But simply purchasing tires is only half the race. Proper maintenance includes rotating them at the recommended intervals to maintain even wear and getting the alignment checked regularly so you can continue to drive on a straight course.

It's important to remember that all-wheel and four-wheel drive are not substitutes for specialized tires. While these drive train systems offer excellent traction during acceleration, your success in slowing down, turning or braking relies on properly performing tires. In fact, it's only when the rubber literally meets the road that your car can stop.

Whichever type you choose, make sure that all four tires on the vehicle are the same. A complete set of tires with the same tread pattern helps ensure the best handling, control, and safety.

TREADING WISELY

Do you know the different types of tires available, and which are the best matches for your vehicle? While all-season tires may seem like an easy default, there are other types that can help your car function at its highest performance while keeping you safe on the road. Let's break a few things down.

Understanding Sidewall Letters and Numbers

First, when shopping for tires, you should know the meaning behind some of the key information molded onto the tire.

- **Tire type:** The letter **P** at the beginning of the tire size means it's made to the standards of a passenger vehicle. **LT** is for light trucks.
- **Tire width:** The three digits following the tire type letter represent the width in millimeters.
- **Load index:** This is the maximum load the tire can support when fully inflated. Always choose a load index that is equal to or higher than what originally came with your car. The information is found in both pounds and kilograms.
- **UTQG:** The Uniform Tire Quality Grade Standards is a rating system for relative traction and temperature resistance provided by the National Highway Traffic Safety Administration (NHTSA).

All-Season

Many people like the appeal of all-season tires as they provide versatile traction for most weather conditions. This makes them a practical option for many sedans. While this might be fine on a dry summer day or a damp winter night, they are not meant for superior performance.

These tires don't meet the U.S. Tire Manufacturers Association (USTMA) standards for handling icy roads and heavy blizzards. Their tread wear warranty can range from 40,000 to 80,000 miles.

Pro Tip: When researching all-season tires, look for tires with low-rolling resistance for better fuel economy. This could represent savings of over $100 a year for an average user.

Touring

If you frequently commute on highways or do long trips, touring tires may be a better option for you as they feature a low profile and wider tread. Touring tires are known for a quiet, smooth ride and responsive handling. Like all-season tires, they function best in moderate temperatures and weather.

Snow

In winter, snow tires are the preferred option for snowy or icy road conditions. On the outer sidewall, look for the three-peak mountain and snowflake symbol, an official USTM mark. This icon confirms the tires meet the stringent industry requirements for severe snow and winter traction typically found under 45 degrees Fahrenheit. When picking your snow tire style, stud-less are preferable because they grip the road without damaging any surfaces.

Regardless of style, snow tires are made with specially formulated tread rubber that stays flexible at low temperatures. This soft compound wears down quickly in the heat, so it's best not to use these tires except in the winter.

All-Terrain

If you have a sport utility vehicle (SUV) and drive on unpaved roads, this durable tire is your best bet. Interlocking, open tread blocks with deep grooves and ridges allow the rubber to grip in any direction on gravel and dirt. As the name suggests, an all-terrain tire's capabilities off-road also apply on smooth pavement. Trade-offs may include a louder ride than other types of tires, as well as shorter tread life and lower fuel efficiency.

Compact Spares

These special-purpose smaller-diameter tires are only meant to be used if you find yourself with a flat tire and need to temporarily replace it. To save space and weight in your trunk, spares are light with shallow treads and often come in compact size. Most spares also have limited mileage capacity and can't handle highway speeds. You should switch out the spare with the new or repaired tire as soon as possible.

For more detailed information about tires, visit:
https://carconfidential.net/tires

HOW TO EXTEND TIRE LIFE

It is easy to understand the three basic tire care essentials: patch a flat tire, replace worn out tires when necessary, and maintain proper pressure levels. But let's go beyond this. Tires are truly unsung heroes of our vehicles and deserve some respect. By giving tires proper TLC, you not only extend their lifespan and save hard-earned cash but, most importantly, you ensure our safety on the road. Let's embark together on this 'tire-tastic' adventure as we cover proper tire maintenance strategies and secrets to their longevity.

 FUEL FOR THOUGHT

PREVENTING PREMATURE WEAR
Improper alignment is a major cause of premature tire wear. With that in mind, it's a good idea to have it checked between 12,000 to 15,000 miles.

The Importance of Proper Alignment

Adjustments made on a vehicle's suspension system — the one connecting its wheels — rather than directly on the tires or wheels themselves is referred to as an alignment. This involves making changes that affect how tires contact the road surface. For an analogy, imagine running with untied sneakers. As a result, the foot might be slipping side-to-side without proper contact and cause injury. Improper alignment has the same effect. It leads to premature tire wear that requires replacing them sooner than expected. Getting this checked can save both hassle and cost down the line. Some of the benefits include:

- **Better Gas Mileage:** When rolling resistance decreases, gas mileage increases. Total alignment sets all four wheels parallel, which, along with proper inflation, minimizes rolling resistance.
- **Safer Driving:** The alignment procedure includes an inspection of the suspension system. This allows technicians to detect worn parts before they cause expensive problems.
- **Improve Handling:** Does your car pull to one side? Do you constantly have to move the steering wheel sideways to keep your car traveling straight ahead? Many handling problems can be corrected by a complete front end alignment service. With all vehicle components aligned properly, you get a smoother ride as road shock is more efficiently absorbed.
- **Tire Warranty:** Alignment is also crucial for tire warranty. When tires are sold, a warranty, covers them from manufacturing defects. But if premature tire wear is due to alignment issues, they will not be replaced.

Heat Is the Enemy of Tires

Heat might be wonderful to cook the Thanksgiving turkey, but it's a disaster for tires. This is why tire covers are a bad idea. They turn wheels into charcoal-cooked marshmallows by blocking air intake and reducing their cooling capabilities. Enclosing them is a surefire way to send them straight to ruin as heat damage is not fixable.

Arizona, Nevada, and Texas can reach temperatures in excess of 110 degrees, which is enough to make tires sizzle.

Just imagine your tires trapped under covers for hours, days, and months, without escape. That is like a one-way ticket to a tire spa with no way out. Trust me; this is a treatment they don't need. Instead, give your tires plenty of air circulation to allow them to breathe and stay cool. It will result in smoother and safer rides.

 PIT STOP LESSON

BURNT RUBBER REGRETS

Covering tires to protect them from the sun might seem like a good idea, but in fact it turns them into a hot sticky mess.

Heat-induced tire damage cannot be fixed. When temperatures are rising, give your tires some space as heat-induced damage cannot be fixed.

THE SHELF LIFE OF TIRES

When increasing car knowledge, one facet often remains obscure: tire expiration dates. Yes, they have one. But, fortunately, it's further away than the jug of milk you just bought. There's no need for speculation here. Tires keep us moving along so it makes sense that they should come equipped with warning labels. Evidence shows us all too clearly that older tires are far more susceptible to failure than their newer replacements.

To understand this phenomenon, one must delve deeper into the nature of tires themselves. Composed largely of rubber, these marvels of engineering don't stand up well against relentless time. Rubber degrades when exposed to extreme climate conditions — such as scorching heat waves or freezing roads — or general wear and tear from everyday use. These factors speed up their breakdown.

Dry rotting treads can crack under pressure from age and wear. This makes tires vulnerable and unpredictable at highway speeds, where their failure could result in injuries, or worse.

Yes, Tires Do Expire

What causes tire ageing in the first place? The answer can be found in the realm of chemistry; specifically, oxidation. When tires meet oxygen molecules, an irreversible chemical reaction takes place that transforms flexible rubber parts into hard, brittle structures. This is akin to an old rubber band breaking under regular stress. It is what will eventually befall tires over time.

At its heart lies an irony: This oxidation process occurs naturally, regardless of whether a tire is actively in use, stored as spare material or sitting innocently on store shelves waiting for an unwitting buyer. Time doesn't stop for anyone, including tires. This is why ignoring an impending expiration date could prove costly in terms of service life and roadworthiness.

As time progresses, tire technology keeps making significant advances. Tread life has seen an exponential increase since 1970. Some cutting-edge tires even boast promises of 100,000 miles. While tread life remains important, the issue of oxidation is prevalent in hotter regions where temperatures often surpass 100F (38C).

Most consumers remain ignorant about their wheels' ticking clock and the hidden risks of driving on expired tires. I will now share the secret for decoding the hidden manufacturing dates that will help you gauge their age. Look on the side of each tire's sidewall where a four-digit code awaits. The first two digits represent the production week number; the following two are the year when it was manufactured. With this knowledge at your disposal, it becomes much simpler to avoid buying rubber that is past its prime.

Some automobile manufacturers have taken steps toward providing warnings in owner's manuals, but deciphering this code remains difficult for most individuals. Should you find yourself lost with those numbers, seek guidance from either your trusted mechanic or local tire shop as they know the solutions to unlock this mystery.

 PIT STOP LESSON

DON'T JUDGE A TIRE BY ITS TREAD

Regulations state that tires must be changed every five years regardless of tread thickness. This means that age is more important than tread wear and tear when considering the fate of tires.

MORE SECRETS ABOUT TIRES

Let's explore some surprising truths and myths surrounding tires. I can vouch that there's more to them than meets the eye. Tires serve as shoes for our cars — faithful companions on life's highways. But are tires really just black rubbery donuts with tread that look nice on our cars? Certainly not. Underneath those treads is an incredible world waiting to be discovered.

Tire Deals: Temptation or Trouble?

Imagine finding an offer for two tires at half the price. Tempting right? Be wary. Don't get stuck into buying tires solely based on price. Consider your car's needs first before making decisions based on sales tactics and hype alone. Tires could be discounted because they've been sitting in a warehouse for a while and will expire sooner than expected. Long wear tires might sound great but if they age out before reaching that mileage mark it could end up wasting your hard-earned cash. Don't fall for the sales trap. Make educated decisions based on your driving habits and needs.

Nitrogen-Filled Tires: VIP or Vexation?

Luxury or just hot air? Nitrogen-filled tires might be hailed as the VIP treatment for your wheels. But is it really? Let me be the one to break the illusion and dispel any notion of luxury associated with nitrogen. The truth is it won't make them last longer or improve performance. It's simply an extravagant marketing push designed to sound luxurious. While race cars need nitrogen for extended laps around a track, do you really need it for daily grocery runs? Plus, filling tires with nitrogen could cost quite a few pennies. Your car won't mind receiving regular air fill-ups. Air already contains 78% nitrogen.

🏁 PIT STOP LESSON 🏁

TIRE QUALITY OVER PRICE

Prioritize value over price when shopping for tires. Ask for the manufacture date to ensure they haven't been sitting around for years.

If you purchase discounted tires, it is crucial that they come with warranty insurance in case of defects.

Insurance and Tire Mishaps: Who's to Blame?

When an accident is caused by a flat tire, insurance companies will quickly move in, looking for someone to blame — perhaps you. If your tires were worn down and contributed to the collision, negligence might be considered to be at play here. To safeguard yourself against future troubles it would be prudent to check with your insurer about liability before these issues arise. But why not just stick with roadworthy tires to stay safe instead and avoid this whole fiasco. Safety first.

Oops or Catastrophe: The Truth About Tire Blowouts

Tire blowouts are no laughing matter. Every year they cause approximately 11,000 collisions and over 700 fatalities. Yikes! Underinflation, overloading the vehicle and speeding are major contributing factors.

The need to check tire pressure and tread depth regularly is often overlooked. This is easily accomplished through purchasing a tread gauge from either an auto parts store or online. Most states set legal minimum tread depth requirements at 2/32 of an inch. Experts suggest replacing tires at 4/32 inch for safety in wet environments. Tires also feature wear bars which raise small bumps at the bottom of their tread grooves. These indicate that the tread remaining is near the recommended safety limit. When reaching these levels, it may be time for a replacement.

Preventive Tire Maintenance: Your Safety Routine

Never take tire inspections lightly. Check them regularly for uneven wear patterns and cracks or bulges that could indicate imminent blowouts if ignored. Always choose safety on the road and err on the side of caution. It is better to be safe than sorry.

Spare Tire: The Long-Lost Brother

This might come as a surprise to some people, but many new vehicles do not have spare tires. The trend is to replace them with either run-flat tires or to provide sealant and inflator kits. This is being done to cut costs, including saving weight and fuel. Most vehicles feature a dedicated space in their trunk to store a spare tire for emergencies.

You should verify that you have a spare and confirm it is in good condition, especially if you purchased the vehicle second-hand. Be mindful of this hidden tire when checking the pressure of its four grownup brothers who carry the weight. Their younger sibling should always be ready if duty calls from the trunk. Become familiar with what to expect should you need to use it to replace a flat or blow out tire.

KEY TAKEAWAYS

- **Beyond the Basics:** Understanding tire sidewall codes and UTQG ratings will help make informed decisions for your driving needs without risking their integrity or your life.

- **Tire Care:** For durability and safety, proper tire maintenance is absolutely necessary. Your checklist should include regular pressure checks, with periodic rotations and alignments.

- **Enhance Safety, Minimize Risk:** Learn to recognize expiration dates found within sidewall codes, be wary of deceptive discount tire deals and pass on nitrogen inflation.

- **Pack a Spare:** Ensure to always have an emergency spare available for your vehicle for maximum road safety.

INFORMATION IN MIRRORS IS MORE EMPOWERING THAN IT MAY APPEAR!

BOTTOM LINE ON MAINTENANCE

It is now time to consolidate all our automotive knowledge into an easily digestible package and highlight its most essential points. A key to being an excellent owner is treating an automobile like it was a child. Even small issues can quickly snowball into major headaches and costs.

Car ownership requires attention and dedication just like taking care of a family member's health. Arm yourself with knowledge to effectively navigate your automobile journey. Reach out for answers from repair shops. Maintaining your car will be easy if you follow a few basic guidelines. Consult the owner's manual as a starting point and pay attention to warning signs as they arise.

While doing it yourself may save money and effort, it is best to use credible mechanics to perform your maintenance services. Always disclose up front if you attempted DIY work.

As always, no automobile maintenance question is too silly, and mechanics are happy to provide their clients with advice on the most vital fixes. Let's work on those automotive parenting skills and keep our four-wheel dependents in great shape.

"Two Laps Aced!

*One Final Victory Lap to
the Podium of Wisdom
O Enlightened One!"*

ROAD SAFETY

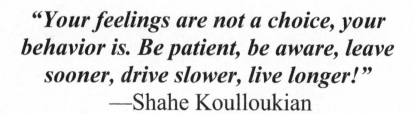

"Your feelings are not a choice, your behavior is. Be patient, be aware, leave sooner, drive slower, live longer!"
—Shahe Koulloukian

Quest for Road Mastery

Christopher has always been very comfortable behind the wheel of a car. It helped that, as a kid, he spent a lot of time on the road with his father, Philip, who drove trucks for a living. He received invaluable lessons about the flow of traffic, keeping safe distances, and anticipating how people might behave. His father had often explained technical concepts, such as steering wheel impact in unexpected situations and how to keep control during emergencies. Much of those concepts were a bit too advanced for a kid who was years away from driving, yet he subliminally absorbed many of them. This experience and unconscious wisdom provided Christopher with a greater sense of confidence and awareness behind the wheel.

Christopher is now trying to repeat the cycle as he strives to pass this driving wisdom to his daughter Cynthia. He feels like this is part of his duty as a parent. Prioritizing safety should be at the top of everyone's list, he thought to himself.

Cynthia quickly learned the importance of proper steering wheel hand positioning, yet she often questioned it as most people she knew always drove with one hand, especially her mom. Christopher went bonkers when he saw his wife drive with one hand to eat, fiddle with her hair, or in extreme cases touch up her makeup at a red light when running late. It was a sensitive topic, so he would usually stay mum on the issue. He now thought they were paying the price as children always emulate their parents. He's hoping to influence Cynthia's perceptions about safety as he won't always be in the car with her.

Their next challenge is to teach her proper merging skills. There's nothing like experience, yet the first few times were nail-biting situations. This was true for both the student and particularly so for the teacher. (The inner door handle still has marks.) Good things Cynthia got from her mother are her laser focus and attentiveness. "This will always be handy on the road," Christopher kept repeating himself.

Chapter 16

DRIVE SMARTER NOT HARDER

I feel that most drivers would fail a driving refresher test miserably. Most of us will humbly admit to the occasional wrongdoing in traffic. (Yes, it also happens to me.) We often become busy or distracted and forget the basics because nobody has the time or the opportunity for review classes on lane changing, merging and other driving skills. For most of us, our driving test was checked off the list years earlier. Our experiences behind the wheel are subconsciously dictated by habits, rather than by the rules of the road. This is a sad fact.

Perhaps you've never been in an accident, and I'm pretty sure you've never gotten a speeding ticket, right? You've been driving for over 20 years. But do you really know how to drive?

🏁 PIT STOP LESSON 🏁

PROPANE TANKS, A RISK YOU CAN'T IGNORE

Whenever you must transport a propane tank, secure it in place. Only transport propane tanks between locations when filling or exchanging them. Never keep one stored in your trunk, with no ventilation.

LIFE IN THE FAST LANE

We are creatures of habit, good and bad. Remember that bad driving habits might result in undue wear and tear on your vehicle, a traffic violation, or a crash. The best time to start again is now. Perhaps it is a good time to get reacquainted with the basics. Most people don't practice what they preach, so allow me for just a moment to get a little poetic with an old Armenian saying, which feels appropriate for the circumstances, "Morality and ethics swing in the wind."

As a refresher, there are the two pillars of road safety:

- The habits of the driver
- Adaptation of the driver to road conditions

Keep in mind that you can unlearn risky driving behaviors and train yourself on the path to mastery. To begin, let's talk about routines. It's time to break free from habits that are holding you back. Put your phone away, slow down, and stop making aggressive moves. Practice concentration, tolerance, and politeness. As you skillfully handle the lanes, you're painting an image of safe driving. Make every trip an example of how seriously you take safety. However, routines by themselves are insufficient. Think of the road as a chameleon. It changes colors constantly and requires you to do the same. Learn to adjust as you go down this path.

The road may present you with unexpected obstacles including severe weather conditions and unexpected traffic delays. But don't fret, with knowledge comes power. Adjust your speed, maintain an appropriate following distance, and be attentive to road signs as they appear. All these create harmony between drivers and asphalt. Anticipation and responsiveness become your allies in finding safe passage through it all. Let's begin this journey and embrace unlearning, reprogramming, and establishing safe driving techniques. Create habits that foster an overall culture of road safety with every mile covered. (Mic Drop... I now conclude this poetic journey.)

 FUEL FOR THOUGHT

PLEASE DONT DRIVE LIKE A MANIAC

As a friendly reminder, you're moving in a metal box that weights about 5,000 pounds. It demands that you treat it with respect and tempered emotions.

First... Hold That Steering Wheel

Let's go back to basics. How do you place your hands on the steering wheel? If it was a clock, where would your hands point? **10:00** and **2:00?** **9:00** and **3:00?** Or **8:00** and **4:00**?

It's time for a fresh look at your steering habits and turn back the clock. We all know about happy hour, but have you heard about safety hour? Most people have been taught to place their hands at the **10:00** and **2:00** position. This 'Safety Hour' allows moving the steering wheel suddenly without jerking it and losing control of the vehicle.

While this has been preached ad-nauseum for years in driver's ed, did you know that this hand positioning may damage your arms during an accident? Yes, that's right. The industry has been taking a second look at this recommendation since airbags came into play in 1989. If airbags get deployed in an accident, the arms are more likely to break when holding the steering at the **10:00** and **2:00** position. (Ouchy!)

This is why some safety experts are now recommending positioning your hands at a position as low as **8:00** and **4:00**. They claim it allows the same control without potentially damaging your tennis arm. While this is still debated between experts, it seems like many crash test dummies agree with this recommendation.

Keep this in mind and decide what feels right for you. We can be flexible after all, what's half an hour between friends?

 FUEL FOR THOUGHT

ELEVATE TO STIMULATE

Experienced long-haul truck drivers have developed many valuable techniques to maintain concentration. An effective one is keeping their left arm (which lies close to the heart) resting firmly against the top of the steering wheel. Anecdotally, it has been said that raising the arm above heart level may help increase blood circulation, alertness and prevent fatigue.

🏁 PIT STOP LESSON 🏁

RUBBERNECKING HAZARDS

Rubbernecking near automobile accidents is one of the worst behaviors any driver can exhibit on the road. This happens when traffic begins to crawl as drivers slow down to watch what may have transpired.

It shows just how hazardous driving can be.

BREAKING BAD HABITS

Let's face it, for most of us, driving lessons happened a while ago. And it often began with parents, an older brother, or a favorite uncle saying, "OK, let's go for a ride." For some it was a 'crash course' to learn the basics about operating a vehicle. This might have covered the seatbelt, the perfect double-handed grip on the steering wheel, turn signals, looking behind before backing up, speed limits, and yada, yada. The rest was usually left unsaid. The assumption was that it would come naturally over time.

You might now realize that it's been a few years since that exciting day. How did you get some of your current habits? (And where has the time gone?) Perhaps it took longer to master some things, such as parallel parking. For many, this is difficult at first, and it takes a lot of concentration. However, once you get accustomed, it becomes second nature. Now most people don't even need to think about it.

The same behavioral principles also apply to speeding, tailgating, rolling through stop signs, distracted driving and so on. Unfortunately, these unhealthy, and sometimes illegal, habits become entrenched in your everyday routine and go unnoticed. Even when a bad habit is the cause of an accident, people quickly dismiss it by blaming the other driver or by saying something ridiculous like, "Well, it's Monday."

It's true that some traffic laws might be difficult to keep in mind. They can also differ from state to state, and even from one municipality to another. Something we might take for granted, like turning right on a red light, might not be permitted somewhere else. The increase in the number of traffic regulations can be a source of confusion. With the evolution of devices, such as GPS, smart phones, and satellite radio, there is a huge distraction problem, which brings even more rules.

The Habits You Should Focus on Breaking

Driving Distracted. When you're driving, stay focused on the road by minimizing distractions. Eating and texting are a couple of examples of habits that can lead to poor driving. Texting behind the wheel is now a leading cause of car accidents and fatalities, especially with teenagers; yet most underestimate the hazard.

Rubbernecking. We're curious by nature, so most people don't even realize that they are slowing down to look at crashes or construction. That is referred to as rubbernecking. The act of staring curiously at an accident, event, or scenery, is not only harmful, but it can cause traffic to slow down causing a chain reaction. Always keep your eyes on the road ahead to be aware of stopped cars, closed lanes or police officers issuing a ticket or directing traffic. While cats have nine lives, you might not be as lucky.

Tailgating. One of the most hazardous and annoying things a driver can do is tailgate. This might be tempting when a stubborn vehicle is hogging the left lane with an empty road ahead. But following an automobile too closely can easily cause an accident as reaction time is reduced. Tailgating may irritate the driver in front to a point of retaliation by brake-checking. This can easily escalate to road-rage incidents. No matter how frustrating or how rushed you might be, it is wise to stay cool and maintain a safe distance until it's possible to pass.

Parking Illegally. When you're in a hurry, it's tempting to park in prohibited places. This decision could put others at risk and result in a large fine for you. Even outside of authorized parking hours, resist the impulse to park in handicap spaces, red zones, or along curbs.

Park Sensibly. Easing into a parking space until you hit the curb can damage tires and potentially causes alignment issues. Make sure to ease into a parking spot until you start getting close to the curb. Look to make sure the lower portion of the driver's side-view mirror aligns with the concrete pad or sidewalk to know where to stop. This will ensure your vehicle is far enough from the curb to avoid damaging your tires, plastic bumper, or the lower engine splash shield. You want to park the vehicle at an average of four inches away from hitting anything to avoid any damages.

Not Checking Blind Spots. Blind spots are inherently risky but failing to check them frequently is even riskier. When changing lanes, make sure to check not only the proper mirror, but also to look over your shoulder to ensure the coast is clear. Drivers who don't look at blind spots tend to get distracted and drift into other lanes, causing knee-jerk reactions when nearly colliding with other vehicles. It is a factor contributing to accidents.

Failing to Signal. It's important to let other drivers, bikers, and pedestrians know your next move so they can slow down and accommodate. Signal at least 100 feet in advance, approximately two to three car lengths ahead of you.

Riding the Brakes. Keeping your foot on the brake pedal might cause strain on your brakes. If you are driving a manual-transmission vehicle (stick shift), try downshifting to remain at safe speeds.

Keep in mind that drivers behind you see your brake lights every time you press the brake pedal. If you keep your foot on the pedal, they might begin paying less attention and miss the moment when you need to make a hard stop.

Running Yellow Lights, Red Lights and Stop Signs. Even if you think the streets are clear, come to a complete stop before turning or proceeding into the intersection. If you don't and the intersection is not an all-way stop, you may cause a crash. When the light turns yellow before you reach the intersection, it's best not to risk it.

Sudden Stops. Keep an eye on your surroundings and anticipate when you might need to stop. Pressing slowly on your brake pedal helps limit the wear on brake pads. It will also indicate to cars following you that you might stop, allowing them to slow ahead or keep more distance.

Fast Starts. Peeling away from a stoplight uses excess gas and it might put a strain on the key components of your engine. Accelerating at a slow smooth rate is better for the car and for people around you.

Driving on Fumes. In older cars, with electric fuel pumps, gasoline acts as a cooling agent. When driving with low fuel, there is less fluid to help cool the engine. In modern vehicles, the fuel pump is encapsulated inside a tube and always surrounded by fuel, even when running low, so it is less of a concern than in older cars. Fuel deposits and safety remain good reasons to keep the tank full.

Disregarding the Speed Limit. Posted speed limits are set by state or municipalities based on various safety considerations, such as pavement, schools, and other factors. Limits will sometimes change due to construction or road conditions, so stay aware. If you miss a sign and find yourself wondering what the limit is, here is a general guide that should help:
- **Residential area:** 15–30 mph
- **Undivided road (rural):** 40–55 mph
- **Divided road (rural):** 55–70 mph
- **Freeway:** 55–70 mph

Improper Merging. Surely you've experienced the annoyance and frustration of seeing someone ahead of you struggling to merge onto an onramp. To properly merge, you need to be patient, observant, and skilled. Learning the theory behind merging can help you in these situations. The objective should be to strike a good balance between doing things quickly, safely, and being kind to others.

Drivers should clearly communicate their intention to merge so others can anticipate their movements and take appropriate action. In the same way, keep your speed constant and stay alert to the surrounding traffic.

Making erratic lane changes or hard stops should always be avoided. Leave plenty of space between vehicles. Extend courtesy to drivers who may be new to merging or who may be navigating hazardous road conditions. Keep in mind that merging is a group activity, and that improving these abilities benefits everyone on the road.

🏁 PIT STOP LESSON 🏁

WATCH OUT FOR ANGLES

Studies reveal that most deaths in automobile collisions result from angle accidents. This typically happens when acting hastily at intersections.

DO YOU TANGO OR WALTZ WHEN MERGING?

According to studies, an estimated 20% of accidents can be linked to merging errors. These range from minor fender benders to severe accidents. Although it might be confusing at first, it is important to master this skill. I like to use the tango metaphor to help drivers understand the intricacies and better convey my suggestions.

Let me explain why I compare a fast merge to dancing a tango. What I mean is that it calls for a combination of calculated risk, quick adjustments and spacial awareness. You're maneuvering your way to find space on the road's dance floor, which could result in bumping bumpers more than stepping on toes. However, if you drive with synchronized movements and flow smoothly, you're waltzing your way into merging traffic. This skill may help you win the most important prize of all, **your safety**.

When entering, exiting, or even changing lanes on busy roadways, never assume that other motorists will make room for you. Some folks may wave you in, but everyone is in such a hurry, or distracted, so don't count on it.

As such, motorists must drive defensively and exercise extra care when passing other vehicles to prevent merging collisions. Be mindful that larger vehicles dragging trailers require extra time for stopping and acceleration due to extra weight. Adjust to their speeds appropriately when maneuvering around them.

While it seems trivial, understand that properly changing lanes can greatly reduce safety risks. Sweet patience is key here.

How to Merge Safely into Traffic

Step 1: Adjust your speed to match the flow of traffic before entering the roadway.

Step 2: Yield to drivers on the freeway but avoid stopping unless absolutely necessary.

Step 3: Find a 3 to 4 second gap in traffic to merge. Never look for the vehicle you want to get ahead of; look for the vehicle you want to be behind.

Step 4: Check for cars around you before entering a lane. And remember to check your blind spot to see if the way is clear. Turn your head. Mirrors only show a portion of the road.

Step 5: Use turn signals early. Signal 100 to 300 feet (three to six cars lengths) before merging or changing lanes.

Step 6: Wait for the dotted line before merging. A solid line indicates that lane changes are prohibited. **Only cross one lane of traffic at a time.**

 FUEL FOR THOUGHT

DEVELOPING HABITS

We are what we repeatedly do.
Excellence is a habit.

How to Safely Exit Traffic

Step 1: Prepare your exit by maneuvering into the far-right lane as you approach the off-ramp.

Step 2: Keep up with the speed of traffic until you exit. Adjust your speed to weather conditions and the design of the exit ramp.

Step 3: If you must pass a vehicle, do so on the left and return to your lane once the vehicle is visible in your rearview mirror. Increase this distance when passing larger vehicles.

- **Re-Learn Road Skills:** Be aware of your driving habits and reprogram any risky behavior picked up over time. Opt for safer hand positioning on the wheel and stay on top of road conditions and new regulations.

- **Eradicate Driving Complacency:** Avoid dangerous behaviors, such as distracted driving, rubbernecking, and tailgating. Return to fundamental practices like proper signaling, parking wisely and blind spot monitoring.

- **Harmonize With Traffic:** Remain smooth, alert, and in sync with the flow by altering speed as necessary. Merge like a waltz and clearly signal your intentions.

INFORMATION IN MIRRORS IS MORE EMPOWERING THAN IT MAY APPEAR!

Safety First

*V*ictoria and Christopher are often in a rush. Like most people, they chase time in order to reach their destinations quickly when they get busy and distracted. Victoria thinks that her positive outlook on life will attract good things, like empty roads. Christopher keeps reminding her that she has yet to fully master the Law of Attraction. Their daughter finds it ironic to see her dad complaining about her mom's lack of planning. He's often so captivated by his phone that he ends up running late to appointments. Cynthia is confident that she will do better.

Regardless of their habits, both parents kept hammering the message that owning a car comes with immense responsibility that should never be underestimated. This is an awareness that grew stronger over time. They have never experienced any major incident on the road, but they both know that some of their behaviors behind the wheel at a younger age could have resulted in difficult situations.

The Smiths made a firm commitment to safety when Cynthia was born, especially when she was present in the car. It's like a switch went on and they understood that driving wasn't just a means of transportation. It could pose a threat to themselves, their passengers, and other motorists on the road.

Victoria rarely criticized Christopher's driving, although she sometimes thought he was a bit quick on the horn. She was particularly happy that he had changed some of his language when Cynthia began to speak. That was until she had her first ride with their daughter and heard her repeat her dad's famous line, "Come on, slowpokes! I have things to do."

The proud parents remained impressed to see Cynthia drive defensively by keeping a safe following distance, using turn signals, and checking blind spots. Thankfully, she was also more patient and considerate on the road than her father. She knows that her goal is not simply to reach her destination quickly but to arrive safely as well.

Chapter 17

DEFENSIVE DRIVING

The saying goes, "It's not you I'm worried about. It's the other drivers." While we certainly cannot control what other drivers do, there is no question that defensive driving techniques can reduce the risks of being involved in a collision. First, you need to understand the basics of defensive driving. The key is acknowledging potentially risky situations and taking action to avoid them before anything happens.

PERFECT THE REFLECTION IN THE MIRROR

Now is the time to learn the art and science of properly adjusting those lifesavers known as side view mirrors. Your primary aim here is to minimize blind spots. Those are the areas not visible from your central rearview mirror. Even if your car has proximity sensors, you shouldn't rely exclusively on them.

Method One: Lean With Grace

Start by sitting comfortably in your driver's seat. This should become your natural driving posture.

To Adjust the Driver's Side Mirror: Most people adjust their mirrors in a way that they see the edge of their car. This will include an area that is already safe, so it is ideal to point them slightly away from your vehicle. A tip to do this adjustment is to lean six inches to the left while seated normally. No bending forward here. Make sure the mirror is carefully adjusted outward until it just barely reveals a glimpse of the far rear corner of the car. We want just enough detail so that the vehicle appears but nothing more.

To Adjust the Passenger's Side Mirror: After returning to your normal position, lean approximately six inches toward the right while remaining seated. Make sure the mirror is carefully adjusted outward until it just barely reveals a glimpse of the far rear corner of the car. Again, you want just enough detail so that the vehicle appears but nothing more.

Final Check: Return to a natural sitting position and ensure you can't see either side of the car in the mirrors without leaning in.

Bonus Pro Tip: Make sure your mirrors are unobstructed and double-check their adjustment during different driving conditions (night or rainy weather for instance) to maximize safety.

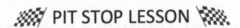 PIT STOP LESSON

ADJUSTING SIDEVIEW MIRRORS

Sideview mirrors are unsung heroes of the road. They should always be adjusted properly.

Adjusting them is quick and should be done before hitting the road to ensure you can clearly see what's around you.

You will find a link in the bonus section for two speedy techniques to quickly adjust mirrors while driving. This might be convenient if you were too busy loading the car and feeding the dog before leaving.

https://carconfidential.net/ccbonus

PREVENTION SKILLS TO MASTER THE ROAD

There are many ways to make conscious choices to reduce risk and keep everyone safe. Here are a few ideas to help you achieve this.

Watch Out for Red Light Runners. Count to three before leaving an intersection on your green light. Look both ways to make sure no one is trying to speed through a red light.

Be Alert and Diligent. Aggressive and unsafe habits, like speeding, tailgating, and running red lights are all part of road rage. Almost 80 percent of drivers in the U.S. have reported seeing this type of behavior at least twice a month.

There's no question about it, it's no picnic to become the target of a driver with road rage. Your first line of defense is to avoid provoking this type of driver in the first place. Pushing their buttons will only cause them to become even more aggressive. It is best to change lanes or direction and give them space by getting out of their way.

If you ever find yourself in a tense situation with an enraged driver, make sure to never get out of your vehicle. Stay calm, smile, wave and drive away. Most importantly, pay attention that they are not following you and call 911 if you feel you're in danger.

It's All About Space. What's your rush? Make sure to keep space between you and other vehicles. This will allow you to be in control and maneuver your vehicle if there is a sudden traffic jam or an unexpected event ahead of you.

A safe following distance is about five to ten seconds from the vehicle in front of you. In city traffic, a full-car length is also a good rule of thumb. The greater the speed, the greater the distance you should keep. Allow for more space if you are under extreme weather conditions, such as rain, snow, wind, or dust storms.

Be sure that you can always see the full rear tires of the car ahead of you when you're slowing down or at a full stop. This way, if you are rear-ended unexpectedly, you won't crash into the car in front of you.

Make sure to play peek-a-boo by glancing frequently at your side and rearview mirrors, even at a stop. It is important to identify threats, like cars swerving in and out of traffic.

Caution Around Large Trucks. Be patient and exercise caution when passing semis. They often lose speed when going uphill and gain speed when going downhill. They are not playing games with you, it's simply gravity at work. Allow ample space before moving in front of them. They are heavy and can't stop as fast as cars.

Truck drivers have a large blind spot on their right-hand side, so be especially careful when driving next to an 18-wheeler. If you cannot see the truck's side mirrors, that driver cannot see you.

Look Out for the Fast and Furious. Keeping an eye on your side and rearview mirrors will help you spot for motorcycles and cyclists swerving between lanes. Be sure to focus on four-way stops as pedestrians and joggers may jump into traffic to cross the street.

Maintaining a three-foot distance between you and cyclists is a good habit. This allows enough space to ensure safety.

Turn Your Head. Physically look before backing up. Remember that your backup camera doesn't cover 100% of what is happening behind your car.

Watch Out for Kids and Animals. Should you be reminded to be super careful and drive slow within school zones and parks?

Keep Your Emotions in Check. Emotions are feelings such as anger, fear, and joy. They can alter the way you perceive risk and affect your driving judgment. When you are affected by powerful emotions, your ability to make sound decisions may be impaired to a point where you might miss critical events or misjudge risk factors.

You must always be in control of your behavior. Practice defensive driving, accept responsibility for your decisions and adopt a safe driving mindset.

Remain conscious of your mental state. Look at yourself and determine if you have the focus and awareness required to operate a motor vehicle safely. If you have any doubts, wait and allow yourself time to relax and focus. Make it a habit to avoid driving when emotions are high. You can expect stress in your everyday driving. Learning to manage it is important for everyone's safety. Consider the following suggestions:

- If you are angry or emotional before getting behind the wheel, take a break.
- No matter what is going on in your life, when you get behind the wheel, resolve to focus solely on driving.
- Allow plenty of time to get to your destination to avoid becoming frustrated by red lights or heavy traffic.
- Recognize that many aspects of driving, such as traffic and other drivers' conduct, are beyond your control.
- Part of having a safe driving attitude is consistently applying defensive driving techniques.
- Make sure your car is in good working order. Wear your seatbelt and ensure your passengers do.
- Travel at a speed that is appropriate for the conditions. Whenever possible, create a space cushion around your vehicle.
- Observe the actions of other road users, including motorcyclists, cyclists, and pedestrians to anticipate their actions early.
- Look at the road ahead, behind, and on both sides of your vehicle.

FUEL FOR THOUGHT

WHEN INTELLECT COMES IN SECOND

Your emotions are the most intense aspect of your life. Intellect comes second. When you get angry, fearful, or frustrated, your emotions are throwing your intellect out the window. This affects your behavior on the road.

EMBRACING MOTHER NATURE'S MOOD SWINGS

In a perfect world, it is best to avoid driving in bad weather. The safest move is to wait out challenging weather conditions. If you must go, have a backup plan and be extra cautious. Heavy rain, fog, ice, wind, and other inclement weather can make it difficult to maintain control of your vehicle. Here are a few points to keep in mind if you need to venture out when conditions are not ideal.

What's Your Rush?

Are you driving or are your emotions driving? If you're angry, excited, sad, mad, or feeling other deep emotions, take a deep breath and bring your mindset back to the road. This is always important but especially so when road conditions are less than ideal.

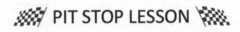

PIT STOP LESSON

DE-ICING WITH HAND SANITIZER

Make it a habit to keep a bottle of hand sanitizer in the car so that you can de-ice a door lock in extreme cold weather.

In case you didn't know, alcohol doesn't freeze.

Learn to Stay Calm

If you hit an icy patch, keep calm. Take your foot off the gas, steer straight, and refrain from braking. If the back end of the car starts to fishtail, turn the wheel gently in the same direction. Still skidding? With antilock brakes, apply steady pressure. For other braking systems, gently pump the brake pedal.

Check the Forecast Before You Go

Get into the habit of checking the weather forecast, especially during seasonal changes. If a monsoon or dust storm is predicted, use the recirculation button on your climate control. This will keep the outside dust from getting into your air vents. When the weather reports predict hail, it is best to park in the garage or under a covered parking. Hail could ding the vehicle to a point where your insurance may consider it a total loss. You might want to install an early warning and extreme weather/hail alert on your mobile device. There is a wide range of apps available.

PIT STOP LESSON

WATCH OUT FOR STRONG WINDS

These winds make it more likely that a car door will swing violently against your vehicle. It could also increase the possibility of trees or branches falling. Plan accordingly when parking in these conditions.

Mind the Wind, Fog, and Rain

In foggy and rainy conditions, use low-beam lights. High beams will increase glare and make it more difficult to see. During strong winds, maintain a firm grip on the wheel and watch for tree limbs and other debris that could blow into your path. Keep an eye on larger vehicles, which can be knocked off course by high winds. Slow down and avoid using the cruise control. If your vehicle begins to hydroplane, calmly steer in the same direction your vehicle is sliding until you stop or regain control.

Handling hazardous conditions deserves more attention. Important details will follow in **Chapter 18 — Adapting to Road Conditions**.

AVOIDING UNCLE DING AND COUSIN DENT

Yes, everyone hates noticing dings and dents on their car. Dings are like unwelcome pimples that appear seemingly out of nowhere and become irritated on the surface. Dents are like unruly wrinkles that you notice when washing your car. So, when life gives you either of these little surprises, remember that your ride deserves special treatment. (It might be time for a Botox touchup.) 😊

Let's face it, dings and dents are hard to avoid, and they don't discriminate based on make, model, or value. Whether you're driving to work, a grocery store or the dental office, chances are you're going to have to park next to other vehicles. And when you're pressed for time, you simply ignore what you know could happen. You might be a master at parking in tight spots, but what about the person next to you? Don't overestimate their skills.

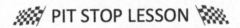

PIT STOP LESSON

SWEET PATIENCE WILL PREVENT SURPRISES

Dings and scratches can be avoided by assessing the situation and taking more time to park.

Everyone is in such a hurry; it is always GO, GO, GO! Yet, patience and simple habits will help prevent many unwelcome surprises.

Crunch vs. Krinkle

There are a few things that can be done to prevent them. The first step is to slow your roll. Your Go-Go-Go habit will invite every ding your vehicle gets. Being patient and assessing your options before choosing a parking spot helps. Here are more ways to avoid them.

Look at the end, not the beginning. The best protection from dings is to park away from carts, cars, and crowded driveways. Try to find a spot further away, rather than taking the first one by the store entrance. If you don't mind walking a bit, park further out, regardless of how

228

many cars are on the lot when you pull in. The end spot is generally the safest bet in a crowded lot. The odds of someone crowding in next to your vehicle are more remote when parking further away.

Measure With Your Eyes Before You Park. When you're pulling into a parking space, look at the length of the doors on the neighboring vehicles. Could they reach your vehicle when they are fully extended? Are they parked in the center between the lines?

How Tall Is Your Neighbor? Look at the height of the vehicle you are parking next to. Most cars have a rubber strip in the middle of the door to prevent damage from neighboring car doors. If your car is next to a taller SUV, these heavier doors could catch your side view mirrors or ding your door at a higher position than usual. This portion of your door has seam lines and curves which are more costly to repair than simple dent removal in the lower part of the door. You're better off moving to another spot.

Be a Detective. Always look at the car next to you and try to determine which side of the vehicle you should park on. Look for clues to see if they might have passengers, especially near shopping centers, parks, or schools. Kids might have less control over holding a door when getting out. If you're at work, parking on the passenger side of cars can be better as these doors are less likely to open. Be sure to pay attention to the door lines and check if they have rubber molding. They will not stop the door from hitting your vehicle but might reduce damage.

Parking opposite direction from other cars can be worse than a traffic infraction. It increases the risk of side-view mirror dings or dents due to improper placement.

Protect both your car and your peace of mind by parking like the others. Consider it advanced car care.

Smack in the Middle. If you must take a parking space where another car is off to one side, choose the side with more space. Always try to park in the middle, between the lines. Otherwise, you will look like the one who can't park if the other car leaves before you.

The first parking space at the end of a row is usually a safe place to protect one side from other cars. The first space next to a handicap spot is also safer. Just remain within the proper lines of a legitimate parking spot. Never park in the extra painted section next to a handicap parking place as it provides space to maneuver wheelchairs.

No matter how much you love your car, please don't park diagonally across two parking spots.

 PIT STOP LESSON

CRACK THE CODE TO COSTCO PARKING

Parking at Costco can feel like a high-speed sport, but a few tips can help. Consider your neighbors when looking for that perfect parking place. Select a spot next to cars that are parked nose in. When cars are parked rear in, it's a danger zone for dings and dents. Owners are likely to push their carts between cars to unload their haul.

Think Like a Parent. Check for child seats in neighboring cars as they may increase your risk of a ding. Remember that for parents to properly secure their child into a car seat, they normally need to fully extend their doors and might not be paying attention. This could be an indication that you might want to find another space.

Door Dents Are a Part of Life.

No matter how hard you try, door dents may be inevitable. If you have minor cosmetic dents that you want to fix, many companies will perform simple repairs. Some are mobile and equipped to do this in your driveway. They use special tools to push dents out from the inside, without a need to paint them. It's a clean fix, and many repairs can be performed while you wait.

If you have multiple clusters of dings and can't stand the sight, you can call your insurance and make a claim under your comprehensive coverage. For dings that cannot be pulled out and appear as minor paint scratches, automotive stores may have products to help you conceal the damage.

 FUEL FOR THOUGHT

THE BALLAD OF THE PARKING TRIO

Before parking, remember the three D's; Damage, Dings and Dents. This short poem can help you pay attention to neighboring cars and prevent unwanted surprises.

Like the Three Musketeers in their prime,
Ding, Dents, and Disaster often chime.
So navigate with care, soft and slow,
To dodge the trio's notorious blow.

KEY TAKEAWAYS

- **Defensive Driving and Blind Spot:** Master the positioning of your mirrors to eliminate blind spots. Practicing defensive driving will help you anticipate unpredictable behavior.

- **Be a Samaritan Vigilante:** Be a vigilante for red-light runners. Set emotions aside to focus on the road and be a good Samaritan by giving ample space for large vehicles. Prevention and patience will keep you ahead.

- **Weather Wisdom and Dent Prevention:** Safeguard your vehicle by selecting suitable parking spots to avoid door dings and costly dents. You can also learn to arm yourself with the knowledge necessary to face Mother Nature's bad days.

INFORMATION IN MIRRORS IS MORE EMPOWERING THAN IT MAY APPEAR!

Losing a Heartbeat

*T*he Smiths were itching for adventure. They badly needed to escape their everyday routine as things had recently been quite hectic. A few days before Easter, Christopher told Victoria, "Why don't we hit the road for the long weekend ahead? We don't have any plans and I think we need it." Victoria initially laughed and then realized he was serious. "Where is this coming from? We haven't done that since Cynthia began school." she exclaimed. It didn't take too long for both to get excited, and they concluded that it was a good time to do it as Cynthia might not want to tag along if they wait too long to do such a trip.

Early Friday morning, the Smiths packed Christopher's car and headed north for an impromptu visit to see Victoria's sister. They all got excited, yet Cynthia was quick to put on her headset when the fantastic duo sitting in front of her started singing.

The roads were surprisingly quiet, and they made good time. That was until they arrived at an unpredictable mountain known to get snowfall up to mid-April. They didn't expect to find bad weather as the forecast for their ultimate destination was good.

It soon became obvious that weather problems were ahead. As rain began pouring, Victoria asked Christopher to slow down. In response, he boasted: "Trust me. This is not my first rodeo!" The weather soon took an unexpected turn and the mountain landscape caused heavy flooding. Christopher believed his SUV could handle every challenge, but two inches of water quickly caused the vehicle to hydroplane for a few seconds in a curve. They all felt it and lost a heartbeat. The car got really quiet for a moment as they all processed what had happened.

Though no serious harm was sustained by anyone, Victoria spilled some coffee on her yellow dress. "Darn!" She yelled. "I told you to slow down; you never listen to me. Now look at this mess." Christopher was quick to explain that it was an unexpected stream of water from a crease in the mountain; yet he knew it had been a close call.

Chapter 18

ADAPTING TO ROAD CONDITIONS

Mother Nature can surprise us with her whimsical outbursts, dousing us in raindrops that awaken rosebuds and invite us to dance in puddles. She brings more delight when letting soft white snowflakes gracefully descend from above, enticing us to ski or just enjoy sliding across its surface. These magical moments allow us to escape stress-laden work environments by snuggling into cozy cabins for hot chocolate while marveling over nature's snowy blanket.

Winter brings with it both excitement and caution. As we head outdoors in search of winter activities, it is wise to be wary of unpredictable weather conditions. Slippery roads can present unexpected difficulties during our travels — particularly if entering unfamiliar territory.

Long-distance excursions require that drivers remain mindful of road conditions ahead. Although practicing driving under extreme weather conditions may not always be possible, you can equip yourself with an understanding of fundamental safety measures. Handling a car competently in any weather is an invaluable skill to possess for peace of mind.

Drivers must understand the challenges associated with driving under less-than-ideal conditions. When Mother Nature makes it more challenging, we need to remain alert and adjust our driving behaviors accordingly. Slowing down and increasing focus are proven strategies for success when facing severe weather.

So, let's embrace the elements and master the art of driving in adverse conditions. Through diligence, knowledge, and some extra cautionary measures, you can safely navigate rain-sodden roads, gusty winds, snow-covered landscapes, and slippery surfaces. It is possible to enjoy every second of the journey and reach your destination safely.

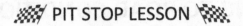

PIT STOP LESSON

SURF'S UP!

Avoid driving through dangerous waterways altogether during a heavy downpour or flooding. Though your vehicle is likely many things, it should never become an aquatic engineering marvel like those seen by ducks.

In all honesty, nobody has ever written a sea shanty about being stuck in the rain in a car. Stay dry while looking good and safe.

EASING ROAD ANXIETY

Learning how to deal with road anxiety is essential as sometimes you just need to get somewhere, and the weather can change quickly. So, I want to cover some factors that cause the most stress behind the wheel. These include rain, snow, fog, ice, and wind. I've put together a list of driving behaviors you should instantly abandon when dealing with these conditions.

Anxiety levels can jump when driving through heavily flooded streets. In the U.S., we see over 900,000 accidents a year due to wet driving conditions. They result in roughly 5,000 fatalities and 350,000 serious injuries.

So, before you open that flimsy old umbrella or grab your grandfather's snow sled and head out into the cold white wilderness, take some multivitamins to boost those rusty memory cells. Driving behind a rain-splattered windshield doesn't have to be a white-knuckle, nerve-wracking experience. Just remember the following tips. When you arrive home with your automobile — and your spinal cord — in one piece, you'll thank me. Let's learn to adapt to Mother Nature.

When the Sky Cries, Steer Wise

It's important to learn how to adapt to wet roads, so buckle up as we brave the dangers of driving in the rain. Be mindful. This is real life and there are no guarantees of making it through torrential storms unscathed. Exercise caution, especially when encountering situations which look like water park attractions with free-flowing rivers of water all around you. You're not auditioning for *Naked and Afraid*. In case my warning got lost somewhere along the way: Here is a quick refresher. **Stay clear — do not even consider driving through.**

Every year, careless drivers believe that crossing a small stream of water no deeper than an inch or two will not harm their vehicles. You'd be shocked how many of these people end up being washed off the road into a raging torrent as they struggle to get out of their car and grasp a tree limb to avoid sinking below the waterline. It's better to wait out the storm and the rain than to risk your life and the lives of those close to you because you thought a little water wouldn't hurt you.

Even if the water isn't moving, you have no idea what's beneath it if the bottom isn't visible. A pothole the size of a swimming pool could be present. There could be shattered glass or nails from a truck. If you can't see the bottom, don't risk your life by driving on submerged pavement. Stop a safe distance from the water's edge or find a method to drive around it, if possible.

Beware of Hydroplaning

Hydroplaning is the most dangerous hazard when driving too fast in the rain. No, this has nothing to do with flying in a Cessna with pontoons on a fishing trip. When your car feels like a boat gliding on water, while still on the highway, it's called hydroplaning.

Tires can normally slice through water while remaining in contact with the road surface. However, if the road is wet and you're driving too quickly, you may float on top of the water, causing the tires to lose contact with the road surface. This is a disaster. **This is a disaster!** Get it? It is a major problem as you can no longer steer when this happens.

You are also no longer able to brake. This is what occurs when you hydroplane. It will feel as if the car was gliding on ice. The worst part is that you may not even realize you're hydroplaning until you press the brakes, or try to steer, and the car begins to slip out of control. Considering this, it's best to avoid traveling at hydroplane speeds in the first place.

While rain may bring peace and serenity for some people, driving in these conditions is quite another matter. Don't let slippery roads, reduced visibility or unpredictable conditions disorient or discombobulate you. I am here to guide you safely through this wet and wild adventure. It is possible to master the art of driving on rain-soaked roads — from maintaining balance between traction and control to staying visible amidst splashing waters. You'll soon be performing, "I'm singing in the rain; singing in the rain…" But just make sure to keep your windows closed so other drivers can remain focused on the road. 😊

 PIT STOP LESSON

CRUISE CONTROL WARNING

Don't use cruise control when road conditions are not ideal as the system might not recognize slipping and may accelerate when it shouldn't.

Navigating Under Stormy Skies

Grab your favorite umbrella and get ready to navigate stormy weather with style and confidence using the following tips.

Be Aretha Franklin. It's crucial that you *THINK* before you drive. Many people drive subconsciously, out of habit, and when it starts raining, they often forget to adjust their thinking. When conditions are less than ideal, drivers need to stay alert and focus on what's going on around them. It's that simple.

Get Back to Basics. It's the law in all states to turn on headlights when visibility is low. Many states also require having them on when the windshield wipers are in use. Make sure you have working wipers and good tires before you attempt driving in subpar conditions. This is especially important when driving on highways or roads with higher speed limits. Check your tire pressure, even your spare, to make sure they will perform at their best in these conditions.

INSIDER FILES

BEHIND EVERY VISIBLE ROAD IS A WOMAN
The Inventive Tale of the Wiper Blade Pioneer

Mary Anderson was the ingenious woman who saw through the rain and changed the way we drive. During a snowy day in New York City in 1903, Mary noticed streetcar drivers manually opening their windows to wipe off snow accumulation. She thought it was quite an inconvenience, and wondered if there could be an easier way to deal with this. With that thought in mind, Mary got busy developing solutions.

In 1905, she designed and patented a swinging arm device with a rubber blade that could be operated from inside the car. This would allow operators to easily clear windshields of rain, snow, or other obstacles. Drivers could simply pull a lever to operate this system.

Mary Anderson's invention ultimately created what we know today as windshield wipers. It may not have had immediate success, but it laid the groundwork for automatic wipers to come. Today when your windshield wipers wipe away rainwater from your windshield remember Mary Anderson who had the vision to enhance the driving experience.

Don't Be Tom Cruise. Turn off your cruise control. Ironically, on rain- or snow-slick surfaces, cruise control may cause you to lose control.

You might think it'll help you stay at one steady speed, but if you hydroplane while you're in cruise control, your car will accelerate.

Learn to Read. This may sound silly but remember to keep an eye out for speed-limit signs. People often assume the limits by following traffic flow or routine. Awareness of speed is important as posted limits are designed for ideal driving conditions. When the roads are busier, and the conditions or visibility are not ideal, these limits should be reduced significantly.

So, lift your foot off the accelerator and allow more time to get to your destination.

 PIT STOP LESSON

DID YOU CHANGE OR DID THE ROAD CHANGE?

Drivers need the wisdom and adaptability to alter the way they drive to successfully traverse highways and byways with precision. No one should expect that roads will magically transform before their very eyes. They should adapt their driving styles accordingly to face the ever-evolving asphalt kingdom.

Don't Play 'Frogger.' Yes, it's raining, traffic is slow and you're running late, but jumping from lane to lane in these conditions is like asking for trouble. Always drive defensively when merging or passing vehicles to prevent collisions. Visibility is often limited by rain and fog. (FYI, if you don't know Frogger, it was a popular video game in the 80s. Explaining this makes me feel old.)

CONQUERING HAZARDS OF THE ROAD

Driving through treacherous roads, unpredictable weather and unexpected obstacles can transform an otherwise peaceful drive into an adventurous journey. I will now unveil the best way to tackle hazardous road conditions. Be ready in case you ever feel like your car is skating on ice, or when your windshield wipers can hardly keep up. Fasten your seatbelt and get prepared as danger might spring at any turn and your driving abilities will quickly be under the spotlight.

Dealing With Snow and Ice

It's freezing outside, so chill out. Please watch out for black ice. That's a frozen area that might appear normal. You can think of it as invisible ice. Remember that bridges and overpasses freeze first, so they are more likely to have black ice. In those conditions, take it slow and avoid sudden changes in speed or direction.

PIT STOP LESSON

KITTY LITTER AND OLD SOCKS

To quickly defrost your windshield, place old socks filled with kitty litter in each corner of your dashboard. Meow, Meow...

You need to be a Clean Freak. Keep all windows clean as visibility is crucial, especially in bad weather. Turn on the lights and wipers and crank up the defroster, if necessary. Scrape the ice off your windows before leaving to ensure a clear view of the road and potential hazards. Remove all the snow off your roof as it may slide down when braking and instantly blind you. If you don't do it for yourself, be considerate of others as at higher speeds patches might fly off on the windshield of the car following you. Make sure that all items are removed from the back window as you need to keep an eye on vehicles following too close in these instances. If the conditions worsen or you're having trouble seeing the road clearly, carefully pull over to a safe location well off the roadway.

Brake Sensibly. Abrupt braking can cause the wheels to lock up and lead to the loss of steering control. If you have anti-lock braking system

(ABS), previously referred to as anti-lock brakes (ALB), apply constant, yet firm, pressure to the pedal. Gauge your stopping distance and let off the accelerator before braking. With vehicles without ABS, you can gently pump the brakes to slow down without locking them.

Stuck, now what? If you get caught in snow, don't 'floor it.' Simply straighten the wheels and accelerate slowly. It is important to avoid spinning the tires. If necessary, use wood blocks, sand, or kitty litter under the drive wheels to increase traction. Be proactive by carrying some of these useful tools when traveling in snowy conditions.

Handle Gliding

What if your car turns into a loose puck on ice? What should you do if you've lost control and notice you're skating or hydroplaning? First, stay calm. Don't slam on the brakes. That will only make things worse. Keep your eyes on the road and slowly let off the gas pedal to allow any leftover traction to slow you down. Make no attempt to turn. Don't fight the automobile if it's going off in a direction you don't want to go; just follow your wheels. Keep steering into the direction where it's gliding. Your goal is to stop safely or regain control. And as the automobile slows, this should eventually happen, almost miraculously.

Driving In Fog

Headlights should be on and set to the low beam when driving in fog. Turn on fog lights if you have them.

If you're having trouble seeing, safely pull over to the right, well out of the traffic lane, and turn on your emergency flashers. Wait until visibility improves before continuing.

Driving In High Winds

Look up and look out to stay alert for flying debris. Use extra caution near trailers, vans or vehicles carrying lightweight cargo as a strong gust could make them sway toward your vehicle. Without speeding, you want to quickly pass them in case they shift lanes.

It's best not to drive a trailer, van, or other 'high-profile' vehicles in high winds. Autos with high centers of gravity, like SUVs and trucks, are more vulnerable in high-wind conditions.

Driving With Big Trucks

Give Trucks Enough Stopping Space. The maximum load capacity of most tractor-trailer trucks is 80,000 lbs. That weight is about the same as 24 Honda Accord sedans, or six African elephants. At 55 miles per hour, these trucks will need 550 feet — the length of 1.5 football fields — to come to a complete stop. In comparison, an average-size Ford Fusion moving at 70 mph can stop within 178 feet. It is nice that the Fusion driver can brake quickly enough to prevent a collision on the highway. However, the important question is whether the truck will have enough room to dodge the Fusion.

🏁 PIT STOP LESSON 🏁

CAUTION AROUND LARGE TRUCKS

When trucks are in the left lane, it's usually to pass obstacles or other trucks. They also shift to the left before turning right, so pay extra attention before going around them.

If a car is tailgating you, stay in the fast lane and pass the trucks before returning to the slow lane.

Don't 'Grillegate!' This term refers to the opposite of tailgating. It happens when a driver passes a truck in the left lane and pulls back in front of it too close and at a similar speed. It's understandable that most drivers don't want to get caught behind tractor trailers but moving within 25 feet in front of them isn't enough of a safety buffer for these 80,000-pound beasts. Their speed will often vary based on the incline of the road. They slow a bit going uphill and gather speed going down, so it is best to give them space so they can leverage gravity.

Always Pass on the Left. If you've ever driven behind a huge truck, you've probably seen these messages: "Passing Side" on the left door, and "Suicide" on the right side. This is good advice. Pass trucks on the left, even if it means waiting a few seconds longer.

Don't Fly Your Car

Speed limits are in place to let you know how safe it is to drive in normal conditions. When the weather is bad and the roads are flooded, these limits are useless. This doesn't mean that you should ignore them as fewer cops might be hiding out in speed traps. It means that you should drive safely, according to the conditions, and the worse the circumstances are, the slower you should go.

 **PIT STOP LESSON**

NEW CAR NOISE MIGHT BE NORMAL

Some noise or issues might come up after changing habits or patterns. Do you have a new commute? Did your kids begin attending a new school?

Various factors might explain the new noises, such as different pavement or speed limits, more stop signs or traffic lights. Those might make tires or brakes noisier.

Stay Off the Side of the Road

Roads are constructed so that they're highest in the middle. That elevation might be slight, but it causes water to run off the center hump (crown) and drain toward the edges. If you're driving in the rain, you want to avoid standing water, which means that you want to be where the water isn't — and that's in the center of the road. Okay, I know this isn't always possible. You might be on a narrow one-lane road and the sides may be the only place you have to drive safely. And no, the center won't be dry either, especially if it's still raining, but it's going to be the driest place around (other than your garage).

I CAN SEE CLEARLY NOW

There are two important details to keep in mind about headlights. First, they help to better see the road ahead. The flip side is that light helps other motorists see you. While both aspects are important, it's easy to forget about sharing the spotlight.

Headlight Etiquette

While headlights help you clearly see ahead, they also assist you in being noticed. That said, you don't want to mistakenly blind people. When using high beams, remember that approaching vehicles might also have difficulty navigating the road, so please be considerate and turn them off when not needed.

It may seem obvious, but it's astonishing how many people appear to be missing common sense. Even if you know the road so well that you could drive it while sound asleep or blindfolded, you shouldn't drive when there's enough water on the windshield to support a goldfish colony.

I also keep reminding clients not to turn off their headlights, even during the day. They help you see other people, and be seen, especially when it's pouring.

  FUEL FOR THOUGHT

WHEN CLEANING DAMAGES TIRES

Petroleum-based cleaners applied directly to tire surfaces may cause irreparable damage to brake pads or rotors, leading to screeching noises when applied directly; more so on hot rotors after it has been driven. Keep in mind that aluminum wheels feature gapped designs with 6–8-inch openings which may allow for overspray to hit your brake system directly.

DID YOU KNOW?

The lack of sunlight makes the world look like one big mass of overcooked oatmeal. In the murky gloom of a rainstorm, even if it's just a light drizzle, seeing a pair of headlights coming out of that bowl will remind other drivers that — whoops! — there's something in that oatmeal and it doesn't look like raisins.

If you can't see ahead, you don't know what's around the corner. You could find stopped cars, wandering animals, or fallen trees in front of you that you're not expecting. It's possible that you're not driving as straight as you think, and that you're heading for a bridge abutment.

When visibility begins to deteriorate, pull over to the side of the road as soon as it is safe to do so. Come to a complete stop. While you wait for things to clear up, take a deep breath and listen to soothing music. Call Mom and apologize for all those times you left the fridge door open for no reason and, most importantly, let them know your current location and situation. If you're not alone in your vehicle, turn to the person next to you and learn more about them. Wonderful partnerships have blossomed from less fortunate beginnings.

GAS FUEL FOR THOUGHT

BREAKFAST ON RAINY DAYS

If rain is as thick as syrup pouring over your windshield and you start craving pancakes, please stop driving!

DID YOU KNOW?

- **Adverse Weather Requires Adaptation:** It is your skills behind the wheel which ensures safe arrivals.

- **Road Anxiety Can Be Overcome with Preparation:** Beat anxiety and road rage by adopting an attitude of readiness, from vehicle preparation to perfecting the art of snow and ice braking.

- **Illuminate Responsibly:** Use your headlights throughout the day and night to illuminate your path and be seen clearly. Dip beams to also ensure clear driving by all.

INFORMATION IN MIRRORS IS MORE EMPOWERING THAN IT MAY APPEAR!

Challenging Conditions

Christopher has faced challenging driving environments throughout his life. His skills and reflexes have been put to the test a few times, but the scare in the mountain on the way to see Victoria's sister caught him off-guard. He knows quite well that cold climate states may still encounter inclement weather in late spring. Yet, hydroplaning on an icy stream after a curve in the mountain made him feel queasy. The weather had been so nice and the road perfect until that curve. It was still troubling him a few miles later as he had never experienced such a queasy feeling with his daughter in the car.

While he tried to keep a straight face, he thought, "This could have been so bad. So bad!" He kept looking at the ditch beside the road wondering, "What if?" Victoria knew him well enough to see that he was more affected than he let show. A part of her still wanted to scream at him, but there was nothing to do at this point. And, ultimately, there was nothing he could have done differently. He wasn't reckless; it just happened so quickly. They still had mountain terrain to tackle, and she was glad to be in the passenger side, even though the conditions were now good, and the scenery magnificent.

Victoria changed the playlist, upped the volume and their mood swiftly shifted. She didn't put the volume as loud as it was earlier, to make sure Christopher remained attentive on the road ahead. But he was fully focused. He looked like he had been infused by a couple of IV drips of espresso coffee. Wondering if Cynthia got scared, she quickly checked in the back and saw her humming to her own tunes. Their daughter seemed oblivious to the slight tension. She wore her big headphones, as usual, half-hypnotized by her phone.

When turning her head forward, Victoria caught sight of a sign indicating that her sister's town was only 30 miles away. She got excited thinking that they'd be there within the next hour. Victoria was already thankful to be spending quality time with family for Easter, hopefully with a mimosa, she thought.

Chapter 19

PLANNING A ROAD TRIP

T he change of seasons is around the corner and changing weather triggers your emotions. You begin to visualize yourself packing the car and getting ready for an adventure. The best part is that you know this reality is only a turnkey of your ignition away. The car is packed solid, yet are you ready to handle an emergency or breakdown? Chances are you're not. Before you get excited and bolt, you need to get prepared.

According to AAA and Department of Transportation, there were over 127,000 car crashes in the U.S. in the last year. That's an average of 348 crashes per day and, unfortunately, almost 30% of those crashes involved injuries.

If you live in a desert state, you won't see many winter storms, unless you're driving up to a northern county. Use extra caution if you plan to visit those regions. Winter driving safety begins before you leave your house. No matter how experienced a driver you are, you are never prepared enough for the unexpected.

 FUEL FOR THOUGHT

GREEN LIGHT ON TRIP SAFETY

Before hitting the road, make sure to visit your trusted repair shop and have them do a 'trip safety check' which includes your battery, fluid levels, and inspecting the wear on your tires.

THE THREE P'S OF A PERFECT ROAD TRIP

As with any adventure, examining our experiences and learning from them are vital to have a worry-free road trip experience. Here's my guide to help prepare, protect, and prevent a stressful road trip. The aim is to give drivers of all skill levels the information they need for a safe journey. Preparing ahead for a road trip is key to handling unexpected circumstances, such as poor weather. Always have an emergency kit at the ready as well as taking measures like routine car maintenance checks to protect both yourself and your car on this adventure. Take control and turn every trip into a safe and exciting journey with these guidelines in hand.

- *PREPARE* for the trip,
- *PROTECT* yourself and
- *PREVENT* surprises on the road.

How to Use the 3 P's

Plan Your Route. Consult weather and traffic reports to plan the safest way to go. Check for any road construction or detours. Give yourself extra time for the conditions and traffic. Make sure to share your travel plans with friends or family.

Stock Up. Charge your cell phone and pack a charger. Assemble a cold-weather kit with blankets, sleeping bags, warm clothes, and boots. Remember to have your usual car emergency kit ready, along with a windshield brush and scraper, traction aid, shovel, and road salt. For electric cars, map out all the charging stations, both regular and express, as you may need more power than anticipated.

Get Your Vehicle Ready. Check the oil. Fill your gas tank and antifreeze. Top up the windshield washer fluid and bring an extra container as usage increases in bad weather. Check your tire condition and pressure, including your spare. Have your battery tested. Ensure your windshield wipers and headlights work. If you have an electric or hybrid car, plug in your vehicle as often as possible when parked.

Make sure to have your repair and tire receipts with you, or pictures of them, in case you need that information. This might be useful, if repairs are required on the road, to see if it is something still under warranty. Write down your repair shop's number in case something happens, and you need their guidance.

Pay Attention. It's easy to get distracted when everyone in the vehicle sings, "Santa Got Run Over by a Reindeer." Use extra caution on bridges and exit ramps, which tend to freeze before other parts of the roadway. Take note of warning signs about areas likely to be slippery in wintry conditions. On long drives, take frequent breaks to help you stay alert.

Wait for Help. If your car stalls or you're in an accident, stay in your vehicle. To improve your visibility, keep an interior dome light on, and either place a reflector or attach a bright cloth to your trunk, window, or antenna.

Practice. If you have an opportunity, sharpen your winter driving skills by practicing U-turns and fast and abrupt braking in an empty, snowy, parking lot. You want to understand how the vehicle will handle in the snow before traveling on such roads.

Leverage Technology. Dust off your owners' manual to get re-familiarized with your vehicle's safety features. Pay particular attention to information that can help prevent accidents, such as anti-lock brakes, electronic stability control, adaptive headlights, and lane departure warning. Before your next trip, make sure you understand how these systems perform on slippery roads. Remember that you can start with G O O G L E...

BE AN EPIC ROAD TRIP MAESTRO

Road trips are always exciting, yet unexpected events or obstacles can throw a wrench at the experience. Fortunately, there are a few things you can do to reduce the risks and be ready if something happens. Here are fun yet straightforward suggestions you can follow to become a road trip master. Though some tasks might appear trivial or irrelevant, with persistence they will bring ease to your next trip. Get ready for adrenaline surges and occasional moments of giggling brilliance.

Be a Navigational Ninja. Hone your map-reading skills and embrace GPS navigation. No more driving in circles like an annoyed squirrel. You will save time, gas and frustration as most GPS software adapts routes to the latest traffic conditions and road work.

Be a Tire Whisperer. It's time to use the ancient art of tire checking. You can master this quick ritual with the subtle use of a magical tire gauge. Checking tire pressure before a long trip will help avoid flat tires and keep your wheels rolling smoothly like ninja stars.

Be a Fluid Connoisseur. Becoming an expert at maintaining essential fluid levels like oil, coolant, and windshield washer fluid, will keep your car hydrated like an oasis. Keep those camels hydrated too.

Be the Master of Basics. By learning the fundamentals of car maintenance — from changing flat tires to jump-starting dead batteries — you'll become the hero if there's trouble on the road. Yes, you can proudly wear that cape on your back and save the journey.

Be a Packing Picasso. Plan your needs ahead and limit your weight by reviewing the stuff you've been hoarding in the trunk forever. Think about what you might need on the way, so you won't have to unload everything to reach it. Embrace your inner 'Tetris champion' (yes, another throwback to the glorious 80s), and master the art of packing.

With a little planning, you can fit all your road trip essentials into your trunk and access them like a magician pulling objects from his hat.

Be a Snackologist Extraordinaire. Can you imagine a Super Bowl party without a game plan for food? You know that bellies will eventually scream, so plan your road trip snacks. You can up your game by selecting tasty and healthy snacks which can be eaten while driving. Avoid stuff that will drip on your shirt or cause choking hazards. The last thing you need is an accident due to your snacks.

Be DJ El Coche. Create the ultimate road trip playlist that will keep everyone singing along. Pick songs that will not only fit your passengers' personalities but tunes that will keep them engaged. The ideal playlist will cater to everyone's tastes. No autographs please.

Be a Pit Stop Pro. You can master the art of efficient pit stops to refuel both you and your passengers by planning bathroom breaks, snack refills, and stretch sessions efficiently. This will lead to optimal road trip enjoyment.

Be a Weather Whisperer: A good ninja is also a master in the art of reading weather forecasts. You need to be prepared for all road trip conditions. With the right gear and some planning, you will conquer your journey like a true weather warrior.

Be an Emergency Jedi. Stock your emergency supplies — including first aid kits, roadside assistance tools, flashlights, and jumper cables. Bring a notebook with emergency contacts, such as your family and doctors. This will help if your cell phone battery dies, and you can't remember 300 numbers off the top of your head. If roadside emergencies arise, you'll be a prepared hero.

- **Essential Preparations:** Before setting out on your journey, ensure your car has an emergency kit. Become acquainted with your car's security systems to make every trip safe.

- **Travel Mastery:** To guarantee that your vacation becomes a positive experience, master the art of preparation.

INFORMATION IN MIRRORS IS MORE EMPOWERING THAN IT MAY APPEAR!

Emergencies

Christopher was driving back from work after a productive day, reveling about spending time on the deck with a cold beer while roasting veggies on the BBQ. He told Siri to call Victoria to make sure they had everything home as he didn't feel like going out again in the evening. While talking on the hands-free system, he noticed a squirrel about to cross the street and hit the brakes. That's when he heard screeching tires and heard a thump on the back bumper.

After a few expletives, he told Victoria that something happened, and he'd call her back. "Are you OK?" she asked, with a worried tone. "Yes, I'm good, let me check the car," he replied while rushing out.

Outside, he found a confused 17-year-old behind the wheel trying to reach his cell phone on the floor between the pedals. Seems like he was engaged in texting while driving, although he claimed that he had just "looked down for a second," without mentioning the phone.

While Christopher was initially shocked and angry about what had just occurred, he couldn't help but feel compassion for the driver who was the same age as their daughter. The damage was barely visible as it was a very low impact mishap. Luckily, they were on a quiet street and they both drove within the speed limit. He gave the young driver a stern warning and decided to let it go. Involving insurance was not worth it, he thought, and he didn't see a need to call the cops.

Back home, he shared the story with Victoria, and she felt he should have reported it to make sure the kid got a stronger lesson. The Smiths both realized that they couldn't rely on the assumptions they held about their daughter's driving habits or those of her friends.

The experience influenced a long chat with Cynthia, over dinner on the patio, about steps to take during roadside emergencies, preparation, but mostly prevention. Christopher was humble enough, for the sake of his daughter's safety, to admit that he should have looked behind him quickly before hitting the brakes. "If I had noticed the car following closely, I might have reacted differently," he openly reflected.

Chapter 20

COLLISIONS AND EMERGENCIES

E ven on a lovely day, when all is good in your world, the unexpected can happen. Just when you thought you were a great driver, you get involved in a collision. You might ask yourself, "How did this happen to me?" It's time to navigate the reasons behind roadside emergencies and car accidents.

No one is immune, so stop blaming yourself. Car accidents are more common than you might think. What is unfortunate is that most incidents are caused by simple human errors that could have been prevented. Knowing this reality, the best thing you can do is to empower yourself before it happens. No matter how experienced you are, in the event of an accident, you are going to be shocked, possibly dizzy with adrenaline or enraged at the person who caused it.

We all know how to be safe when we get behind the wheel. You trust yourself and other motorists to drive carefully and defensively to prevent accidents. Unfortunately, car crashes still happen every day. It's important that you mentally train yourself to understand the basics.

Let's take a moment and chat about the logistics of how and why accidents happen. I want to help you be your own first line of defense. Don't learn safety by accident.

🏁 PIT STOP LESSON 🏁

PLAN FOR THE WORST

Keep a car escape hammer under your driver's seat in case you must break your window in an emergency. A knife or scissors could also be handy to cut a seatbelt.

CRASHOLOGY 101: DEMYSTIFYING CAR COLLISIONS

When we get in our cars and drive away from our problems, we have a profound sense of liberation. Cars serve as more than just a method of transportation; they are also an outlet for our feelings. They were originally invented to transport us from one location to another, not as a vanity item to be displayed like a Rolex. What the heck is going on? That can't be real. Can it? That original idea died when people began letting their egos dictate their car needs.

Driving is one of the riskiest things people do every day, yet it's easy to overlook the need for practice and improvement. As a reminder, to keep things in perspective, accidents involving motor vehicles cause as many deaths and injuries every year, in the United States, as firearms.

It's hard to describe the feeling of pure exhilaration and joy that you get when you're listening to your favorite music and gazing out the window at the open road. You start feeling the invisible butterflies of happiness as you get near your destination. Can we agree that feelings make up to eighty percent of the driving experience? If this wasn't the case, there wouldn't be such a thing as road rage, right?

Understanding the Three Main Types of Accidents

Car accidents are among the leading causes of serious physical harm or even death; yet we seldom discuss how they can be avoided. Let's take a closer look at three categories of vehicle accidents as well as when and why they typically happen.

Rear-End Collisions. Accidents in which one vehicle collides with the rear of another are known as rear-end collisions. Distracted driving, following too closely, and unexpected stops are common causes of rear-end incidents.

T-Bone Collisions. When one car smashes into the side of another, it causes serious damage and is sometimes referred to as a 'T-bone.' Running a red light or stop sign, failing to give the right of way, or driving under the influence are all common causes of side-impact collisions.

One-on-One Collisions. Accidents involving a single vehicle happen when it collides with another stationary object, like a tree, pole, or guardrail, or when it rolls over. Loss of control, intoxication, and high speeds are common factors in single-vehicle collisions.

 FUEL FOR THOUGHT

SOMEONE MADE A MISTAKE
Accidents do happen. For a moment, let's dismiss the myth that car crashes are accidents. Someone made a mistake.

When Are Accidents More Likely to Happen?

After Daylight Saving Time Begins. Believe it or not, areas observing Day Light Saving Time see an increase in car accidents the day after they turn the clock forward. It is unclear why these accidents occur more often. Some research points to sleep deprivation due to the time change and the unfamiliar darkness in the morning as possible culprits.

Reckless Driving. Speeding, changing lanes too fast, not watching traffic ahead, and ignoring red lights or stop signs are all examples of reckless driving that commonly lead to accidents. Acting aggressively behind the wheel is another noteworthy one. This is why it's so important to stay alert for these behaviors.

Distracted Driving. It's very easy to get distracted when driving. It can happen when fiddling with the radio or with an impromptu call on your cell phone. It often occurs when eating or fussing with the kids. Studies show that distracted driving is getting worse every year and is responsible for many accidents, some of them fatal. It is important that you pay attention to your driving and to the road, not your friends, phone, or children. If you must deal with any urgent problem, it's best to pull over, take care of the problem, and then get back on the road.

Impaired Driving. No one needs reminding how dangerous drinking and driving are. Commercials, news media coverage or personal conversations all emphasize it repeatedly as drunk driving is a leading cause of car accidents. It remains one of the deadliest behaviors.

What needs to be highlighted are the hazards of driving under the influence of anything which could affect your cognition or alertness. These include such things as recreational marijuana or prescribed medications, which can make you drowsy or foggy. If you ever feel incapacitated in any way, or plan to have some drinks, please designate a sober driver, or take an alternative form of transportation. It might be a good idea to consider downloading a taxicab service or ride-sharing app on your phone ahead of time.

According to the Centers for Disease Control and Prevention (CDC) in the U.S., alcohol-impaired driving accounts for an estimated 28 deaths every day. This statistic demonstrates that anything can happen within seconds. Drivers, passengers and even pedestrians are constantly at risk. It is vitally important for everyone to know the rules of the road and be able to handle various emergency scenarios.

Any initiative to prevent impaired driving is worth considering. Lives depend upon it.

Animal Crossings. If you see an animal crossing sign, slow down and be alert. There are various animal crossing signs in areas where they have been seen in the past or where they have a large population. While these signs will vary based on your location, from deer or moose to frogs and turtles, and sometime alligators, they remain a hazard regardless of their size. Most drivers know that swerving into oncoming traffic to prevent hitting an animal darting into the road is a bad idea. Yet it's an instinct to attempt not to hurt another living thing.

INSIDER FILES

THOUGHTS ABOUT CAR SAFETY

Road safety remains a primary concern, yet no significant improvement has occurred over time. According to the Association for Safe International Road Travel (ASIRT), 37,000 people die each year in car accidents in the United States while 2.35 million are injured or disabled from these collisions.

Approximately 1,600 American children under the age of 15 and 8,000 between 16–20 are killed yearly in motor vehicle crashes.

Keep in mind that most of these fatal accidents still result from driver impairment.

THE PHYSICS OF COLLISION: ENERGY AND FORCE

It's always good to understand some physics. This begins with a grasp of Newton's Law of motion. It states that a body in motion will remain in motion until an equal but opposite force is applied. Basically, if you strike anything while going at a particular speed, you and all passengers will continue to move toward the crash point, even if the car has slowed or stopped. Simply put, you and your passengers will be injured.

While most people have been too preoccupied with eating Fig Newtons to study Newton's Law, now is an opportune moment for refocusing on the task of staying alive on the roads. Let's review the two types of force crashes and their devastating impacts.

Colliding With a Wall. Car crashes are clear examples of Newton's Law of motion. Sure, cookies are more exciting than reviewing theories… but we'll keep it basic. You need to understand that an object in motion will stay in motion unless an external force acts upon it.

Conversely, if an object is at rest, it will remain at rest until an unbalanced force act upon it. **In simpler terms, you hit something or something hits you.**

Colliding With a Car. If the cars are similar in size and weight, both will bounce back, like rams having a disagreement. In a head-on collision, it would be like hitting a brick wall at 50 mph. Broadly speaking, when you hit a wall, pretty much all the energy goes into deforming the car. The wall will not significantly change.

For example: A 3,200-pound vehicle traveling 30 mph will compress one foot upon impact. At 60 mph it would collapse two feet upon impact.

It's been said many times over that the biggest concern is not for your driving, but it's about the other drivers. Guess what, when that advice is provided, it works both ways, so who are we really fooling?

It's easy to point fingers at other drivers or blame the weather. But in reality, every one of us is responsible for our own and for others' safety on the road. The time for excuses has passed; it is now about being accountable.

Safe driving requires nothing more than paying attention. Make sound decisions by always maintaining a heightened state of awareness. It means never driving while impaired by drugs or alcohol. The actions of other motorists are never predictable, so it is your duty to act responsibly and in a secure manner. Set an example and trust that like attracts like.

Now is the time to develop the habit of driving safely if you haven't already. Make safety your priority. Pay attention when driving. No one is too old to start learning again. We can all do our part to avoid accidents and save lives if we each put safety first.

TOP CAUSES OF ROADSIDE EMERGENCIES

It is impossible to avoid all road risks. Yet there are steps you can take to prioritize safety and decrease the possibility of an emergency. The top list of incidents includes:

Flat Tire. Unexpected road hazards can cause sudden blow outs, but many other tire issues can be avoided with basic, old-time 'Mechanic

101' lessons. Develop the habit of regularly checking tire pressure and looking for abnormal bulges on the sidewalls. Notice how much tread the tires have and if they are worn evenly. Pay attention to the date they were manufactured as old tires can dry and are more likely to blow when they get hot. And if your steering wheel isn't straight while you're driving, it may be a sign of alignment issues and impending problems. (Check Chapter 15 for more details about tires.)

Empty Fuel Tank. It's as basic as it gets. When your fuel gauge is at half or less, you should fill up so that you don't accidentally get stranded. This is a good habit overall as the fuel pump is inside the tank and the fuel surrounding it keeps it cool. When you're taking a long road trip and enjoying the road, it's important to pay attention to the road signs informing you of the distance to the next filling station. They can sometimes be few and far apart. Remember the potential danger of driving on empty. (This is covered in greater detail in Chapter 6.)

Locked Out. It can happen to all of us, yet prevention is simple and inexpensive. The first thing you should do, right now, before an emergency, is to locate your vehicle key code. This information will be in the owner's manual, or on a small sticker inside your glove box. Sometimes you will notice a tiny metal dog tag attached to your original or spare key. If you can't find it, you can call your dealer's parts department and give them your VIN and they will provide you with the key code. Once you know that number, write it down and keep it in a secure place. This code will be useful in case you need to give it to a locksmith to cut a new key. If you frequently forget the key in your vehicle, get into the habit of manually locking your car with the key instead of using the remote.

Dead Battery. Out of sight and out of mind. Most drivers rarely think about their car battery until it's too late and their vehicle will not start. When it comes to prevention, you simply need to understand that batteries can be adversely affected by extreme heat or cold. Most new batteries are maintenance free; this means that you don't need to top off cells with distilled water.

It is a good idea to occasionally check your battery to make sure it looks OK. Grab the cables and jiggle them to see if they are loose. Pay attention for chia-pet-like corrosion that might build up. If it does, clean it with either soda or cold coffee. (Check the battery section in Chapter 13 for more details about maintenance.)

YES, MY DEER, NATURE CAN BE SURPRISING

While traffic rules make road interactions more predictable, wildlife won't blink an eye at those regulations. It's possible to encounter animals, small or large, wherever you go, from urban streets to remote wilderness. While all defensive driving suggestions apply, such as following speed limits, and looking far in the distance, I have three simple suggestions to prevent wildlife incidents.

Be an Eagle Eye on the Road. Always remain alert during dawn, dusk, and night. Wildlife does not obey crosswalks and traffic laws. Slow down in areas with abundant forest and wildlife and keep an eye out for Bambi and his pals.

Showtime. When there's no approaching traffic, use high-beam headlights as they will allow you to spot party crashers from a safe distance. Keep an eye out for approaching cars and lower your beams so you won't blind them.

Stay the Course. If an animal darts in front of your vehicle unexpectedly, stop hard but do not veer off course in response. Doing so could result in more serious mishaps, like flipping the car or colliding into trees — all serious party fouls.

Stay aware and keep two-legged, four-legged and occasionally no-legged friends safe. Driving wisely keeps everyone alive.

 PIT STOP LESSON

NOT SO SECRET MAGNETIC KEY BOXES

Thieves commonly hunt for keys hidden in magnetic boxes, so they often check for them first. A more secure strategy would be to consult your local repair shop and ask about securing a key in an unexpected place. They might be able to suggest a location where a lock box can be bolted safely and inconspicuously.

WHAT TO DO WHEN AN EMERGENCY HAPPENS

It's never fun being stranded on the side of the road but it could happen. If it does, wouldn't you like to know what to do? To begin, let's acknowledge that there are many reasons you may have an emergency:

- You hit a massive pothole and hear your tire pop.
- You're on the highway and smoke starts billowing from your engine.
- Your check engine light comes on and something smells funny in your car.
- You hit a huge prehistoric bug and it clogs your air intake valve.

The Smart Way to Handle Roadside Emergencies

This stuff happens all the time (OK, maybe not the prehistoric bug). When it does, you can react in one of two ways; you can panic and spill your expensive Starbucks all over your car or you can be smart and calmly finish your latte. Here are a few ideas to follow in an emergency.

Get Off the Road. First things first. If you're driving and something happens to your car, move off the road quickly and safely. Get out of the flow of traffic. Look for a wide shoulder, emergency lane, rest stop, exit, or parking lot. You always want to move toward the furthest lane or shoulder to the right. Even if it means destroying a blown tire and rim or wheel well in the process, you need to pull over. Just remember to never stop in traffic. Avoid places that are hard to see for oncoming traffic, such as blind corners, hills, or on narrow roads and bridges.

Let People Know There's Something Wrong. Find the hazard button in your car (it's the big one with a red triangle on it) and press it on. This'll let people know you've got car issues and you're not just taking a little mid-trip snooze.

Don't Leave the Car Until You're Out of Traffic. Never get out of the car until you've safely moved it out of the flow of traffic. If you can't get your car out of harm's way, don't get out, even if you're tempted to pop the hood or check out the damage.

Safely Exit the Car. If it's safe, get out of the car on the opposite side of traffic, even if you must crawl over the passenger seat. Once you're out of the car, go ahead and pop the hood, check out your tire, examine the damage and attempt minor repairs (if you know what you're doing). Generally speaking, it's safest to ensure that everyone stays clear of the car and wait for help to come.

Increase Your Visibility. You may want to mark your location with flares or triangles. At the very least, you'll want to raise your vehicle's hood. This will let everyone know that you're having car problems and need help.

Call Your Roadside Assistance Program. If you don't have it, get it. You will be surprised how inexpensive it is to add roadside assistance to most insurance plans. Or consider other programs, such as the American (or Canadian) Automotive Association (AAA/CAA) or OnStar. Some wireless providers also offer this service as an add-on to mobile plans. They are there to help, 24/7. Store this number in your cell phone and inside your glove box so you're not scrambling to find it during a time of need. (This is also a great holiday gift idea.)

Stay With Your Car. It's important not to leave your car. It may take some time, but it's more practical to meet help, a tow truck or the police, at the scene of your disabled vehicle than at a nearby burger joint.

Keep Emergency Supplies in Your Car. Take a lesson from the Boy Scouts and always be prepared. Keep some water, a blanket and a first aid kit in your car. It's also wise to have a spare tire, jack, fix-a-flat, and other simple repair tools. A good Samaritan may help in times of need, yet knowing how to change a spare tire is a valuable life skill.

Put Your Hood Down. Once you're done changing the tire or when a tow truck is on the way, you can put the hood down and store any flares or other emergency signals. Otherwise, a driver may put themselves at risk by trying to slow down and help.

Be Green. Clean Up the Scene. Clean up whatever packaging, trash, and debris you left around the area. Littering is bad news, and abandoning broken car parts is wasteful and could be a road hazard.

 PIT STOP LESSON

HOW MANY PHONE NUMBERS DO YOU KNOW?

Keep important numbers, such as family members, doctors, and vets, in your wallet in case your phone dies and you have no way to remember them.
This could also be useful in case of an emergency.

STEERING THROUGH THE COLLISION REPAIR JUNGLE

Finding a collision repair shop demands that you have an awareness of how each service provider is unique. Estimates may vary from center to center. Despite this, it shouldn't be too difficult to choose a center that is able to fulfill all your requirements. Look for a shop that can do high-quality collision repairs.

Road Map to Finding a Quality Collision Repair Shop

Seek Recommendations with a healthy dose of skepticism. Suggestions from friends or loved ones tend to be more trustworthy than those made by businesses. Keep in mind that most companies provide quality service.

Location and Specialization. Consider the location and avoid sacrificing quality. The cost of labor might vary greatly from one region to another, but the real worth rests in skill and precision.

Obtain Multiple Estimates. Gathering various estimates before deciding on the one with the lowest price can help you avoid being overcharged. When considering whether to accept a bid, it is important to exercise caution if the price seems unusually low. Low bids might indicate that quality or adherence to standards is lacking.

Collaborate With Your Insurance Partner. After an accident occurs, insurance plans become of vital importance. Understand the benefits included in your policy and ensure either comprehensive or collision coverage will cover repairs as soon as needed.

Inquire about your rental coverage as some policies may only include short periods, such as 10 to 15 days. Who is responsible for paying rental car fees after the initial coverage provided by insurance has expired? Will the rental coverage continue if repair components are delayed, and facilities fall two or three months behind in scheduled repairs? If unsure, have your policy reviewed immediately to ensure your rental will be paid by the insurance for the duration of the repairs.

Exercise Due Diligence. Before making repair choices, carefully weigh all available options. To prevent nullifying a warranty inadvertently, check details regarding specific repair warranty coverage. Note its validity, any associated limits and whether OEM parts have been substituted. Unfortunately, to increase profitability, some shady shops will occasionally use aftermarket components, while invoicing OEM parts. When picking up the vehicle, ask for an itemized list of parts used. This will help ensure that you got the OEM parts and associated warranty coverage.

Opt for Certified Collision Centers. Be wary of collision facilities which cannot be independently confirmed as legitimate. You will get better service this way.

Trust Your Instincts. You should give some thought to heading in a different direction if your gut tells you there may be something fishy in the repair estimate.

KEY TAKEAWAYS

- **Conscious Competence:** Automobile catastrophes are often due to human error, so proactive education and strategic planning are crucial. Each driver is responsible for maintaining road safety. The privilege of driving comes with responsibility to drive safely with sobriety, caution, and vigilance.

- **Cause and Effect:** Accidents reflect Newtonian physics in terms of their physical effects and long-term psychological ones.

- **Vigilance in the Wild:** Your attention must always remain laser focused. Wildlife tends to be most active at dusk and dawn; so, headlights are essential. In case of sudden encounters, apply brakes decisively while maintaining your path.

- **Crisis Navigation:** When car problems strike — whether a tire blowout, smoking engine, or warning lights appear — promptly guide your vehicle toward safety. Call for professional help while staying with your auto.

INFORMATION IN MIRRORS IS MORE EMPOWERING THAN IT MAY APPEAR!

Buckle Up, Co-Pilot!

While Cynthia got her driver's license, Christopher took additional steps to make sure she had experience and confidence at the wheel. She thought her father was overzealous and hated getting up early on Sunday morning to practice reverse parking and master side view mirror use, yet complied as it was the price to pay for borrowing the car. She might later appreciate these father and daughter moments in sprawling shopping mall parking lots, but she wasn't there yet.

Christopher enjoyed passing on what he had learned while spending time on the road with his dad. Considering the rising rates of teenage car crashes and fatalities, he believed that parents should all step up and teach their teens about responsibilities behind the wheel, not only for themselves, but for everyone on the road.

One night, Victoria was cleaning a drawer in the living room and found an old map of the city. Cynthia laughed and found it hard to believe that people used to rely on this archaic tool when driving around. Christopher told her it was still good to have one handy in case her phone died, and ultimately, it was important to have a general understanding about local geography and cardinal points. He explained that a GPS can sometimes play tricks due to lack of updates or inaccurate maps, so having a general knowledge of an area can be helpful. But, ultimately, even Christopher was forced to admit that technology is incredibly useful and convenient, especially for updates on traffic and road work. The Smiths thought it somewhat ironic that the use of GPS and smartphones for road directions was so convenient, even though they can occasionally decrease concentration.

Before reaching for more merlot, Victoria told her husband how happy she was that their daughter was open to learning and practicing basic things such as backing up, using hand signals, or even changing a spare tire. They both knew that these habits help create safe drivers who act responsibly and respectfully.

Chapter 21

EMPOWERING TEEN DRIVERS

Y ou're at a family gathering or at an adult party chatting when all of a sudden, the subject of parenting comes up. The stories about children often start with, "Oh, how I remember the terrible twos," and they quickly get to, "I can't believe they are about to drive."

Parents do their best based on what they know or what they have been taught. Unfortunately, most of us weren't taught well. It's not really any generation's fault. It's what we learned in the times we were living in. With so many teen drivers on the road today, we can't help but reminisce how we were once teenagers and very eager to drive a very cool-looking car to show our friends. Yet people tend to forget that there are not only more cars on the road, but more distractions than ever. The younger generation also needs to understand that safety is more important than the look of the car.

Over 80% of car purchases are based on emotional value and, for that reason, car washes are very successful. People worry and will often apologize to friends and family about their car being dirty and messy. Yet, they will never admit that they haven't changed the oil in a long time, or that they drive with balding and unsafe tires. They might ignore oil leaks or squealing brakes for a long time. Instead, they feel guilty that their vehicle doesn't look good. Unfortunately, this is the sad example that children see and repeat.

Adults and parents need to know more about safety beyond repeating, "Put your seatbelt on," and preach, "Be careful on the road." There is so much more to understand about being a safe car owner than we ever imagined.

Empowering Teens to Drive Confidently

Teen drivers must understand safety basics, even if that is not as exciting in their eyes. Considering that auto accidents are the leading cause of death for children ages 15 to 20, safety education is paramount. And, for older folks, it's never too late to get back to basics. Being humble and young at heart are good traits to keep throughout a lifetime.

When you get down to it, the only thing new drivers really need is a safe and reliable ride. Yes, your kids will beg for something fancy and trendy. They will tell you that their friends have nice cars. You will hear relentless groans and moans if it doesn't have that 'Sick' ('Dope' or any other cool generational word) factor. Stand your ground and do what you know is right, they will thank you in the future.

Before you even think of purchasing a vehicle for them, make sure they understand and respect the car and safety issues first.

GETTING EMPOWERED TOGETHER

Navigating roads with young drivers can be both exciting and intimidating. Be not concerned. We have you covered with strategies designed to enable both teens and parents to tackle roads confidently. This includes everything from mastering defensive driving techniques to developing responsible habits behind the wheel. These tips will help our future road warriors have safe journeys ahead.

Tip 1: Practicing with new drivers is honestly the best way to start. Share stories of your first experiences driving and how nervous you were. Acknowledge the mistakes you may even continue to make today.

Tip 2: Remember, you are not responsible for making your teen a great driver, they are. Accept the fact that you're not the master, you are just initiating them.

Tip 3: Explain that distractions are the main reasons for accidents. Teach them about the three types of distractions.

- **Manual distractions** happen when you move your hands from the steering wheel.
- **Visual distractions** happen when your eyes are not focused on the road.
- **Cognitive distractions** are when your mind wanders away from the task of driving.

Tip 4: Let them practice parking and turning in an empty lot before allowing them to drive on the road. They should practice repeatedly until they feel confident. Be sure to spend at least 10 hours with them so they master parking and turning. Relax, you'll still have plenty of time for happy hour and your favorite TV shows. Besides, you can spread it out over more than one session. A good rule of thumb is to commit to 30-minute segments, for roughly two hours a week. After they master parking and turning, you can slowly start driving in low-risk situations. Start with 15 hours on that. Then work up to more risky situations for at least 10 hours.

Tip 5: No friends or passengers, other than parents, should be in the vehicle while they learn. There should also be no radio or music for the first 20 hours of driving. They can sing and "get jiggy with it" anytime in the future.

Tip 6: Monkey see, monkey do. Teens whose parents drive distracted are two to four times more likely to do the same thing. Remember, teens might not openly admit it, but they see their parents as role models and learn by their example. That fact doesn't change when they get their license. When you are behind the wheel, don't do anything you wouldn't want your teenagers to do. If they catch you — admit to your mistakes. It shows that it is never too late to start driving safely.

Tip 7: Sign them up for driving school and leave them alone. They need to focus on learning from a non-biased third party. You can consult with them later.

Tip 8: The most important step after they have completed a driving school course is to sign your teen and yourself up for the amazing B.R.A.K.E.S. program. (https://putonthebrakes.org/shop) They travel all around the country to teach advanced driving skills. You simply sign up using a credit card to hold your spot. If you show up, it's FREE. If you flake out and stay in bed that morning, you get charged for your saved spot. It's that simple.

Tip 9: When you're ready to purchase a vehicle for a teenager, stay away from models that have all the bells and whistles in terms of safety features, such as backup cameras, side motion sensors and cruise control. These can cause bad habits if they learn to rely on them without actually paying proper attention.

We did fine as drivers, way before any of these features existed. Sure, ABS, stability control and airbags are now standard. But they could prevent new drivers from developing good habits. They should make it a habit to always move their head before turning or changing lanes. They shouldn't wait for a beep from a sensor. It is important for them to develop the habit of fully turning their head when backing up instead of just looking into a camera or waiting for a sensor to chime.

Here Are Some Disturbing Facts

- Fifty percent of parents have knowingly texted their teen while they knew they were driving. About a third of these parents expect a response before the teen reaches their destination. Of all the folks in a teen's life (friends, siblings, or other adults), they tell us in their own survey that when driving they are most likely to respond quickest when a call or text comes from a parent.

- Fifty-five percent of parents say they use apps while driving. Nearly a third of teens have asked them to stop. And 95% of teens in the survey acknowledge that app usage is a danger behind the wheel. Sadly, 68% of teens will admit to using apps while driving. Monkey see, monkey do...
- Sixty-two percent of parents say they use their phone to check incoming calls or talk while driving. Seventy-five percent of teens say they have seen their parents do this, and 50% have asked them to stop.

 PIT STOP LESSON

TEXTING IS SERIOUS WORK

Texting requires more attention than you might think. It involves three types of distraction: **Manual, Visual, and Cognitive.**

If you need to text, stop and park first so everyone is safe while you give it your full attention.

Consider These Other Dangerous Behaviors

- Forty-five percent of parents admit they speed while driving — and 43% of teens have witnessed it.
- Thirty-four percent of parents say they drive while drowsy or tired — and 35% of teens have witnessed it.
- Twenty-five percent of parents report they drive aggressively — and 47% of teens have witnessed it.

This is not a pretty picture.

 PIT STOP LESSON

LEAD BY EXAMPLE

If you don't want your teens to text while driving, don't text them when you know they're behind the wheel.

Driving is one of the most beloved activities we engage in each day. From carpooling with friends to solo travel, driving is something most people cannot avoid. But once a certain level of comfort has been reached, vanity overtakes safety as attention focuses more on adorning this rolling 3,000-pound box.

Modern cars boast many safety features which are great. However, for new drivers these features may not prove so useful. It might be better to help them develop good driving habits without relying on the new technology. Teach them how to adjust both side and rearview mirrors. They should also be accountable for recognizing any unfamiliar sounds or smells. Have them replace tires so they understand the process. It's simple stuff, yet so important.

SAFE PASSENGERS INCREASE SAFE JOURNEYS

Teens typically learn to drive around the same time as their friends do, increasing the chances that they will ride with an inexperienced driver. Over half of all teens killed in car accidents were not driving at that time. Therefore, riding with young drivers significantly increases the chances of fatal crashes.

Limiting distractions and respecting the driver will help reduce risks for teen passengers. A few more aspects can help keep everyone safe:

- **Talk about how to be a safe passenger.** Distracted driving is a leading cause of car accidents, and passenger distractions are especially risky for inexperienced drivers. Discuss beneficial passenger behaviors, including reading directions, when asked, and respecting the driver by not talking loudly, texting, listening to loud music, or being disruptive.

- **Insist on seatbelts.** Most adolescent passengers killed in car accidents are not wearing seatbelts. Explain that by fastening their seatbelts, they will be helping to safeguard their friends, as well as their own lives. In the event of a collision, an unrestrained body can cause harm to others in the vehicle.
- **Don't let your child ride with a driver who has less than a year of experience.** Most teen car accidents are caused by beginner mistakes. Even the most mature adolescent requires adult supervision to obtain driving experience. It is wise to prevent your teen from driving with their younger brothers or sisters for the first six months, as siblings can be more distracting than peers.
- **Pay attention.** Keep the lines of communication open to assist them in making appropriate safety decisions. Know where they're going and why. Ask how they plan to get there and when they'll come back. Offer them alternatives, such as rides, so they can avoid dangerous driving situations.
- **Create a code word.** Allow kids to call or text you with a previously agreed-upon code word that indicates a danger situation. This could help them get out of difficult circumstances without losing face in front of their friends. This is like friends asking for a check-in call during a first date. Be attentive for the term as soon as you hear or see it. You may want to change the code word after it's been used.
- **Lead by example.** Always fasten your seatbelt. While driving, don't talk on the phone or text. Observe traffic laws, especially speed limits.

- **Safety Over Style:** Help your teen drivers realize the value of safety when selecting their first car. They may want something eye-catching, but what really matters are unglamorous yet vital safety features and driving practices.

- **Monkey See, Monkey Do:** Set a good example by emphasizing safety, eliminating distractions, and demonstrating defensive driving tactics.

- **Practice Makes Perfect:** Before teenagers get behind the wheel, encourage them to perfect the art of driving by investing time in practical training.

- **Back to Basics:** Opt for core driving instruction that emphasizes hands-on experience over reliance on technical features, such as parking sensors or backup cameras.

INFORMATION IN MIRRORS IS MORE EMPOWERING THAN IT MAY APPEAR!

Confidential Information

Victoria was stunned when the grocery teller announced that her card was declined. "What? Impossible!" she said. The young cashier has heard it all before and asked if they should try another card. Victoria felt insulted and wondered if rubbing the card in her hair would make a difference, yet the "Declined" message on the terminal was clear.

Upon returning home, she called the bank to complain and found out that her credit card was full... "No way!" she said, until they both realized that several purchases were unusual. Things got worse when the teller pulled Victoria's credit score and noticed that someone had established two credit cards in her name and purchased a car out of state using her identity. "Oh My God, there's more..." the agent exclaimed. Upon further inquiry, it turned out the scammer had also obtained two loans with high APR rates using Victoria as collateral.

After realizing that she was a victim of identity fraud, Victoria called Christopher to share the bad news. "How is that possible?" he asked. She had no idea but thought it might have happened after following a link on a bad website or a purchase from a bad sales terminal.

In the evening, the Smiths went to the local precinct to report the identity theft. Officer Stanley, the agent assigned to their case, reassured them that it was more common than they might think. In fact, he explained that they recently had several similar cases which were later tied to an astute car wash employee. The malicious individual was copying and scanning personal information, like receipts and registrations, left in glove boxes. Christopher asked Officer Stanley where that happened, and the Smiths were stunned when they heard him mention it was at the car wash next to Victoria's office.

Alarmed, Victoria said, "I often left my car there so they could clean it while I work." They might never really know what happened, Officer Stanley seemed to think it was a good possibility that criminals obtained information from her glove box while getting it clean. Christopher claimed, "You even gave them the key!"

Chapter 22

KEEPING YOU AND YOUR CAR SAFE

When the economy goes down, crimes go up. No one is immune to this reality. We never expect to be a victim until it happens. If you've ever returned to a parking spot only to find that your vehicle is gone, you know how terrifying auto theft can be — not to mention the logistical headache that comes with it. Car theft is unfortunately on the rise, but there are steps you can take to safeguard your vehicle.

IN A DEN OF THIEVES

Many car thefts are opportunity crimes, which means that if you take basic precautions, like locking the doors, rolling up the windows, taking the keys with you, removing temptations from view, and parking inside or at least in well-lit areas, you've likely put-up effective deterrents. The number of people who do not lock their automobile doors is astonishing.

You should also investigate your vehicle's make and model, as some are famously easy to break into and, as a result, are more commonly targeted by thieves. The list of the most stolen vehicles includes Honda Civic and Accords, Toyota Camrys and Corollas, and Nissan Altima. Pickups are also hot, particularly Ford, Chevrolet, Dodge, and GMC trucks. If you own one of these vehicles, take extra precautions to protect it, such as adding a vehicle immobilizer system that only allows you to start your engine with the correct key or a steering wheel lock. **The difficulty of stealing your vehicle increases as you add layers of protection.**

It's a solid strategy. Anything that a burglar encounters as a deterrent decreases the likelihood that they will steal your vehicle. If all else is equal, criminals will take the path of least resistance. Thus, increasing the efforts required to steal your vehicle will lower your risks.

While a GPS tracker might not stop the theft from happening in the first place, it could help you recover your vehicle faster with fewer parts missing. Your car will be easier to recover if you have a vehicle GPS tracking system like OnStar or LoJack.

Installing a GPS monitoring system in your automobile is one of the finest ways to maximize the chances of your car being recovered. LoJack, for example, claims a 98 percent recovery rate. Unfortunately, most statistics simply state, 'recovered.' They do not specify the condition of the vehicle when it comes back.

INSIDER FILES

AIR QUALITY CONCERNS

While definitive evidence may not yet exist, studies suggest that benzene, an unstable chemical found in some cars' interiors, may become a hazard when exposed to extreme temperatures. Rolling down windows before starting your vehicle and turning on the air conditioning could reduce exposure.

Those with respiratory limitations should be particularly aware of the health risks, although everyone should remain mindful of this.

It might also be possible to reduce air quality concerns by replacing cabin air filters every 15,000 to 20,000 miles.

PROACTIVE WAYS TO SAFEGUARD YOUR VEHICLE

With so much technology and convenience, it is easy to become complacent and forget about the fundamentals. Something as simple as a cartoon sticker, showing how many family members and pets you have, puts you at risk. A thief could know if every family member is home because of this sticker. The one on your bumper that reads, "My child is an honor student at…" could allow criminals to track your child's whereabouts during the day. Keep in mind that a prestigious school might attract more attention. Instead, consider installing those cartoons and honor roll stickers on your fridge or in your heart instead of your automobile. It might also be better for trade-in value.

Gated Access

People living in gated communities might have a false sense of security. That laser sticker on the front of the vehicle, allowing quick access in and out, can often be scanned with a cell phone, printed, and used to get easy access. Ask your homeowner's association (HOA) if you can put your gated community quick access sticker somewhere else or come up with a safer option.

Proactive Safeguarding

Here are a few more tips to help safeguard your car and belongings.

Common Sense. Always remove the keys from the ignition or take your key fob before exiting the vehicle. Lock all doors, roll up the windows, and park in well-lit places or indoors when possible.

Warning Devices. Aftermarket alarms are available for all makes and models. Alarms that are both visible and auditory are excellent warning tools. Column collars, steering wheel locks, and brake locks are effective visual warning devices.

Immobilizing Devices. Smart keys, fuse cut-offs and kill switches are third-tier security options that prohibits thieves from bypassing the ignition and hot-wiring the vehicle. Other options include wireless ignition authentication, or starter, ignition, and fuel pump disablers.

Tracking Devices. Tracking devices are quite helpful in assisting authorities to recover stolen vehicles. Several systems integrate GPS and Wi-Fi technologies to allow for remote vehicle monitoring. If the vehicle is moved, the technology will alert the owner, and the vehicle may be tracked using a computer.

Personal Information. Make sure to keep all car repair receipts that have your home address, credit card information, email, or phone numbers in a folder in the trunk of your vehicle. Place it under the floor mat or next to your spare tire if you have one. It's a good idea to keep your insurance card and registration in your wallet or purse since they contain your personal information.

LOCKED, SHOCKED, AND STOLEN

New technology brings new challenges. To avoid having your car broken into and stolen, follow these tips for safeguarding your keyless entry system:

- Don't lock your keyless entry remote in your car or keep it near a glass surface. Car thieves will have an easier time picking up your fob's signal in this situation.
- Keep your keyless entry fob inside the house and at least 10 feet from the door. Your fob's signal will be harder for thieves to pick up.
- For better protection from signal theft, keep the fob in a faraday bag, a signal-blocking pouch. These will shield the signal or radio waves emitted from your key fob. Some thieves use high-tech frequency scanners to steal the signal, allowing them to duplicate it remotely.
- Put your car in a garage or behind a parking post to prevent it from being stolen. Even if car thieves circumvent the electronic protections, these physical barriers will make them think twice before attempting to steal your vehicle.
- Be on the lookout for any unusual or suspicious behavior in your area. Tell the police right away if you see anyone acting suspiciously near your car or house.

- Don't put all your faith in your car's electronic safety features. Thieves can still steal your car if they use high-tech tools.
- Avoid complacency. Thieves who are intent on stealing your vehicle will find a way, even if you've parked your car in a garage or in a seemingly secure area.
- Never give your keyless entry fob to someone you don't know and trust.

How Keyless Fob Scanning Leads to Auto Thefts

As an expert in the automotive field, I can't stress enough the need for car owners to take the initiative to learn about the potential dangers posed by keyless fob transmitters. When it comes to protecting vehicles from theft, car owners must be at the forefront. Preventing keyless fob theft is a new and important reality, so you need to know some basics.

Yes, it is true that the more advanced our technology becomes, the easier it is for thieves to steal vehicles. As a consumer, it is natural to feel frustrated and powerless in the face of this threat. You can't just shrug it off and say, "Well, I have insurance, so it doesn't matter." There is no substitute for being a careful and conscientious motorist, and insurance can only do so much to help you.

Everyone should take a deep breath and make a pact to be safe drivers. Purchasing signal-blocking pouches or faraday boxes to store keyless fobs safely is the first step.

WHEN YOUR RIDE VANISHES INTO THIN AIR

What to do if everything else fails? Despite our best efforts, theft may still happen. If your vehicle ever goes missing unexpectedly, take a deep breath and remember that it wasn't your fault. The following suggestions will help you deal with the situation.

Unraveling the Aftermath of a Stolen Vehicle

The first step is self-evident: call the police right away. Prompt reporting will help law enforcement to locate your vehicle. Be prepared to provide them with the description, license plate number, suspected time of the theft and information about your vehicle's last known location. Follow the directions provided by your local law enforcement as the processes and policies for submitting a stolen vehicle report will differ based on where you reside.

Step two is to contact your insurance company within 24 hours after realizing that your car has vanished. With comprehensive insurance, any damage to your car should be covered if it is promptly identified as stolen. If your vehicle isn't recovered, they'll satisfy your claim for the loss. Your insurance agent will demand a copy of your police report, so make a copy for yourself and one for your insurer. You're more likely to get your automobile back without damage if you report it within a few hours of it being stolen. If it's been a few days, your vehicle may have been wrecked from a joy ride, or it may have been dismantled and sold for components. It could even be on its way to another continent.

Exhaust and catalytic converters are commonly missing from recovered vehicles because they contain valuable metals. Tires and wheels are difficult to track and sell, so they are often the first items to be removed from a stolen vehicle. Your personal information is also at risk if you have receipts containing phone numbers, emails, or credit card receipts in your glove box. Unfortunately, this information is sold to perpetrate ID theft, which adds a new dimension to the implications of stolen vehicles.

When your vehicle is returned, complete a thorough walk-through inspection, taking notes and photos of everything you notice. Call your insurance agent and have your vehicle examined for missing or damaged parts to guarantee it's safe to drive.

IS YOUR CAR A CERTIFIED INFORMANT?

The vehicles we once hailed as the pinnacle of innovation now feel like state-sponsored snooping devices. Mozilla experts now claim that the latest and best cars from the industry's leading manufacturers have flunked their privacy exams.

Tales of Auto-Spy Rendezvous

From Ford Fiestas to Tesla Model S, our four-wheel transportation partners appear to be engaging in nefarious data harvesting. This exposes personal information about us, including our facial expressions, our body measurements, and even our sexual activities, although no details have been provided by manufacturers about how this data is collected.

It seems that some cars, or technology companies involved in the manufacturing process, even keep tabs on private conversations. Oh, humanity! Some automakers may be breaking the once-sacred understanding between humans and machines by selling our preferences, views, and abilities to every Tom, Dick, or Harry with an ID badge or license. It looks that the right to privacy has boarded a train to its own demise.

You might be wondering about those whom we revere as car tycoons. Unfortunately, many pose as protectors of our privacy while selling off private data at auction for profit. Car parties are big events and unwitting drivers are honored guests.

So, my friends, keep in mind that your vehicle knows more about you than you think. What happens in the car might not always stay in the car.

KEY TAKEAWAYS

- **Enhance Vigilance:** Adopt a tiered approach to vehicle security by employing obvious deterrents, like steering wheel locks, immobilizer devices, and GPS trackers. While no safety precaution can guarantee complete protection, it's possible to make your vehicle less desirable for theft.

- **Protect Personal Information:** Hide documents containing your information to minimize identity theft or similar crimes.

- **Tech Caution:** Modern automobile technology presents greater concerns for privacy as vehicles can reveal private facts about us to organizations, without our knowing. Remain mindful of new technologies and services included in your vehicle and periodically review privacy controls.

INFORMATION IN MIRRORS IS MORE EMPOWERING THAN IT MAY APPEAR!

Congrats, You Pedal-to-the-Metal Scholar! Your Final Lap was an Intellectual Victory Tire Burnout! You Didn't Just Cross the Finish Line, You Lapped It in Genius!

SAFE JOURNEYS

Esteemed readers, as we've reached the final pages of *Car Confidential*, I can't help but reflect on our journey together. Through the eyes of the Smith family, we've explored many unspoken truths and hidden secrets about car ownership. I hope this was a shining light about empowerment, making responsible choices, and becoming our own best advocates.

The Smiths served as guides as their triumphs and trials provided invaluable lessons. They've demonstrated the value of prioritizing practicality over emotion to make informed decisions, rather than succumbing to impulsive desires. Finally, they have proven the value of taking responsibility for a vehicle.

Thank you so much for choosing to begin this adventure with me. Your decision to read this book demonstrates your dedication to taking control of your car ownership experience rather than being a passive victim of circumstances. Together we are changing narratives, reclaiming power, and transforming our involvement with vehicles.

However, our journey does not end here. My hope is that this book will serve as an indispensable source of wisdom for future generations when embarking on their car ownership journeys. *Car Confidential* is more than a book; it's a call to action. It urges everyone to become conscious consumers, mindful drivers, and responsible guardians of vehicles. We are creating a society which embraces car ownership's true essence: safety and practicality.

Your support and enthusiasm have fueled my passion to continue sharing these unspoken truths with the world. Let us stand united, committed to reshaping the future of car ownership.

With heartfelt appreciation and utmost regard,
Shahe Koulloukian

RECOMMENDED PRODUCTS

Here is a list of products I have mentioned throughout the book and others that I often recommend to friends and clients. I am not affiliated with any of these companies, but I may receive compensation from Amazon if you purchase anything using these links.

Air freshener	carconfidential.net/freshener
Animal/rodent repellant	carconfidential.net/rodentrepellant
Baby car seat	carconfidential.net/babyseat
Blanket	carconfidential.net/blanket
Bungee cord	carconfidential.net/bungeecord
Car cover	carconfidential.net/carcover
Car headrest hooks	carconfidential.net/hooks
Car phone holder	carconfidential.net/phoneholder
Car ride audio for anxiety	carconfidential.net/audioanxiety
Car seat cushion	carconfidential.net/seatcushion
Car seat lumbar support	carconfidential.net/lumbarsupport
Car sickness wellness	carconfidential.net/sicknesswellness
Car sunvisor extension	carconfidential.net/sunvisorextension
Car trunk/rear hatch organizer	carconfidential.net/hatchorganizer
Car vacuum	carconfidential.net/carvacuum
Car wash mop kit	carconfidential.net/mopkit
Car washing soap	carconfidential.net/washingsoap
Cordless upholstery cleaner	carconfidential.net/upholsterycleaner
Emergency roadside flare alert	carconfidential.net/flarealert
Faraday bag	carconfidential.net/faradaybag
Folder for glovebox	carconfidential.net/gloveboxfolder
Headrest safe	carconfidential.net/headrestsafe
Night glare driving glasses	carconfidential.net/nightglare

Pet seat cover	carconfidential.net/petseatcover
Rubber floor mats	carconfidential.net/rubberfloormats
Safety kit	carconfidential.net/safetykit
Security hammer	carconfidential.net/securityhammer
Steering wheel cover	carconfidential.net/steeringwheelcover
Sun shade	carconfidential.net/sunshade
Tire gauge	carconfidential.net/tiregauge
Travel pillow	carconfidential.net/travelpillow
Trickle chargers	carconfidential.net/tricklechargers

ACKNOWLEDGEMENTS

How can we begin when recognizing and thanking those who have inspired us, even unknowingly? Those small but mighty moments in our lives that included fun, laughter, fear, fright, celebration, care, encouragement or simply being there when needed are often all it takes. Allow me to name those who have played an integral part in shaping the character and personality that enabled me to write *Car Confidential*.

My late father Hagop Koulloukian had amazing inner strength that always left me curious and open to learn new things. He traveled the globe, always keeping our family close by his side. He taught me to shake every hand and listen to every voice. According to him, people will see when you become the man you were meant to be. They may perceive you as unique but won't fully comprehend that you took bits from each person you encountered in life to form yourself into who you are today — someone who people love and appreciate. Thank you, Dad. You remain at my side even after 36 years have gone by.

My dearest mother Azadouhy Koulloukian immediately took over my father's role just like a powerful lioness. She transformed herself into the superpower of love, care, and strength that was my family. There are no words to express the depth of maternal love. Only God can describe such a gift. When it's like this, the mother loves her child unconditionally. I received this from her and now I share it with my children. Thank you Sireli Myres for being the rock that laid my life's foundation!

Alex, my big-hearted brother. After our father's passing, it was hard for me to watch over you when you were a 15-year-old boy. It made me feel guilty for having taken on an authority or father figure role rather than simply being your brother. Over time I realized that having someone focus on grieving was essential in helping us through it all. Years later, I finally got to meet the brother I knew was always there and adore him for teaching me humility and grace. Love you always for being my number one fan.

My loving wife Lena has been my companion and inspiration for three decades. You always tell me there's more out there than meets the eye, while reminding me to remain humbled by it all. Your incredible motherhood inspired me to be a caring father. Thank you for always showing support, patience and understanding during those late-night writing sessions. Love you always Hokis.

My two beautiful and adoring sons, Hagop and Janno, bring such immense joy to my heart. Your presence keeps me inspired to share all I know with pride while pushing me forward in every task at hand. Thank you both for always treating me like an amazing rock star. Love always.

My dear uncle Mesrob was responsible for my entrance into the automotive industry at age 13. Your work ethic and discipline provided key advantages; stay focused, put in effort, and avoid taking the easy way out. Thank you, Keri, for always showing kindness and providing guidance. You will always remain in my heart.

My dear Uncle Haig was always my go-to person for anything my father wouldn't give me. You taught me to see the world from all perspectives rather than viewing things through just one lens. You shared my first beer with me, showed me how to drive, introduced me to the Timex Sinclair 1000 computer for the first time ever and helped me perfect my tennis skills. Very importantly, you kept me connected to my Armenian heritage. Your guidance has been an integral part of my life. Thank you, Keri, and love always.

My dear late Uncle Sahag was an exceptional example of hard work and devotion. This started during our early days together, as he demonstrated genuine work ethic and the true definition of diligence. Thank you. You remain in my thoughts and prayers always.

To my loving late Uncle Sarkis, thank you for always filling me with laughter during our times together. Your presence was like a goldmine, always inspiring the humor that ignited my career as a stand-up comedy professional. Love you forever in my prayers.

My late and loving grandparents, Elizabeth, Chuchri, Mary and Iskender, will always be remembered fondly. Your grandparenting instilled me with love and taught me to respect family first. Your care and guidance as the pillars of our family taught me everything I needed to know about its true meaning. Thank you for always watching over me from up above. I miss you all dearly.

Time spent with my uncles Levon, Zaven and Hratch as a child will always remain special to me. Your influence was crucial at that time in my development even as our lives have taken different turns since those early years. For that, I remain immensely appreciative.

My dear Aunt Virginia, thank you for showering me with such extraordinary love since the age of five. Your care and love have never wavered, even during those early years when I just wanted to have fun and perform poems and sing songs for your pleasure. Your encouragement to do so ignited within me a spark that fueled strong resolve and determination. I will forever be grateful for that inspiration. Love always.

To Abe and Many Bekelian, you were more than mentors. You became family. Having you take me under your wings as an apprentice wasn't simply professional courtesy. It was more like life insurance during one of the most turbulent chapters of my life: grieving the loss of my father. Your patience, care, and brotherly love provided an anchor that kept me grounded during those trying times. Your dedication to keeping me on the right path was more than mere guidance: it provided the impetus necessary to help fill the gap left by my father's absence. Your support allowed me to believe in myself once again. I extend my sincerest appreciation and thanks to everyone with the Bekelian family, brothers and sisters alike. Your hospitality allowed me to find strength within myself at a time when my world seemed to be crumbling around me. Your example taught me the value of both biological and chosen family relationships. For this I will remain eternally grateful and express my everlasting affection and deep thanks.

James Bauer and Christopher Hutson, my dearest brothers who came from other mothers. I met them during my early days of stand-up comedy. In those days, I was struggling to cope with the loss of my father. Both of them filled that void with brotherly guidance and love. Those days of heart-wrenching laughter kept me on the straight and narrow, allowing me to face life's challenges with humor. You gave me the strength to reach my current life destination. My brothers, I love you.

Sal, my late brother from another mother. I still vividly remember our first meeting as though it were yesterday, our friendship was instantaneous and its depth immeasurable. Your sudden absence left an empty spot in my life, but your memory continues to guide my journey. It taught me the beauty of brotherly respect and love. I miss you dearly.

Certainly not to be overlooked is my deep gratitude to my wonderful brother-in-heart, Michael McEniry, for his impact in the early days of Mazvo Auto Repair. Our paths in life shifted but the lessons you taught me, without even knowing it, will live with me forever. I will always be thankful to you for the early friendship and collaboration that helped define my future.

To the late Dr. Ralph Herro, whom I was blessed to call a friend, provided guidance when I opened Mazvo Auto Repair. Your advice about what and what not to do for my business proved invaluable. Your love and respect were something I will never forget and not one day goes by that I don't remember your visits of support and care. Thank you for always being there in that fatherhood role. Forever grateful.

Armen Hagopian, Adeeb Shamhat and Carlos Sayegh — my three original Musketeers from my high school glory days. Our incredible friendship has persisted through the years; I can't tell you how often I think back on those innocent but meaningful gestures and brotherly respect. You have always been there when needed as a source of strength to get me through any challenge that life throws my way. Thank you always, my brothers. Thank you for illuminating my life.

Thank you to all these incredible individuals — family, friends, mentors — for being the cornerstones of my life's tapestry, my soul. Without you all as part of my story, I would not be who I am today, or tomorrow. Your love and lessons remain at the core of who I am now and always will be.

ABOUT THE AUTHOR

Shahe Koulloukian (pronounced SHA-HAY) embodies the essence of what it means to be a modern-day renaissance man. Shahe was born into an Armenian family in Beirut, Lebanon and has experienced life across four continents, having lived in such cities as Lyon, Hanover, Milan, Damascus, Toronto, Philadelphia, and Los Angeles.

Shahe experienced many diverse cultures while traveling, and eventually settled in Phoenix, Arizona. Along the way, he became fluent in six languages. This is thanks to his mother who served as a part-time translator.

Although not born with a wrench in hand, Shahe's love of auto repair was fostered under his uncle who is an expert. This early exposure led him to explore opportunities within dealerships as well as starting his own business venture, Mazvo Auto Repair. But don't be fooled by Shahe's car expertise alone. Other interests lie far beyond automobiles.

Shahe was an in-demand stand-up comedian across North America before turning his full focus toward Mazvo. Not content to rest on his laurels, Shahe also earned a professional culinary degree while wowing audiences at Hilton Resorts. Eventually he started providing tasty delights from his food truck for several years. But that wasn't where his story ended. Shahe has also dabbled in acting, appearing in over eight feature films and numerous television series.

At the core of all his endeavors lies Shahe's genuine enthusiasm for autos, and the people who drive them. Not your average shop owner; Shahe is more like a teacher with his wealth of automotive wisdom.

Invited as guest lecturer to colleges nationwide, he uses car tips as life lessons.

Since opening Mazvo Car Care Center, in Phoenix, Arizona, in 1995, it has become known as the Mayo Clinic of auto repair. Shahe is passionate about educating car owners about responsibility, fundamental knowledge, and accountability. Evidence of his commitment to upholding industry ethics while steering car owners toward responsible care practices earned him the reputation of Ethics Guru. This has been recognized in the community through four consecutive nominations for the Better Business Bureau's Torch Awards for Ethics. His goal is simple, yet profound: instill in every driver an attitude of responsibility, fundamental knowledge, and accountability.

ABOUT MAZVO AUTO CARE

How my Mom's Auto Repair Nightmare Fueled the Birth of Mazvo Car Care

The summer of 1994 was one that I'll never forget, though not for the reasons you might expect. While I was away on vacation, soaking in moments of rest, my mother was facing a situation that would redefine my career and purpose. When she heard a concerning noise coming from her car and, not wanting to disturb me during my time off, she took it upon herself to get it checked out at the dealership where I worked.

She was initially told that it would be a $50 repair. Simple enough, right? But soon after, they manipulated her fears by painting a picture of catastrophic failures and safety risks. By the time they were done, my mom's repairs had totaled $2,300.

When I returned from vacation and learned of this situation, I was devastated on multiple fronts. First, I had always been the one to look after her car and knew very well that it had no such issues. Secondly, and more heartbreakingly, this unethical behavior had happened at the very dealership where I was employed and carried out by people I had to face every day.

The realization hit me hard: if this could happen to my mother, in a dealership where her own son worked, then it could happen to anyone. It was a turning point for me. I decided then and there that my career had to stand for something more than just repairs and maintenance; it had to be about integrity, education, and above all, trust.

From that moment on, every repair, service, and interaction in my professional life carried the weight of this personal experience. I made a commitment not just to excellence in the automotive field, but also to safeguarding my customers' trust and well-being. In a world where shortcuts are often taken at the expense of others, I strive to be the person who stands in the gap for honesty and fairness.

This story is the cornerstone of my professional journey. It's the reason behind every piece of advice I offer and every piece of information in this book. It's a lesson that, while painful, has instilled in me a deep sense of purpose that goes beyond the nuts and bolts of auto repair. And for that, I'm eternally grateful.

MAZVO
AUTO CAR CARE CENTER
4610 N. 7th Street | Phoenix, AZ | 85014
602.248.8711 | mazvo.com

IMPORTANT RESOURCES

As much as websites provide valuable knowledge for car ownership, relying solely on them may prove insufficient when the time comes for wrenching on a vehicle. So, bookmark these sites and visit them like pit stops on your journey. By having these resources at your fingertips, you will enjoy driving with peace-of-mind while saving money.

Kelley Blue Book (KBB.com) is your invaluable resource for gaining insights into the resale value of vehicles. With it you can assess their precise value based on condition, mileage, and other pertinent factors allowing you to make informed purchases or sales decisions. Plus, their annual awards honoring vehicles with excellent resale values will help keep you abreast of current market leaders.

Edmunds (Edmunds.com) is a great site to use when seeking detailed car valuation insights. The platform features the "True Market Value Tool" which provides estimates based on factors like condition and mileage as well as other pertinent criteria.

Automotive Lease Guide (ALG.com) is famed for their annual residual value awards. ALG recognizes vehicles across various segments with predicted residual values that maintain the greatest proportion of their Manufacturer's Suggested Retail Price (MSRP), or those predicted to keep holding substantial residual values over their lifespan.

TrueCar.com is your go-to site for precise car pricing details and value determinations, both brand new and pre-loved alike. They measure values based on recent deals as well as supply and demand trends. Their calculations offer insight that you would not receive anywhere else.

Consumer Reports (ConsumerReports.org) is your ultimate pit crew. It is your one-stop resource for honest reviews of new and used cars. You will find information about pricing, fuel efficiency, reliability, and depreciation rates for every make and model available on the market today. Their road warriors strive to give impartial opinions to help you avoid being misled when purchasing an undesirable ride.

NADA Guides (nadaguides.com) offers information with an edge. Dive into the exciting world of car price checkers which provide accurate resale values tailored to wear-and-tear mileage for specific makes and models. Think of them like your very own "what's my car worth" book.

CarGurus (CarGurus.com) is a site that uses an algorithm to reveal the instant market value of local vehicles. It's like having your very own expert advisor. This handy tool plays detective to assess whether you are getting value for your dollar compared to similar listings in your area.

National Highway Traffic Safety Administration (NHSTA.com) is the revered alcove of the National Highway Traffic Safety Administration. Discover an astounding cache of safety recalls, vehicle ratings and crash test results. While you might wonder about the cost, don't worry. The NHSTA provides its information for free. Have a browse and enjoy some automotive enlightenment while driving safely.

FEEDBACK

Friends, allow me to share something personal. While writing Car Confidential, *I found myself often regretting that certain sections weren't included. While words have their place, some narratives need to stand alone before readers and fans can fully appreciate them. So, I encourage all of you to explore* **carconfidential.net/ccbonus** *where you may even discover additional fascinating articles — or perhaps chapters which unfortunately couldn't fit.*

Every journey must begin somewhere, and Car Confidential *was my inaugural step on the literary highway. If you enjoyed and learned something from it, please leave a review on Amazon. Your opinion will encourage me to keep writing and sharing my passion for cars with the rest of the world. Thank you and keep driving with passion.*

Share your feedback, stories, or insights here:
https://carconfidential.net/review

Made in the USA
Las Vegas, NV
29 February 2024

86486668R00204